KINGS OF JUDAH & ISRAEL

Christopher Knapp

LOIZEAUX BROTHERS
Neptune, New Jersey

FIRST EDITION, 1909
PAPERBACK EDITION, 1983
SECOND PRINTING, MARCH 1988

LOIZEAUX BROTHERS, Inc., PUBLISHERS
*A Nonprofit Organization, Devoted to the Lord's Work
and to the Spread of His Truth*

ISBN 0-87213-461-X

PRINTED IN THE UNITED STATES OF AMERICA

CONTENTS

PREFACE.

THE field covered by the present volume has been practically unworked hitherto. The author knows only of a brochure of less than a hundred pages on the Hebrew kings, and treating but of the kings of Judah as types of Christians when the subject permitted.

The volume in hand was begun several years ago, but laid aside in the hope that some one better qualified might take up the work. As nothing has appeared since, the writer resumed his work, and the result is now before the reader.

No claim whatever is made to what is called scholarship, though references to Hebrew, etc., in the body of the book, might suggest, to some, the contrary. Scholarly *helps* have, however, been freely used, the principal of which are Strong's " Exhaustive Concordance " (English, Hebrew, and Greek); Fausset's "Bible Cyclopedia " (a work too little known); J. N. Darby's most excellent translation of the Old Testament (designated N. Tr.); also, Josephus, and the already mentioned little volume on the kings of Judah; besides, of course, the indispensable, and best-beloved authorized version of the English Bible. This last has been quoted from freely, though not always *fully*, and the reader is therefore urged upon to read the passages for himself in their entirety, both in Kings and Chronicles, as referred to under each one of the thirty-eight kings named at the head of their separate biographies.

The Author's Introduction was found to be the most difficult part of the undertaking, and is, of course, open to criticism, correction, or amplification. Some one of more leisure and competency may some day, it is hoped, undertake this improvement. If, under God, the present effort shall lead to further researches, and fuller development of the subject, the author shall feel amply rewarded for what he has, from the beginning, sought to make "a labor of love," as also "a work of faith."

May our Lord, the "King eternal," be pleased to use it for the blessing of His people.

C. KNAPP.

Bethlehem, Pa., 1908.

AUTHOR'S INTRODUCTION.

IT is the author's purpose in the following pages to review briefly the histories of the kings of Judah and Israel, as recorded in the inspired books of the Kings and Chronicles. These histories are given us in more or less detail, and do not read exactly the same in each book. God has surely a purpose in this, and it is the glory of saints to search out these matters, and to discover, if possible, why these differences exist. Contradiction there cannot be, for "there is one Spirit," and He who inspired the historian of the Kings controlled also and directed the pen of the chronicler.

These two historical books of the Old Testament bear a relation one toward another somewhat similar to that existing between the four Gospels of the New. In the latter we have a quartet of evangelical biographers, all giving glimpses of that manifested Life, no two in just the same way, or even recording harmoniously any single event of that marvelous life of God incarnate, or reporting verbatim any discourse of the divine "Master of assemblies." The Evangelists Matthew, Mark, Luke, and John, are somewhat like the four parts in some sublime musical composition. Each part differs, the one from the other, yet together they form a most perfect harmony, because arranged by one master musician. Each part is perfect in itself, yet requires the others to give the fulness intended. The one part expresses sweetness; the other, strength; another, pathos; and still another, profundity; and each several part is essential to the proper expression of the other three; and it is in the combination of the four that we have the full, grand harmony. So the four Gospels, though differing, are all the compositions of one Author—the Holy Spirit. Each, also, is in itself perfect, yet requires what the others contain to give to the fourfold record that surpassing beauty which every anointed eye beholds in the four Evangelists: each record being perfectly proportioned to the others, they together produce that sublime anthem of praise to "Heaven's beloved One" of whom they speak.

And He was *the* King. In the two books into which we are about to glance we have kings—some comparatively good, and others exceedingly bad; some who made fair beginnings, and foul endings; others, again, who commenced badly, but made a good finish. All, however, came short of God's glory and the divine ideal of what a king should be. He that was, according to the expectation of the Gentile magi, "born King of the Jews," and was to the Jew Nathanael "the King of Israel," fulfilled that ideal perfectly. So He is called by Jehovah "*My* King." And in the fast-approaching day of His kingdom and power He shall be known and owned as "King of nations." See Matt. 2 : 2 ; John 1 : 49 ; Ps. 2 : 6 ; Rev. 15 : 3, margin.

Let us now seek to discover, if we can, what are the

real differences between the Kings and Chronicles, and their significance.

In the LXX., 1st and 2d Kings are called "The third and fourth of the Kingdoms." Originally, in the Hebrew, they were, like 1st and 2d Samuel, but one book.* Its opening word, "Now," indicates that it is really a continuation of Samuel. Its history of the kingdoms is carried on past the middle of the captivity, and ends with Jehoiachin restored to liberty, and his throne set above that of the other kings that were in Babylon—a beautiful, though perhaps faint, shadow of Israel's restoration and exaltation in the coming millennial day. This, as some one has said, is "in happy consonance with its design." It is as "the first ray of God's returning favor," a slight pledge that David's seed and kingdom should (as God said), in spite of past failure, endure forever. Fausset says, in reference to its relation to Chronicles, "The language of Kings bears traces of an earlier date. Chaldee forms are rare in Kings, numerous in Chronicles, which has also Persicisms not found in Kings." The writer of the book is not known. The Talmud ascribes it to Jeremiah, which seems somewhat unlikely, as the thirty-seventh year of Jehoiachin (the last date in the book) would be sixty-six years after his call to the prophetic office; besides, the prophet probably died in Egypt, with God's rebellious people, whom he so deeply loved, and with whose "sins" his

---

* "Samuel and Kings, as we name them, should be, however, as they were originally, but one book each."—*Numerical Bible*, Vol. II., page 287.

devotion to them caused him to " serve " (Isa. 43 : 24).
On the other hand, as the above-quoted author states,
" The absence of mention of Jeremiah in Kings, though
he was so prominent in the reigns of the last four
kings, is just what we might expect if Jeremiah be the
author of Kings." He remarks further : " In favor of
Jeremiah's authorship is the fact that certain words
are used *only in Kings and in Jeremiah : baqubuqu*,
cruse (1 Kings 14: 3 ; Jer. 19 : 1, 10); *yagab*, husband-
man (2 Kings 25 : 12 ; Jer. 52 : 16) ; *chabah*, hide
(1 Kings 22 : 25 ; Jer. 49 : 10); *avar*, to bind (2 Kings
25 : 7 ; Jer. 39 : 7)."

But whoever the inspired penman may have been,
he evidently wrote with a different purpose in view
from that of the author of the Chronicles, who was
probably Ezra, the priest. Two names, Akkub and
Talmon, found in 1 Chron. 9 : 17, 18, and mentioned
in Neh. 12 : 25, 26, as being porters "in the days of
Nehemiah, and of *Ezra* the priest," and Zerubbabel's
name, with that of others, in 1 Chron. 3 : 19, prove the
writer lived and wrote after the restoration. The fact
of the close of Chronicles and opening of Ezra over-
lapping, indicates one common author—as Luke and
the Acts. Both 1 Chron. 29 : 7 and Ezra 2 : 69 mention the Persian coin *daric* (as "dram" should be
translated). "The high priest's genealogy is given in
the descending line, ending with the captivity, in
1 Chron. 6 : 1–15; in Ezra 7 : 1–5, in the ascending
line from Ezra himself to Aaron, abridged by the omission of many links, as the writer had in Chronicles
already given a complete register." (Fausset.) So if a
prophet (Jeremiah) wrote the Kings, and a *priest* (Ezra)

the Chronicles, it would readily account for the ministry of the prophets being so prominent in the former
book, and that of the priests and Levites in the latter.
It might furnish the key, too, as to the meaning of
the marked differences in many portions of the two
records.

1st and 2d Chronicles, like Samuel and Kings, were
originally one book. They are called in the LXX. *Par-
aleipomena*, or "Supplements"; in Hebrew, "Words,"
or "Acts of Days." Its real history (after the genealogies) begins with the overthrow of Saul (1 Chron. 10),
and reads, almost word for word, like the concluding
chapter of 1 Samuel, with this marked difference:
Saul's body is mentioned in Samuel; in Chronicles
his *head* alone is spoken of. There is also, in Chronicles, a comment on the cause of his death, not found
in Samuel, which would appear to indicate the author's
desire to point out moral lessons in his "supplements."
These practical reflections are frequent in Chronicles;
in Kings they rarely occur.

There are other marked differences between the two
books, and all, of course, in perfect keeping with the
design of each—divergent, though not contradictory—
historian. Let us note a few of the most prominent.
2 Sam. 24 : 24 says "David *bought* the threshingfloor
(of Araunah) and the oxen for fifty shekels of silver";
1 Chron. 21 : 25 says, "David *gave* to Ornan for the
place (not the threshing-floor and oxen merely) six hundred shekels of gold by weight." The molten sea made
by Solomon, 1 Kings 7 : 26 says, "contained *two* thousand baths." 2 Chron. 4 : 5 says "it received and
held *three* thousand baths" (its capacity). Frequently

Chronicles has "God" where Kings has "Lord" (see 2 Sam. 5 : 19–25; 1 Chron. 14 : 10–16; 2 Sam. 7 : 3, 4; 1 Chron. 17 : 2, 3, etc.). "House of *God*" is found seven times in Chronicles; in Kings, not once. In 1 Chron. 14 : 3 there is no mention of David's concubines, as in 2 Sam. 5 : 13. Nor does Chronicles mention his sin with Bath-sheba, nor his son Amnon's crime against Tamar, nor Absalom's rebellion, nor Sheba's revolt. The idolatries of Solomon and some of the early kings of Judah are less detailed in Chronicles than in Kings; Chronicles, in fact, scarcely hints at Solomon's sin. Nor does it mention his somewhat questionable act of offering incense "upon the altar that was before the Lord," as 1 Kings 9 : 25 (see on UZZIAH). Hezekiah's failure, too, is only briefly touched upon in Chronicles. Yet we must not think that there was any attempt made on the part of the writer of Chronicles to pass over, or wink at, the sins of the house of David. He records Hanani's reproof of Asa, on which Kings is silent; also, Jehoram's murder of his brethren, and his idolatry. Nor does Kings mention Joash's apostasy and murder of Zechariah, Amaziah's sin of idolatry, nor Uzziah's sin of sacrilege. On the other hand, the refreshing account of Manasseh's repentance is peculiar to Chronicles; yet no mention is made in that book of the liberation of the captive Jehoiachin.

Kings gives only seven verses to Uzziah's reign, and but five to righteous Jotham's. Chronicles, on the other hand, summarizes Jehoiakim's reign in four verses, and Jehoiachin's in two. Israel is in the background in Chronicles; Judah and Jerusalem are (with the priests and Levites) its principal subject; while in Kings, Israel, with her prophets (as Ahijah, Elijah, Elisha, Jonah, etc.), is prominent.

Another marked distinction between these two interesting books is the sources from which their writers obtained their material. In Kings it is always derived from state records, evidently, as "the book of the acts of Solomon" (1 Kings 11 : 41); "the book of the Chronicles of the kings of Judah" (1 Kings 14 : 29); "the book of the Chronicles of the kings of Israel" (1 Kings 14 : 19), etc. Chronicles embodies more the writings of (or selections from) individuals, as "Samuel the seer," "Nathan the prophet," "Gad the seer," "the prophecy of Ahijah the Shilonite," "the visions of Iddo the seer," "the book of Shemaiah the prophet," "the story of the prophet Iddo," "the book of Jehu the son of Hanani," "Isaiah the prophet," etc. (1 Chron. 29 : 29; 2 Chron. 9 : 29; 12 : 15; 13 : 22; 20 : 34; 26 : 22).

The explanation of all this seems to be that the author of Kings wrote his book in Judah, where he would have access to the national archives; while the writer of Chronicles probably compiled his histories from the writings of the above-mentioned seers, prophets, etc., carried with the exiles to Babylon, or obtained after their restoration to the land. This would make the Chronicles peculiarly the *Remnant's* book; while the Kings would be more for the nation at large, particularly Israel. And if this be so, it would explain why the sins of the earlier kings are veiled in Chronicles, and those of some of the later ones detailed (see above). Being under Gentile domination, they were more or less in communication with them, and they would, in all probability, come in contact with these records of the Hebrew kings. Their later history would be better known to Gentiles, and it would be well for them to know just why they were permitted to destroy Jerusalem and hold the nation in bondage; hence the record of the sins of Josiah, Amaziah, Uzziah, and others. There was no need to record the sins of David, Solomon, and their immediate successors, as this did not in any way concern the Gentiles. It was probably in view of Gentile readers that "God" is so frequently used in Chronicles, instead of His covenant name Jehovah,* that they might know that He is "not the God of the Jews only, but of the Gentiles also." It is the branches of the blessing of Joseph beginning to hang over the wall (Gen. 49 : 22). Hence, too, perhaps, the genealogies of some not of Israel, and all extending back to Adam, common father of us all (1 Chron. 1). Note, too, in view of this, Asa's crushing defeat of Zerah the Ethiopian, recorded *only* in Chronicles, and his reproof by the prophet for relying on the king of Syria; Jehoshaphat's triumph over the vast allied forces of Moab and Ammon; *God's* (not "Jehovah's," note) helping Uzziah against the Philistines, Arabians, and Mehunims, and the Ammonites giving him gifts; Jotham's victory over the Ammonites, and their tribute of silver, and wheat, and barley, rendered to him; and Manasseh's repentance

---

* Israel being given up to Gentile dominion at the time that Chronicles was written, God's covenant name with them could hardly be used.—[*Ed.*]

(that the Gentiles might know God's grace)—all peculiar to Chronicles. On the other hand, Hezekiah's weakness in first yielding to, and afterward rebelling against, Sennacherib, as recorded in 2 Kings 18, is carefully excluded from Chronicles. God never needlessly exposes the faults of His servants to the stranger. "Tell it not in Gath, publish it not in the streets of Askelon," is His beautiful principle of action in such cases.

Then as to Kings, the sins of the house of David in its earlier history are faithfully and minutely recorded, that both Judah and Israel (for whose reading the book was primarily intended) might know the reason of their debased and divided condition. The book gives mainly the history of the northern kingdom, and it is delightful to see that though the terrible sins of its rulers are exposed, any acts of grace or goodness on the part of them or the people are carefully recorded (see 2 Kings 6 : 8–23, etc.). Prophets are prominent among them, because they had cut themselves off from the ministry of the priests and Levites (which naturally connected itself with the temple at Jerusalem), and God made merciful provision for their spiritual needs by the prophetic ministry of such men as Elijah, etc.

These, I believe, are the real differences between the Kings and Chronicles. They are by no means so easily defined as those existing between the four Evangelists, and I do not profess to explain all of the many and marked variations that have been pointed out. What has been offered in the foregoing as a solution of the question may not be entirely satisfactory to all, but if it affords the reader any real help or clue to further discoveries in this direction, the author's main object will have been accomplished. What both writer and reader most need in these studies is to be more in touch with that blessed Master who of old, in the midst of His disciples, "opened their understanding, that they might understand the Scriptures."

Ere closing this Introduction, it might be well to say a word as to the authenticity of these books of Kings and Chronicles. As to the first, our Lord stamped it with His divine authority by referring repeatedly to it, as in the cases of the widow of Sarepta and Naaman the Syrian. Paul refers to Elijah's intercession against Israel; while his earnest prayer in connection with drought and rain is mentioned by James. Heb. 11 : 35 alludes to the raising of the Shunammite's son; and Jezebel is mentioned by our Lord in Rev. 2 : 20. Christ stamped the book of Chronicles with the seal of inspiration by alluding to the queen of Sheba's visit to King Solomon, and the martyrdom of Zechariah, "slain between the temple and the altar" (Matt. 23 : 35)—"altar and temple," (Luke).

The histories as given in these books are likewise confirmed by both Egyptian and Assyrian monumental records; Rehoboam being represented on the former, and Omri, Jehu, Menahem, Hoshea and Hezekiah on the inscriptions of the Assyrian Tiglath-pileser, Sargon, Sennacherib, and Esarhaddon. But Scripture, like its great subject, Christ, neither receives nor requires "testimony from men." The monuments do not prove Scripture to be true; it is only proved, when they agree with the Bible, that *they* are true, and not lies. As we read God's word, "we believe and are sure," because "holy men of God," who wrote these records, "spake as they were moved by the Holy Ghost" (2 Peter 1 : 21). True, it is called "prophecy" in the quotation given, but it has been aptly said that "*history* as written by the prophets is retroverted *prophecy*." "Moses and the Prophets" means (like "the Law and the Prophets"), the Pentateuch, the Old Testament historical books, and the writings generally designated as "the Prophets." And "the prophecy came not in old time by the will of man." So we unhesitatingly declare ourselves, like Paul of old, as "believing *all* things which are written in the Law and in the Prophets" (Acts 24 : 14). "And he that believeth shall not be ashamed"—no, "neither in this world, nor in the world to come." Amen and Amen!

INTRODUCTION.

BY H. A. IRONSIDE.

IN complying with the request of the writer of this series of papers for an introduction to his truly practical opening up of the major part of the books of Kings and Chronicles, I shall but attempt to go briefly over the histories of the three kings of the undivided monarchy, and that only so far as they are set before us in these particular portions of Scripture. The lives of Saul and David are much more fully dwelt upon in the books of Samuel, but others have written at length upon them as there portrayed, and their writings are still available.

Chronicles opens with the genealogies of the children of Israel, tracing the chosen race right back to Adam. With his name the record begins, and, so far as nature is concerned, every name that follows is but another addition of the first man. "The second man is the Lord from heaven." For His coming the world was yet waiting. Man according to God had never been seen upon earth all through the centuries covered by the history and the genealogies of these books, and indeed of the entire Old Testament. God was indeed quickening souls from the first. There can be no manner of doubt that Adam himself had thus obtained divine life when he took God at His word; and, receiving the declaration made to the serpent as to the Seed of the woman, as the first preached gospel, he called his wife's name Eve, "Living"; believing that God had found a way to avert the terrible doom their sin had justly deserved. Faith was in exercise; and where there is faith, there is of necessity eternal life, and thus a new nature. In many of his offspring, therefore, the same blessed truth is manifested; and so, throughout these lists which God has seen fit to preserve, and which will be forever kept on high, we see in one and another the fruit of the new life manifested to the glory of Him who gave it.

There is something intensely solemnizing to the soul in thus being permitted to go over such a record of names long since forgotten by man, but every one of which God has remembered, with every detail of their pathway through this world. Some day *our* names likewise will be lost to mankind, but neither we nor our ways will be forgotten by God.

Esau's race, as well as that of Israel, is kept in mind; a race from which came mighty kings and princes before any king reigned over Israel; for "that is not first which is spiritual, but that which is natural, and afterward that which is spiritual." Then, too, some in Israel are only remembered, one might say, because of some fearful sin that was the ruin of themselves, and often of those associated with them; such as Er, and Achan the troubler of Israel (called here Achar); Reuben, who defiled his father's bed; and the heads of the half tribe of Manasseh, who "went a whoring after the gods of the people of the land."

On the other hand, it is sweet and edifying to the soul to trace out the brief notices (which, if this were

but a human book, would seem so out of place in the
midst of long lists of names) of what divine grace had
wrought in one and another as they trod their often-
times lowly ways, with faith in exercise and the conscience active. Of this character is the lovely passage
as to Jabez, who was more honorable than his brethren because he set the Lord before him. His prayer,
"Oh that Thou wouldest bless me indeed, and enlarge
my coast, and that Thy hand might be with me, and
that Thou wouldest keep me from evil, that it may not
grieve me!" tells of the longings of his soul; and we
do not wonder when we read that "God granted him
that which he requested" (1 Chron. 4 : 9, 10). The sons
of Reuben, too, with their allies who overcame the Ha-
garites when "they cried to God in the battle, and He
was entreated of them, *because they put their trust in
Him*," are cited as another instance of the power of
faith (chap. 5 : 18–20). Nor does God forget Zelophe-
had, the man who had no sons to inherit after him,
but who claimed a portion for his daughters, and
learned that the strength of the Lord is made perfect
in weakness (chap. 7 : 15).

There are precious lessons too of a typical character that become manifest as we patiently search this
portion of the word of the Lord, which, like all other
Scripture, was written for our learning. Who can fail
to see the lesson of "the potters, and those that dwelt
among plants and hedges: there they dwelt with the
king for his work"? Surely it has a voice for all who
seek to care for the tender plants of the Lord's garden, as also for those who minister to the hardier ones
that constitute the hedges, and who are set for the

marking of the boundaries in divine things. It is only
as the servants dwell *with* the King that they are fit
to carry on His work (chap. 4 : 23). The lesson of
chap. 9 : 26--34 is similar.

Saul's genealogy is given in chap. 8, beginning with
verse 33 ; but his whole life is passed over in silence,
and only his lamentable end recorded in the 10th
chapter. He it was of whom God said, " I gave them
a king in Mine anger, and took him away in My wrath."
It was a desire to be like the nations that led Israel to
ask for a king ; and in giving them their request the
Lord sent leanness into their souls. Saul was the
man of the people's choice, but he was a dreadful dis-
appointment. His dishonored death is on a par with
his unhappy life, which is only hinted at in the closing
verses of the chapter, as all the sorrowful details have
been left on record in the books bearing Samuel's
name—the prophet who loved him so dearly, but who
could not lead him in the ways of God. As another has
well described him, he was " the man after the flesh."
This tells the whole story. In all his life he seems
never to have truly been brought into the presence of
God. His activities were all of the flesh, and his way
of looking at things was only according to man, and
the garish light of man's day. Defeated on Mount
Gilboa, he is a suicide at last, and after his death becomes the sport of the enemies of the Lord. " So
Saul died for his transgression which he committed
against the Lord, even against the word of the Lord,
which he kept not, and also for asking counsel of one
that had a familiar spirit, to inquire of it ; and inquired
not of the Lord : therefore He slew him, and turned

the kingdom unto David the son of Jesse" (chap. 10 :
13, 14).

Upon the fall of the people's choice, God's man appears upon the scene.   There is no word here of the
early experiences of David, save that the mighty men
are those who went down to the rock to him when he
was in the cave of Adullam, and others also who came
to him when he was at Ziklag, and kept himself close
because of Saul the son of Kish.

The account here given begins with the coming of
all Israel to David unto Hebron to make him king.
The seven years' reign over Judah is not mentioned.
Owned of the whole nation as the ruler of God's appointment, he begins at once the work of enlarging
their borders and delivering them from their enemies.
Jebus, the fortress of the Jebusites, is taken and converted into the city of David, where he reigns in power,
waxing greater and greater ; thus manifesting the fact
that the Lord of hosts was with him.   The mighty
men who had shared his rejection are now the sharers
of his power, and the glory pertaining thereto.   It is
a picture of the true David, God's " Beloved," who is
yet to be manifested in authority over all the earth,
when those who now cleave to Him when set at naught
will have their part with .Him when He takes His
great power and reigns.

The ark is brought up to the city of David, but only
after the lesson has been learned that God will be
sanctified in them that come nigh Him, and that,though
Philistine carts may do for those who know not the
mind of God, where His word is given it must be
inquired of and obeyed.   Great are the rejoicings of

the people when the symbol of the covenant of the Lord is installed in the place prepared for it, and burnt sacrifices and peace offerings ascend in a cloud of fragrance to God. But when the king would build a house for the God of Israel, though encouraged by the prophet Nathan in his pious purpose, both king and prophet have to learn that the thoughts of God are above the thoughts of the best and most devoted men. Nathan has to inform him that it cannot be for him to build the house, because he has been a man of blood: when, however, his son is established in peace upon the throne, he shall build the house, and all will be in keeping with the times. David thus is seen to picture the establishment of the kingdom in the destruction of the enemies of the Lord, while Solomon sets forth the reign of peace that is to follow for the thousand years. Bowing in obedience to the word of the Lord, David begins to prepare for the work of the temple by gathering in abundance all the materials that he is able to obtain.

But it is made evident that the ideal King has not yet come, for even in the man after God's own heart is found failure ere he resigns his crown to his son. His personal sin, that left so dreadful a blot upon his character, is here omitted, as befits the character of the book. But his official failure in numbering the people is told in all faithfulness, as also the fact that it was Satan who provoked him to act as he did. But in amazing grace God overrules all to make David's very sin the means of manifesting the site for the future temple of the Lord. Finally, having set all in order, and arranged even the courses of the priests and

Levites who are to officiate in the glorious house of
Jehovah, the aged monarch appoints Solomon his son
and the son of Bath-sheba to be king in his stead;
and after solemnly charging him both as to the kingdom and the house that is to be built, "he died in a
good old age, full of days, riches, and honor: and Solomon his son reigned in his stead."

In the opening chapters of 1 Kings we see that his
last days were not all bright.   His failure to properly
control his household brought him much sorrow, and
embittered his cup when he was too feeble to exert
himself as he would have desired.   Adonijah's effort,
however, to secure the crown for himself results in disaster, and eventually in his own death, and Solomon's,
title is indisputably established.

Solomon's reign begins most auspiciously.   Having
gone to Gibeon, where the altar still remained with
the tabernacle, to offer sacrifice, God appeared to him
in the night with the wondrous message, "Ask what
I shall give thee."   It was as though He placed all
His resources at the disposal of faith.   The young
king prays for wisdom and knowledge in order that he
may care for the flock committed to him.   It was a
most remarkable prayer for one placed in his position,
and the Lord manifests His pleasure in it by confer-
ring upon him exceeding abundantly above all that he
asked or thought.   His wisdom is celebrated to this
day, and in his own times was the admiration of his
people and the surrounding nations wherever his fame
was carried.

The main part of the chapters devoted to Solomon,
in both Kings and Chronicles, is occupied with the ac-

count of the temple, every whit of which was to utter
the glory of the "Greater than Solomon" who was
yet to come. The symbolism of this magnificent
structure has been gone into at length by others, and
would not properly belong to this introductory notice.
At the dedication of the temple, which had gone up so
silently, Jehovah came in in a manner that none might
misunderstand, and took possession of the house as
His own. Solomon's prayer on that occasion is prophetic of the sad history that these books record as to
later years. He seems to see all that his people would
yet have to pass through.

But light and gift are not sufficient of themselves to
keep one in the path with God. For a time all goes
well with Solomon. His power is unprecedented.
His fame is carried into all lands penetrated by the
trader's caravan or touched by the ship of the voyager.
The queen of Sheba comes from the uttermost parts
of the earth to prove him with hard questions concerning the name of the Lord, and goes away with
every question answered and her heart swelling with
the glorious things that she has both seen and heard.
The king's knowledge in all matters seems to be limit-
less. "And all the earth sought to Solomon to hear
his wisdom, which God had put into his heart" (1 Kings
10 : 24). Sad it is that so glorious a record has to be
blotted by the tale of failure that the book of Kings
records, but which is passed over in Chronicles.

"*But* King Solomon loved many strange women . . .
and when Solomon was old, his wives turned away his
heart." Such is the terrible fall of the man who was
most privileged of all the rulers that history, sacred

or profane, tells us of. He failed to keep his own
heart. The Lord lost the place He had once had, and
the result was that Solomon sinned grievously after
all that he had known and enjoyed of the things of
God. Idolatry was established in the very sight of
the holy temple of the Lord. God was dishonored by
the very man who, of all others, had received the most
from Him. What a warning to every subject of His
grace! May reader and writer lay it to heart!

As a result of his sins the Lord stirred up adversa-
ries against him, and in the days of his son rent the
kingdom from the house of David, with the exception
of the two tribes. But of all this the following pages
will treat.

We would only add a few remarks to trace the
roots of the division that took place at the death of
Solomon, rending the kingdom in twain, never to
be reunited till that day of Israel's regeneration yet
to come, when "the envy also of Ephraim shall depart, ... Ephraim shall not envy Judah, and
Judah shall not vex Ephraim" (Isa. 11 : 13).

As descendants of Joseph, who (in Jacob's and
Moses' blessings) was exalted above and "separate
from his brethren," Ephraim seems ever to have
aspired to leadership in the nation. Already, in the
time of the Judges, that pride had twice broken out in
haughty demeanor. After the mighty victory of Gideon's little band over the Midianites that had invaded
and ravaged the land, the men of Ephraim sharply
chided Gideon because he had not called *them* to the
war—envying the fame of such a victory. Gideon's
most gracious answer to their haughty chiding averted

a catastrophe (Judg. 8 : 1–3); but their still more haughty chiding of Jephthah on a later occasion brought upon Ephraim a terrible, though deserved, retribution (chap. 12 : 1–6).

When the Theocracy (God's direct rule in Israel) gave place to the kingdom by Israel's impious request, Saul, taken from "little Benjamin," is acclaimed by all Israel. Benjamin having been nearly annihilated for their sin some time before, and being Joseph's full brother, may on that account have been more welcome to Ephraim. But when David, of the tribe of Judah, is manifested as God's anointed in the place of rejected Saul, and at Saul's death is made king in Hebron *by Judah*, he is not acclaimed, but opposed, by the other tribes, of whom Ephraim was chief, and a seven-years' war ensues, until the weak pretender of Saul's house gives way before the rising power of David and Judah, and Israel is reunited in one kingdom under David's godly and righteous rule. The jealousy and strife that broke out on previous occasions is for the time forgotten and out of sight.

But as David's sin, and his son's wicked conduct, brought about upheavals in the kingdom, so, later on, through Solomon's departure from God and oppression of His people, occasion is found at his death to make demands upon the new king coming to his father's throne. His insolent and foolish answer brings about the crisis in which the unthankful and heartless cry is heard, "What portion have we in *David?* neither have we inheritance in the son of Jesse : to your tents, O Israel! now see to thine own

house, David" (1 Kings 12 : 16). Ephraim, headed
by Jeroboam—an Ephraimite—then takes leadership
of the ten tribes revolted from the house of David,
and a new kingdom is formed, in which *every one* in
the line of their nineteen kings is an apostate from
Jehovah.

I now leave the reader with what my beloved fellow-
servant has penned, praying that as he passes on he
may have the hearing ear, the anointed eye, and the
subject heart that alone makes the truth living and
real in the soul.

H. A. IRONSIDE.

CHRONOLOGICAL TABLE

of the kings of Judah and Israel subsequent to the reigns of Saul, David, and Solomon, each of which lasted forty years; from B.C. 1095 to B.C. 975.

(After Ussher.)

Length of reign in years	Kings of JUDAH.	B.C.	Kings of ISRAEL.	Length of reign in years
17	Rehoboam.	975	Jeroboam I.	22
3	Abijah.	958		
41	Asa.	955		
		954	Nadab.	2
		953	Baasha.	24
		930	Elah.	2
		929	Zimri.	Seven days.
		929	Omri.	12
		918	Ahab.	22
25	Jehoshaphat.	914		
		897	Ahaziah.	2
		896	Jehoram.	12
8	Jehoram.	891		
1	Ahaziah.	885		
6	(Athaliah.)	884	Jehu.	28
40	Jehoash.	878		
		856	Jehoahaz.	17
		841	Jehoash.	16
29	Amaziah.	839		
		825	Jeroboam II.	41

Length of reign in years	Kings of JUDAH.	B.C.	Kings of ISRAEL.	Length of reign in years
52	Uzziah.	810		
		773	Zachariah.	Six months.
		772	Shallum.	One month.
		772	Menahem.	10
		761	Pekahiah.	2
		759	Pekah.	20
16	Jotham.	758		(Interregnum of 9 or more years.)
16	Ahaz.	742		
(Interregnum of 5 or more years.)		730*	Hoshea.	9
29	Hezekiah.	727		
		721	Samaria taken.	
55	Manasseh.	698		
2	Amon.	643		
31	Josiah.	641		
3 months.	Jehoahaz.	610		
11	Jehoiakim.	610		
3 months.	Jehoiachin.	599		
11	Zedekiah.	599		
Jerusalem taken.		588 or 587		

*Five or more years should be, from here, added to these dates of Ussher's. See on Hezekiah.

REHOBOAM

(Liberator, or enlarger, of the people.)

(1 Kings 12 : 1–24 ; 14 : 21–31 ; 2 Chron. 10–12.)

Contemporary Prophet, SHEMAIAH.

"In the multitude of people is the king's honor : but in the want of people is the destruction of the prince."— *Proverbs 14 : 28.*

REHOBOAM was not what we call a strong character. He was, in the beginning of his reign at least, as his own son Abijah said to Jeroboam, "young (inexperienced) and faint-hearted, and did not show himself strong" against the troublers of his kingdom (2 Chron. 13 : 7, N. Tr.). Why Solomon should have chosen him as his successor is not clear. It is difficult to believe that he had no other sons ; yet it is a fact that Rehoboam is the only one mentioned (1 Chron. 3 : 10). His father seems to have had misgivings concerning his ability to rule the kingdom (see Eccl. 2 : 18, 19 ; 4 : 13–16, N. Tr.). And it was probably not a question of favoritism ; for Pharaoh's daughter, and not Naamah the Ammonitess (Rehoboam's mother), appears to have been his preferred wife. But if Rehoboam was his only son, he had no choice ; so we read, "Rehoboam his son reigned in his stead."

Weakness and vacillation marked his reign from

the beginning.   His going to Shechem to be crowned
was evidently a concession to conciliate the already
disaffected tribes to the north.   He might have succeeded in his efforts to allay the dissatisfaction caused
by the enforced levy of labor by his father (see 1 Kings
11 : 28), had he wisely and humbly heeded the advice
of the aged men who had been his father's honored
counselors.   They, from long experience, knew the
temper of the people well; and in petitioning for the
lightening of their burdens, they were only doing what
any people not reduced to the condition of slavery,
or serfdom, might have asked.   And had the newly
crowned king granted them their reasonable demands,
and been "kind to them," and "pleased" them, and
spoken "good words" to them, they would, as the old
cabinet ministers said, have been his loyal subjects
forever.   But he forsook their wise counsels.   Influenced by a handful of callow novices and young court
favorites, who, like himself, thought more of the rights
of the king than of his responsibility to govern
righteously he replied with as rash and insolent a
speech as was, perhaps, ever uttered from the throne
to a civilized nation.   The outraged people answer in
the same spirit as the king; and we have the sad, por-
tentous cry, "What portion have we in David? and
we have none inheritance in the son of Jesse : every
man to your tents, O Israel: and now, David, see to
thine own house." (See also 2 Sam. 20 : 1.)

Though truly thankful to God that we are privileged to live under a form of government which gives
us fullest freedom, we have no quarrel with absolute
monarchy.   But while God enjoins subjection to the

powers that be, *tyranny* over the souls and bodies of
men is nowhere countenanced in His word; and rulers
who attempt it must learn the results to their cost.
There are many proofs of this in Scripture, as in history. Government is of God, and therefore of divine
appointment; but God's frown is upon all abuse of
power.

Rehoboam found it hard to believe that the ten
tribes had really refused his yoke. He flattered himself, no doubt, that they would not dare to rebel
against his authority. It could not be possible, he
might think, that these provincials should not readily
and meekly submit to his chastening with scorpions.
So he confidently sent to them Hadoram to collect the
imposed assessment. This ill-advised act brings matters to a crisis, and the old collector-general, who had
served in this office under his father Solomon and his
grandfather David is stoned by the exasperated people. So the king, who had boasted so haughtily that
his "little finger" should be "thicker than his father's
loins," ingloriously "made speed to get him up to his
chariot to flee to Jerusalem."

It must have been evident to him now that the rebellion was a very real and formidable one, and not a
mere passing wave of discontent that would quickly
die away of itself and be forgotten. But such an immense loss, such terrible results occurring so unex-
pectedly, are not so easily submitted to. Force may
yet avail. There is the army, one hundred and eighty
thousand strong : these malcontents should soon be
made to feel the effect of its invincible power. Might
must make right, if right cannot be demonstrated in

any other way. But "the God of peace," who loves
His people even when misguided and in error, warns
the king of Judah (note the intentional limit of his
title, 2 Chron. 11 : 3) by the word of the man of God,
Shemaiah, saying, "Ye shall not go up, nor fight
against your brethren : return every man to his house;
for this thing is from Me."

Under the government of God this division of
the kingdom was the punishment of the sins of Solomon (1 Kings 11 : 33), occasioned by the folly of Rehoboam; it must therefore stand. To fight, then, to
bring back the unity of the nation, good as the purpose might seem, was to fight against God. Rehoboam ought to have been thankful that God's love
to David had left him even two tribes. And he
appears to have been, for "they obeyed the words
of the Lord, and returned from going against Jeroboam." He now betakes himself to make sure
what had been left him. He built, or garrisoned,
fifteen cities within his decreased territory, "and he
fortified the strong holds, and put captains in
them, and store of victuals, and of oil and wine.
And in every several city he put shields and spears,
and made them exceeding strong." The successful
rebel may sometimes turn *invader*, and Rehoboam
(wiser now) will guard against this. There was war
between him and the insurrectionist leader Jeroboam all their days, and the son of Solomon had to
guard vigilantly what remained to him.

The priests and Levites remained faithful to Jehovah, to His house and worship at Jerusalem, and to
the house of David, which was by the election of God

the royal one.   They left the land of Israel, to dwell
in Judah and Jerusalem.   Others too, who had set
their hearts to seek the God of Israel, deserted the
cause of the secessionists, and flocked to Rehoboam's
standard.   For three years all went well, and they
walked "in the way of David and Solomon."   But
their goodness (like all that is of the creature merely)
was as the early dew and like the morning cloud, and
passed quickly away.   Subdued, no doubt, and humbled, by the loss of the greater portion of his kingdom,
Rehoboam walked for a time in fear and dependence.
But alas, even serious lessons like this are soon forgotten by most, and before five years had passed both
king and people had lapsed so far into idolatry as to
be brought to the very verge of apostasy from Jehovah.   "And Judah," we read, "did evil in the sight
of the Lord, and they provoked Him to jealousy with
their sins which they had committed, *above all that
their fathers had done.*   For they also built them high
places, and images, and groves, on every high hill, and
under every green tree.   And there were also sodomites (men consecrated to impurity) in the land: and
they did according to all the abominations of the nations which the Lord cast out before the children of
Israel" (1 Kings 14: 22-24).

And for this cause God sent Shishak king of Egypt
against them.   Solomon had joined affinity with Pharaoh by taking his daughter to wife; and whether this
was merely to please himself, or that he expected to
strengthen his kingdom by an alliance with so powerful a country, it all comes to naught, as do all such
expedients where God's word is disobeyed or ignored.

Shishak overthrew Pharaoh, the father-in-law of Solomon, thus ending that dynasty, and Shishak became the "new king," who "knew not" Solomon, nor his successor. Influenced probably by Jeroboam, he marched against Jerusalem with a vast army of twelve hundred chariots and sixty thousand horsemen, besides an innumerable host of footmen. Realizing the utter hopelessness of his position, and not having faith in God, Rehoboam offered no resistance to the advance of Shishak. Huddled with the princes of Judah at Jerusalem, he awaited with them, in fear of his life, the coming of the Egyptian army.

It is now God's time to speak to their consciences; and Shemaiah the prophet appeared before them with this message of conviction: "Thus saith the Lord, Ye have forsaken Me, and therefore have I also left you in the hand of Shishak." They humbled themselves, then, and said, "The Lord is righteous;" and a partial deliverance was promised them. God says, "I will not destroy them." "The princes of Israel and the king humbled themselves," says the Word. The princes took the lead, it would seem (from their being mentioned first), in this humiliating, yet becoming, confession; the king was slower, the roots of his former haughtiness still lingering unjudged within his heart.

Note what God says: "*I* will not destroy them." Shishak was only His whip, like the Assyrian at a later date, whom God, by His prophet Isaiah, calls "the rod of Mine anger," and "a razor that is hired." It is necessary, for blessing, in calamities like these, to see beyond the instrument, and know the hand that

uses it.   But though their lives were spared, they
must become servants (tributary) to Shishak, "That
they may know," God says, "My service, and the
service of the kingdoms of the countries."   Where
true submission is, the Lord's yoke is easy ; and if His
saints refuse to wear it, they must learn by humiliating and painful experience what the yoke of the
enemy is like.   So Shishak took away all the temple
treasures, and those of the royal palace.   He also
took with him the five hundred shields of gold that
Solomon had made ; and Rehoboam made in their
stead shields of bronze, and with these pathetically
tried to keep up former appearances.   It is like souls,
who, when despoiled of their freshness and power
by the enemy, laboriously endeavor to keep up an
outward appearance of spiritual prosperity ; or, like a
fallen church, shorn of its strength, and robbed of its
purity, seeking to hide its helplessness, and cover its
nakedness, with the tinsel of ritualism, spurious
revivalism, union, and anything that promises to give
them some appearance of justification for saying,
" I am rich, and increased with goods," etc.

There is little more to say of Rehoboam.   Whatever was in his father's mind when naming him
"Liberator," or "Enlarger of the people," he failed
utterly to become either.   He enslaved the nation to
Shishak by his sins, and decreased the numerical
strength of his kingdom by more than three millions
through his folly at the very outset of his reign.   He
followed his father's shameful example in taking
many wives.   He displayed wisdom, however, in
distributing his sons over the countries of Judah and

Benjamin, placing them in the garrison towns, and providing them food in abundance. He probably remembered and was desirous to avoid such scenes as had occurred at the close of his grandfather David's life in connection with his sons. Would God that Christians had always as much *spiritual* wisdom as Rehoboam manifested *natural* wisdom in this. Were God's people well fed with truth, and well taken up with the affairs of Christ in the various services of His kingdom, there would be less strife among us. But alas, it is still too often true that "the children of this world are in their generation wiser than the children of light." Rehoboam's wisdom was rewarded when, at the end of his seventeen years' reign, his son Abijah quietly assumed the crown without opposition from his many brethren.

Rehoboam died at the age of fifty-eight. The Spirit's last comment on his character is significant: "And he did evil because he prepared not his heart to seek the Lord." There we are told in a single sentence the whole secret of his failure, both as king of Judah, and servant of Jehovah, who gave him this exalted position, *he applied not his heart to seek Jehovah.* May God in His grace, help us to apply our hearts to seek first and always His kingdom and righteousness. Only so shall we be kept from evil, and preserved from making the record of our lives read anything like Rehoboam's—one sad succession of decline and failure.

ABIJAH

(Jehovah is my Father.)

(1 Kings 15 : 1–8 ; 2 Chron. 13.)

Contemporary Prophet, IDDO.

"Great deliverance giveth He to His king ; and show-eth mercy to His anointed, to David, and to his seed for-evermore."—*Ps. 18 : 50.*

ABIJAH'S reign was a brief one. He outlived his father Rehoboam by only three short years. His mother Maachah was a daughter (or grand-daughter)* of Absalom. Abijah was thus descended from David on both his father's and his mother's side. His mother, however, turned out to be an idolatress (1 Kings 15 : 13). The form of her name Maachah, which means *oppressor*, is altered in Chronicles, in the account of Abijah's reign, to Michaiah—*Who is like God?* She is said here, too, to be a daughter of Uriel, meaning *light*, or *fire of God*. The reason for this will be understood by referring to the Author's Introduction. There is, also, no account of Abijah's wickedness in Chronicles. In Kings, on the other hand, there is nothing recorded of him but his sin. "He

---

* We should remember that family relations are not so punctiliously mentioned in Scripture as it is our custom now to do. Thus blood-relations are often mentioned as "brother" and ancestors as "father" or "mother." [Ed.]

walked," it says there, "in all the sins of his father, which he had done before him: and his heart was not perfect with the Lord his God, as the heart of David his father" (1 Kings 15 : 3).

He was evidently a man of considerable spirit, for he had barely settled himself in his throne before he began a war with his father's old adversary Jeroboam (2 Chron. 13 : 3, N. Tr.). His army numbered 400,-000 "chosen men," while Jeroboam's was just as large again, 800,000, "mighty men of valor," it is noted.

It was a wonderful battle; and it was preceded by a very wonderful speech from Abijah. He stood on the top of Mount Zemaraim, in Mount Ephraim, somewhere along the northern border of his kingdom. For terseness, accusation, warning and appeal, the address is unsurpassed by anything in any literature of any time. Its merit was recognized even in his own day, for the prophet Iddo, in his "treatise," did not neglect to record the eloquent king's "sayings" (2 Chron. 13 : 22, N. Tr.). We shall not attempt to analyze it. Nor does it require any analysis; for it is simple as it is weighty and powerful. Though true in all its statements, it lacks frankness. He says, "Hear me, thou Jeroboam, and all Israel! Ought ye not to know that Jehovah the God of Israel gave the kingdom over Israel to David forever, to him and to his sons by a covenant of salt? But Jeroboam the son of Nebat, the servant of Solomon the son of David, rose up and rebelled against his lord." The gathered hosts who listened to him knew well the truth of this. But, either intentionally or unconsciously, he ignores the root of all this strife—his grandfather's sins; he

also ignores the fact that God had forbidden his father
Rehoboam to make war on the separated tribes, saying, "This thing (the schism) is from Me." He knows
how to put forth that which makes his position right
and good, but he wholly ignores the judgment of God
upon his own tribes and upon the house of David because of its own sins. How unlike the humble and
confessing spirit of his father David all this is! It is
wisdom, but cold wisdom, without the spirit of grace
so becoming their actual circumstances.

But he goes on: "And vain men, sons of Belial,
gathered to him and strengthened themselves against
Rehoboam the son of Solomon." Strong words these,
spoken before an army of valiant men twice the size
of his own!—he is bent on making them realize
that, however strong they are, their origin in separation from his own tribes is not of God. This, of
course, would also greatly strengthen his own adhe-
rents, and he was doubtless speaking for *their* ears as
well as for those of his enemies. Ignoring the judgment of God upon the nation, he makes the plea that
his father Rehoboam "was young and faint-hearted,
and did not show himself strong against them. And
now ye think to show yourselves strong against the
kingdom of Jehovah in the hand of the sons of David."
He seems to say, You might deter my faint-hearted
father from punishing you, and reducing you to submission, but you have a different man to deal with
now.

Then follows that which, together with Jehovah's love
for the house of David, secures the victory he got, and
the awful defeat of Jeroboam: "And ye are a great mul-

titude, and you have with you the golden calves that
Jeroboam made you for gods. Have ye not cast out
the priests of Jehovah, the sons of Aaron, and the Levites, and made you priests as the people of the lands?
Whoever comes to consecrate himself with a young
bullock and seven rams, he becomes a priest of what
is not God (or, ' to no-gods': see Gal. 4 : 8). But as
for us, Jehovah is our God, and we have not forsaken
Him." (However true this might be *outwardly*, we
have seen already the Spirit's testimony as to the *in-
ward* or real condition in Judah as declared in 1 Kings
14 : 22–25.) "And the priests that serve Jehovah are
the sons of Aaron, and the Levites are at their work :
and they burn to Jehovah every morning and every
evening burnt-offerings and sweet incense; the loaves
also are set in order upon the table; and the candle-
stick of gold with its lamps to burn every evening; for
we keep the charge of Jehovah our God; but *ye* have
forsaken Him! And, behold, we have God with us
at our head, and His priests, and the loud-sounding
trumpets to sound an alarm against you." Then he
closes with a brief but eloquent appeal, "Children of
Israel, do not fight with Jehovah the God of your
fathers; for ye shall not prosper!"

On the one hand, all this is sublime ; on the other,
had it been true in their *heart*-relations with Jehovah
as it was true in the *outward* sense, they would likely
not have been found there, facing their brethren for
battle, and about to be engaged in dreadful carnage.
But while God could not have put His seal upon the
state of soul in Abijah and the tribes with him, He
must vindicate the righteousness of all that is said

agai⁻ ͟⁚ Jeroboam and his followers.   So, also, though
"orthodoxy" be away from God in *heart*, yet its battle against antichrists must for the time being be acknowledged and helped. The house of David is loved,
and must be sustained—Christ is dear to God, and all
who fight for Him must be upheld, though God may
have something against them too. So Abijah wins a great
victory, and Israel suffers a most humiliating defeat.
More than half their army is slain, and it was more
than sixteen years before they again attempted to
make war upon the house of David. "And the children of Israel were humbled at that time, and the children of Judah were strengthened, because they relied
upon Jehovah the God of their fathers." God owns
whatever good He can find among His people.

Abijah also took three cities, Bethel, Jeshanah, and
Ephron, with their dependent villages, from Israel.
Neither did Jeroboam ever recover from the effects of
his defeat; and soon after, struck by Jehovah, he died.

When not more than forty years old, probably, Abijah died. Like his father before him, he was unfortunate in not having a good mother. He is called Abi-
jam in Kings. God would not let His name be called
upon him there, because there it is only the dark side
of his life which is told. He is jealous of His name.
It is a holy name; and He would not have it dishonored by the sins of those upon whom it has been
called. May all His people everywhere give heed to
this. The holy name of Christ ("Christian") is given
us. May we never by any act of ours bring a stain of
reproach on it!

ASA

(*Healing*, or, *Cure*.)

(1 Kings 15 : 9–24 ; 2 Chron. 14–16.)

Contemporary Prophets:

AZARIAH, son of Oded;

HANANI;

JEHORAM.

" Better is a poor and a wise child, than an old and foolish king, who will no more be admonished."—*Ecclesiastes 4 : 13*.

" AND Abijah slept with his fathers, and they buried him in the city of David. And Asa his son reigned in his stead. And in his days the land was quiet ten years " (2 Chron. 14: 1).

His name, "*healing*," or "*cure*," reads like a prophecy of the reformation, and consequent rest, effected by him during the earlier portion of his reign. He made a most excellent beginning. " And Asa did that which was good and right in the eyes of Jehovah his God: for he took away the altars of the strange gods, and the high places, and brake down the images, and cut down the groves: and commanded Judah to seek the Lord God of their fathers, and to do the law and the commandment. Also he took away out of all the cities of Judah the high places and the images: and the kingdom was quiet before him." But he did not stop there; he did more: "He built fenced cities in Judah: for the land had rest, and he had no war in those years; because the Lord had given him rest. Therefore he said unto Judah, Let us build these cities, and make about them walls and towers, gates and bars, while the land is yet before us; because we have sought the Lord our God, we have sought Him, and He hath given us rest on every side." He was no mere iconoclast. If he had the zeal to break down the images, he had also the wisdom to build fortified cities. To expose evil is very well, but to furnish the soul with truth is what protects it from the invasion of the enemy. They redeemed the time, as we are bidden to do in Eph. 5 : 16, "Redeeming the time, because the days are evil." So God was with them. Encouraged by the king's words and example, the people entered heartily into the blessed work of building and fortifying.

Well would it have been for the sixteenth-century churches had they been as wise after the Reformation, during the rest that followed, and built and fortified themselves in their position of defence of "the faith once for all delivered to the saints." But alas, they slept; and when the hosts of worldliness, ritualism and rationalism appeared at their borders, they were utterly unprepared, and powerless to repel them. They were not, like Judah, prepared and able to resist the enemy when he came.

"And Zerah the Ethiopian came out against him with a host of a thousand thousand, and three hundred chariots; and he came to Mareshah. And Asa went out against him, and they set the battle in array in the valley of Zephathah, near Mareshah. And Asa cried unto Jehovah his God, and said, Jehovah, it maketh no difference to Thee to help, whether there be much or no power: help us, O Jehovah our God, for we rely on Thee, and in Thy name we come against this great multitude. Jehovah, Thou art our God; let not man (*Enosh*, frail, mortal man) prevail against Thee. And Jehovah smote the Ethiopians before Asa, and before Judah; and the Ethiopians fled. And Asa and the people that were with him pursued them to Gerar; and the Ethiopians were overthrown, that none of them was left alive; for they were crushed before Jehovah and before His army. And they carried away very much spoil."

The monuments do not make clear just who this Zerah was. A king called *Azerch Amar* was reigning over Ethiopia about this time, and the inspired chronicler may have given the Hebrew form of his name. "The greatness of Egypt, which Shishak had raised, diminished at his death. His immediate successors were of no note in the monuments. . . . Zerah seems to have taken advantage of Egypt's weakness to extort permission to march his enormous force, composed of the same nationalities (Ethiopians and Lubians) as those of the preceding invader, Shishak, through Egypt into Judah" (Fausset). Others identify him with Osorkon II., one of Shishak's successors. He was son-in-law to Osorkon I., king of Egypt, and reigned in right of his wife. He was, if this be true, an Ethiopian ruling his own country jointly with that of his wife's (Egypt). And the invasion would then probably be caused by Asa's refusal to continue paying the tribute imposed upon his grandfather Rehoboam by Shishak. But it was one thing for Shishak to invade the land of Judah "because they had transgressed against the Lord" (2 Chron. 12 : 2), and quite a different matter when Zerah came against them unprovoked, "at his own charges," as it were. He met his just punishment from God, who loves and defends His people; he was defeated therefore, and his immense army, numbering more than a million, utterly destroyed.

Asa's faith rises to blessed heights on this occasion. Though himself in control of a fine army of over a half million "mighty men of valor," he takes the place of entire dependence on God, and makes the conflict a matter between God and the enemy. Such faith can never be disappointed.

On Asa's triumphant return to Jerusalem the Spirit of God came on Azariah ("*whom Jehovah helps*") the son of Oded, and he went to meet him, not as a court flatterer, but with a solemn yet cheering word of admonition. "Hear me, Asa, and all Judah and Benjamin," he says; "The Lord is with you, while ye be with Him; and if ye seek Him, He will be found of you; but if ye forsake Him, He will forsake you." It was "a word in season"; for it has been truly said that we are never in greater danger than immediately after some great success, even though it be truly from God, in answer to genuine faith. David is a sad example. In the chapters preceding that which records his sin with Bathsheba (2 Sam. 11) he has one continued series of brilliant victories over his enemies. He defeated and subdued the Philistines, Moab, Hadarezer king of Zobah, the Syrians, the Ammonites, and Amalek. Then, as if resting in these victories, the watchfulness is relaxed, and "the mighty" falls. And Asa, his descendant of the fifth generation, is graciously warned of God lest he should also fall into similar condemnation.

Azariah then reminds them of how, in days gone by ("hath been," verse 3, should be "was"—in the days of the Judges, evidently: compare Judges 5), when, in apostasy and distress, the people turned to Jehovah, God of Israel, and sought Him, He was found of them. "Be ye strong therefore," he says, "and let not your hands be weak: for your work shall be rewarded." "But as for you, be firm," the New Translation says. Asa had probably met with opposition in his reformatory work, and was in danger of failing to continue it to its completion. So he was exhorted to be firm, for there should be a sure reward for his deeds of restoration of the uncorrupted worship of Jehovah in his realm. "And when Asa heard these words, and the prophecy of Oded the prophet (Alex. MS. and Vulg. read, "Azariah son of Oded"), he took courage, and put away the abominable idols out of all the land of Judah and Benjamin, and out of the cities which he had taken from Mount Ephraim, and renewed the altar of the Lord, that was before the porch of the Lord." This was the altar on which Solomon offered burnt-offerings when he brought his Egyptian bride into the house that he had built for her (2 Chron. 8 : 12). It had evidently been removed, or allowed to fall into disuse, or decay, before being "rebuilt" by Asa.

His great victory over Zerah had its effect on many among the revolted tribes (for nothing wins God's people like God's blessing), and "they fell to him out of Israel in abundance when they saw that the Lord his God was with him." Stimulated, as it would seem, by these accessions to their ranks, the people entered into a covenant "to seek the Lord God of their fathers with all their heart and with all their soul." The tide of reformation ran high—too high, it is to be feared; for they determined "that whosoever would not seek the Lord God of Israel should be put to death, whether small or great, whether man or woman." This severity hardly became a people who had only a short time before been themselves guilty of just such omission. They were excessively demonstrative also. "And they sware unto the Lord with a loud voice, and with shouting, and with trumpets, and with cornets." Such demonstrations were no new thing in Israel. They had been heard before at Sinai, and elsewhere; and always with like results—more saying than doing; much promise, and little performance; great anticipation, and scant realization. But there was evident sincerity, and even reality, though mixed with much that was superficial; and God, who can discern what is of Himself, even when mingled with what is only of the flesh, rewarded them. "And all Judah rejoiced at the oath: for they had sworn with all their heart, and sought Him with their whole desire; and He was found of them: and the Lord gave them rest round about."

Asa was no respecter of persons. He spared not his own mother (or grandmother), but deposed her for her idolatry. "And also concerning Maachah the mother of Asa the king, he removed her from being queen, because she had made an idol (or, horror) in a grove: and Asa cut down her idol, and stamped it, and burnt it at the brook Kidron." It is in a man's own family circle that his faithfulness is put fairly to the test. Levi was "proved at Massah," where he "said unto his father and to his mother, I have not seen him; neither did he acknowledge his brethren, nor knew his own children" (Deut. 33 : 8, 9). Gideon too began his work for God by breaking down the altar of Baal which his father had set up. And in the apostolic church men could not serve as elders or deacons if they had not properly regulated homes. And He who was called "Faithful and True" said, when occasion required, "Who is My mother? and who are My brethren?"

"And in the six and thirtieth year of the reign of Asa, Baasha king of Israel came up against Judah, and built Ramah, to the intent that he might let none go out or come in to Asa king of Judah" (2 Chron. 16 : 1). This verse, when compared with 1 Kings 15 : 33 and 16 : 8, presents a chronological difficulty. Baasha must have been dead ten years before the thirty-sixth year of Asa's reign, according to the above references. And we cannot be always falling back, in these seeming discrepancies, on a supposed error in transcription. The only apparent way out of the difficulty is to take "the six and thirtieth year" to date from the beginning of Judah as a separate kingdom from Israel. This would make the event to occur in the sixteenth year of the actual reign of Asa, and shortly after the occurrences of the preceding chapter. Ramah was on the high road from the northern kingdom, and it would be but natural for Baasha to take immediate steps to fortify this key city on the frontier, and thus check any further secessions to Asa from his dominion.

"Then Asa brought out silver and gold out of the treasures of the house of the Lord and of the king's house, and sent to Benhadad king of Syria, that dwelt at Damascus, saying, There is a league between me and thee, as there was between my father and thy father: behold, I have sent thee silver and gold; go, break thy league with Baasha king of Israel, that he may depart from me." It is difficult to account for this sudden defect in Asa's faith. He had only recently, with God's help, completely destroyed the immerse army of Zerah the Ethiopian; now, before an enemy not half so formidable, his faith fails, and he depends for deliverance upon an arm of flesh. Had not his father Abijah, in dependence on the Lord, defeated a former army of Israel double the size of his own? It was the beginning of Asa's downfall; for though the desired deliverance was obtained (for "Benhadad harkened unto King Asa," and Baasha "left off building of Ramah, and let his work cease"), it cost him the rebuke of God and wars to the end of his reign. "And at that time Hanani the seer came to Asa king of Judah, and said unto him, Because thou hast relied on the king of Syria, and not relied on the Lord thy God, therefore is the host of the king of Syria escaped out of thy hand. Were not the Ethiopians and the Lubim a huge host, with very many chariots and horsemen? yet, because thou didst rely on the Lord, He delivered them into thy hand. For the eyes of the Lord run to and fro throughout the whole earth, to show Himself strong in the behalf of them whose heart is perfect (or sincere) toward Him. Herein thou hast done foolishly: therefore from henceforth thou shalt have wars."

"Therefore is the host of the king of Syria escaped out of thy hand." Instead of calling upon Benhadad for help, he might have been subdued by Asa, as "escaped out of thy hand" implies. David had reigned over Damascus, and only in the days of Solomon's degeneracy did Syria begin to exist as a separate and independent kingdom. (See 1 Kings 11 : 23–25.) Its first king "was an adversary to Israel all the days of Solomon: . . . and he abhorred Israel, and reigned over Syria." This continued to be the attitude of Syria toward Israel; but it was in God's heart to use Asa to destroy this heathen power, which in future days caused His people so much sorrow and distress. (See 2 Kings 8 : 11–13.) But he missed his opportunity; and when charged by Hanani with folly, he committed the seer to prison for his faithfulness. "Then Asa was wroth with the seer, and put him in a prison-house; for he was in a rage with him because of this thing. And Asa oppressed some of the people the same time"—the seer's sympathizers, probably. His petty anger (at what he knew only too well to be the truth) betrays a low condition of soul from which he never evidently recovered; and his end was humiliating as his beginning had been brilliant. "And Asa, in the thirty and ninth year of his reign, was diseased in his feet, until his disease was exceeding great: yet in his disease he sought not to the Lord, but to the physicians." In all this record, let us hear and take to ourselves the Lord's word, " He that hath an ear to hear, let him hear."

It is easily seen why the chronicler should write of his acts "*first* and *last*" (2 Chron. 16: 11). "Ye did run well: who did hinder you?" might be asked of many besides the Galatians and Asa. Important as a good beginning is, it is not all: we are called to run with *endurance* the race that is set before us. But when God's people become diseased in their feet, they cease to run well; and though they may try various expedients, such as ritualism, revivalism, the union of churches, etc., to recover themselves, they are every one of them "physicians of no value." " Restore unto me the joy of Thy salvation," wrote a notable back-slider. It is Jehovah who says through His prophet, " *I* will heal their backslidings."

There was a great funeral made over Asa, and he appears to have been sincerely lamented by his people. "And Asa slept with his fathers, and died in the one and fortieth year of his reign. And they buried him in his own sepulchres, which he had made for himself in the city of David, and laid him in the bed which was filled with sweet odors and divers kinds of spices prepared by the apothecaries' art : and they made a very great burning for him."

Asa's *history* reveals his weaknesses : God, in His comments on his character, gives no hint of them (2 Chron. 20: 32 ; 21: 12). He loves to commend whatever is lovely in His servants' lives, and only when necessary exposes their failures and follies. May we in this, as in all things else, be "imitators of God"! (Eph. 5 : 1.)

Jeremiah 41 : 9 refers to a pit (or cistern) made by Asa "for fear of Baasha king of Israel." God would thus, in this incidental way, remind us by this late and last historical notice of king Asa what was the beginning of his decline—"the fear of man, which bringeth a snare."

JEHOSHAPHAT

(He whom Jehovah judges.)

(1 Kings 15 : 24 ; 22 : 41–50 ; 2 Kings 8 : 16 ; 2 Chron.
chaps. 17 : 1 to 21 : 3.)

Contemporary Prophets:

JEHU son of Hanani;
JAHAZIEL the Levite;
ELIEZER son of Dodavah.

"Mercy and truth preserve the king : and his throne
is upholden by mercy."—*Proverbs 20 : 28.*

THE first thing recorded of Jehoshaphat is that
he "strengthened himself against Israel. And
he placed forces in all the fenced cities of Judah,
and set garrisons in the land of Judah, and in the cities of Ephraim, which Asa his father had taken"
(2 Chron. 17 : 1, 2). He began his reign with a determined opposition to the idolatrous northern kingdom. This was in the fourth year of Ahab. A few
years later all this opposition ceases, and, we read,
"Jehoshaphat made peace with the king of Israel"
(1 Kings 22 : 44). This peace was brought about, evidently, by the marriage of Jehoshaphat's son Jehoram
to Athaliah, daughter of Ahab and of the notorious
Jezebel. Alas for Jehoshaphat, and his posterity, that
he ever gave his consent to this unholy alliance, and

made peace with him "who did evil in the sight of the
Lord above all that were before him " (1 Kings 16 : 30)!
But such is man, even at his best: "wherein is he to
be accounted of ? "

But like Asa his father, he made a bright beginning : "And the Lord was with Jehoshaphat, because
he walked in the first ways of his father David" (i. e.,
before his sin in the matter of Uriah the Hittite), "and
sought not unto Baalim ; but sought to the Lord God
of his father, and walked in his commandments, and
not after the doings of Israel. Therefore the Lord
established the kingdom in his hand ; and all Judah
brought to Jehoshaphat presents ; and he had riches
and honor in abundance. And his heart was lifted up
(encouraged) in the ways of the Lord : moreover he
took away the high places and groves out of Judah"
(2 Chron. 17 : 3–6). This last statement does not contradict what is said in 1 Kings 22 : 43. The high
places and groves used for the worship of Baalim were
removed ; "nevertheless the high places (dedicated to
Jehovah) were not taken away ; for the people offered
and burned incense (to the true God) yet in the high
places." Compare 2 Chron. 20 : 33. He abolished
idolatry, but the people could not be brought to see
the unlawfulness and danger of offering sacrifices elsewhere than at Jerusalem. Deuteronomy 12 condemned
the practice ; and it was probably to instruct the people as to this and kindred matters that he inaugurated
the model itineracy described in 2 Chron. 17 : 7–9.
"Also in the third year of his reign he sent to his
princes, even to Ben-hail, and to Obadiah, and to Zechariah, and to Nethaneel, and to Michaiah, to teach in

the cities of Judah. And with them he sent Levites;
. . . and with them Elishama and Jehoram, priests.
And they taught in Judah, and had the book of the law
of the Lord with them, and went about throughout all the
cities of Judah, and taught the people." By this little
band of princes, Levites and priests, sixteen in all, Jehoshaphat did more toward impressing the surrounding nations with a sense of his power than the largest
and best-equipped standing army could have secured
to him. "And the terror of Jehovah was upon all the
kingdoms of the lands that were round about Judah,
and they made no war against Jehoshaphat. And
some of the Philistines brought Jehoshaphat gifts and
tribute-silver. The Arabians also brought him flocks,
seven thousand seven hundred rams, and seven thousand seven hundred he-goats." This was the promise
of God, through Moses, fulfilled to them. If they dili-
gently obeyed and clave to Jehovah, He would, He
said, "lay the fear of you and the dread of you upon
all the land," etc. (Deut. 11 : 22–25). When the patriarch Jacob ordered his family to put away the strange
gods that were among them, "the terror of God was
upon the cities that were round about them" (Gen.
35 : 5). And it was when the infant church at Jerusalem "continued steadfastly in the apostles' doctrine
and fellowship, and in breaking of bread, and in
prayers," that "fear came upon every soul"(Acts 2 : 42,
43). In obedience is power, and only right makes
might in the nation or church that has God for its
help.

"And Jehoshaphat waxed great exceedingly; and he
built in Judah castles, and cities of store. And he

had much business in the cities of Judah." It was an
era of great commercial prosperity, and the kingdom
was in the zenith of its power and glory. He had an
organized army of over a million men "ready prepared
for the war" (2 Chron. 17 : 12--19).

Then comes the cloud over this noonday splendor
of the king and kingdom. "And Jehoshaphat had
riches and honor in abundance; and he allied himself with Ahab by marriage. And after [certain]
years he went down "—yes, it was "down" morally,
as well as topographically, "to Ahab, to Samaria. And
Ahab killed sheep and oxen for him in abundance,
and for the people that were with him, and urged him
to go up against Ramoth-gilead. And Ahab king of
Israel said to Jehoshaphat king of Judah, Wilt thou
go with me to Ramoth-Gilead? And he said to him,
I am as thou, and my people as thy people; and I
will be with thee in the war" (2 Chron. 18 ; 2, 3. N. Tr.)
It was a sad come-down for the godly king of Judah.
Think of him saying to a wicked idolater like Ahab,
"I am as thou." And he not only puts himself down
to Ahab's base level, he must needs compromise his
people also, and say they were as Ahab's, all of whom,
excepting seven thousand men, were bowing the knee
to Baal. Such conduct and language from a man
like Jehoshaphat seems almost incredible. But "who
can understand his errors?"—his own; much more
difficult to see, often, than those of others.

Ahab evidently had fears for Jehoshaphat's scruples
of conscience, and was prepared to meet them; so
the feast prepared for him and his retinue was given a
religious character (the word for "killed" is "sacri-

ficed"). An apostate people or church will go to almost any length of seeming compromise to entice and draw the faithful into fellowship or alliance with them. What must have men like Elijah thought of all this? It is little wonder that when fleeing from the murderous wrath of Jezebel he feared to trust himself anywhere within the realm of Judah. See 1 Ki. 19: 3, 4. ("Beersheba" was on Judah's southern border.) Many would, no doubt, loudly praise the king of Judah for what they would term his large-heartedness and freedom from bigotry. The four hundred false prophets (Israel's clergy), could also quote from the Psalms, "Behold, how good and how pleasant it is for brethren to dwell together in unity!" and say how the world was growing better, and the millennium soon to come. Yes, and the cry to-day is for "union" (*unity* they know little of, and care less for), amalgamation, good fellowship; away with dogma (Scripture they mean, really), let doctrine die the death, and let twentieth century enlightenment make us ashamed of the conduct of our forefathers who fought, suffered, and died for the truth. "What is truth?" was Pilate's idle question—the answer to which he had neither heart nor conscience to care for—while before him was witnessed that good confession, declaring what men of to-day would condemn as bigotry of the most pronounced kind: "To this end was I born, and for this cause came I into the world, that I should bear witness unto the truth. *Every one that is of the truth heareth My voice*" (John 18: 37). But it is come to pass to-day that "truth is perished in the streets."

But to return to Jehoshaphat. He is not altogether at ease in his mind about this contemplated attack on Ramoth-gilead ("A fortress commanding Argob and the Jair towns, seized by Ben-hadad I. from Omri." *Josephus*, Ant. IX. 6, §1). His consent to accompany Ahab was, no doubt, hastily given, and probably during the warmth and excitement of the good fellow-ship at the banquet tendered in his honor. It is impossible not to violate a godly conscience, once we accept the fellowship of the wicked.

Now, when too late, he would inquire of Jehovah. A prophet, Micaiah, fearlessly foretells the failure of the enterprise. But he was only one against four hundred; "so the king of Israel and Jehoshaphat the king of Judah went up to Ramoth-gilead." But for God's mercy Jehoshaphat would have lost his life. Jehovah heard his cry for help, and delivered him; "and Jehoshaphat the king of Judah returned to his house in peace to Jerusalem," a humbler, a wiser, and, we trust, a grateful man.

But God has a message of rebuke for him. "And Jehu the son of Hanani the seer, went out to meet him, and said to king Jehoshaphat, Shouldest thou help the ungodly, and love them that hate the Lord? therefore is wrath upon thee from before the Lord. Nevertheless there are good things found in thee, in that thou hast taken away the groves out of the land, and hast prepared thy heart to seek God" (2 Chron. 19; 2, 3). This man's father had gone to prison for his faithfulness to Asa on a similar occasion, "not fearing the wrath of the king," like him whose laws he would see kept by king and people. The son of

Asa, unlike his father, did not persecute his reprover; but much humiliated by his late experience, it would seem, from what immediately follows we gather that he profited by the rebuke. "And Jehoshaphat dwelt at Jerusalem: and he went out again through the people from Beer-sheba to mount Ephraim, and brought them back unto the Lord God of their fathers." He "went out *again*." This implies that he had lapsed spiritually, and was now restored, repentant, and doing the "first works." The work of reformation is resumed on his recovery. Like his great progenitor David, he will, when the joy of God's salvation is restored to him, "teach transgressors His way, and sinners shall be converted unto Him."

Jehoshaphat also set judges in all the fortified cities of the land. He charged them solemnly, saying, "Take heed what ye do: for ye judge not for man, but for the Lord, who is with you in the judgment. Wherefore now let the fear of the Lord be upon you; take heed and do it: for there is no iniquity with the Lord our God, nor respect of persons, nor taking of gifts." He established in Jerusalem what was probably a court of appeals ("when they returned to Jerusalem," implies this, 2 Chron. 19: 8), composed of Levites, priests, and chiefs of the fathers of Israel. To these he also gave a wholesome charge: "Thus shall ye do in the fear of the Lord, faithfully, and with a perfect heart. And what cause soever shall come to you of your brethren that dwell in their cities, between blood and blood, between law and commandment, statutes and judgments, ye shall even warn them (i. e., enlighten, teach, see Ex. 18: 20), that they trespass not against the Lord, and so wrath come upon you, and upon your brethren : this do, and ye shall not trespass. And, behold, Amariah the chief priest is over you in all matters of the Lord ; and Zebadiah the son of Ishmael, the ruler (prince) of the house of Judah, for all the king's matters : also the Levites shall be officers before you. Deal courageously, and the Lord shall be with the good." "Matters of Jehovah" related to His word or precepts, doubtless ; "the king's matters" to the civil things ; and "controversies" which came under the jurisdiction of the crown. "The Levites were to be *shorterim*, 'officers,' lit. *scribes*, keeping written accounts ; assistants to the judges, etc." (Fausset). All this would make for righteousness, and truly, "righteousness exalteth a nation," or any other body of people.

Satan could not stand idly by and witness this without making some attempt to disturb or destroy. "It came to pass after this also, that the children of Moab, and the children of Ammon, and with them other beside the Ammonites, came against Jehoshaphat to battle" (2 Chron. 20: 1). It was he, no doubt, who moved these neighboring nations to invade the land of Judah—whatever their motive may have been, whether jealousy, envy, greed, fear, or any other of the inciting causes of war among the nations of the earth. Scouts detected the movement and reported it to Jehoshaphat. "Then there came some that told Jehoshaphat, saying, There cometh a great multitude against thee from beyond the sea, on this side Syria ; and, behold, they be in Hazezontamar, which is En-gedi." They might well exclaim,

"Behold," for En-gedi was only twenty-five miles south of Jerusalem. The allies were almost upon them; "and Jehoshaphat feared." But though so nearly taken by surprise, the startling news did not create panic among the people. They were in communion with Jehovah. The king "set himself to seek the Lord, and proclaimed a fast throughout all Judah. And Judah gathered themselves together, to ask help of the Lord: even out of all the cities of Judah they came to seek the Lord."

A great prayer-meeting was held in the temple enclosure. The king himself prayed; and a most wonderful prayer it was. "And Jehoshaphat stood in the congregation of Judah and Jerusalem, in the house of the Lord, before the new court, and said, Jehovah, God of our fathers, art not Thou God in the heavens, and rulest Thou not over all the kingdoms of the nations? And in Thy hand there is power and might, and none can withstand Thee. Hast Thou not, our God, dispossessed the inhabitants of this land before Thy people Israel, and given it forever to the seed of Abraham, Thy friend? And they have dwelt therein, and have built Thee a sanctuary therein for Thy name, saying, If evil come upon us, sword, judgment, or pestilence, or famine, and we stand before this house and before Thee—for Thy name is in this house—and cry unto Thee in our distress, then Thou wilt hear and save. And now, behold, the children of Ammon and Moab, and those of mount Seir, against whom Thou wouldst not let Israel go when they came out of the land of Egypt, (for they turned from them, and destroyed them not), behold, they reward us, in coming to cast us out of Thy possession, which Thou hast given us to possess. Our God, wilt Thou not judge them? for we have no might in the presence of this great company which cometh against us, neither know we what to do; but our eyes are upon Thee!"

If they did not know what to do, they were then certainly doing the right thing when they cast themselves on God, and their expectation was from Him. "And all Judah stood before the Lord, with their little ones, their wives, and their children." Nor did He disappoint them. "Then upon Jahaziel the son of Zechariah, the son of Benaiah, the son of Jeiel, the son of Mataniah, a Levite of the sons of Asaph, came the Spirit of the Lord in the midst of the congregation: and he said, Hearken ye, all Judah, and ye inhabitants of Jerusalem, and thou, king Jehoshaphat, Thus saith the Lord unto you, Be not afraid nor dismayed at this great multitude; for the battle is not yours but God's. To-morrow go ye down against them; behold, they come up by the cliff of Ziz; and ye shall find them at the end of the valley, before the wilderness of Jeruel. Ye shall not need to fight in this battle: set yourselves, stand ye still, and see the salvation of the Lord with you, O Judah and Jerusalem: fear not, nor be dismayed; to-morrow go out against them: for the Lord will be with you."

How these words must have cheered the distressed king and his trembling people. "And Jehoshaphat bowed his head with his face to the ground: and all Judah and the inhabitants of Jerusalem fell before the Lord, worshiping the Lord." What a sight, to see the

king and all his subjects bowed in worship before
God for His promised mercy! And the prayer-meeting becomes a praise-meeting. "And the Levites, of
the children of the Kohathites, and the children of the
Korhites, stood up to praise the Lord God of Israel
with a loud voice on high."

They rose early on the morrow, and as they went
forth to meet the foe, Jehoshaphat said to them, " Believe in the Lord your God, so shall ye be established ;
believe His prophets, so shall ye prosper." He was
not a haughty sovereign ; for he "consulted" with his
subjects. Then singers were appointed, and those
that should praise " in holy splendor," as they marched
along at the head of the army, saying, "Give thanks
to Jehovah ; for His lovingkindness endureth forever."
It is no longer prayer for deliverance, but thanksgiving for assured victory over the enemy. "And when
they began the song of triumph and praise, Jehovah
set liers-in-wait against the children of Ammon, Moab,
and mount Seir, who had come against Judah, and
they were smitten. And the children of Ammon and
Moab stood up against the inhabitants of mount Seir,
to exterminate and destroy them ; and when they had
made an end of the inhabitants of mount Seir, they
helped to destroy one another" (2 Chron. 20: 22, 23,
N. Tr.). Never was a foreign invasion so easily re-
pelled. An ambush set in some mysterious way by
the Lord caused a panic amongst the allies, and they
turned upon one another to their mutual destruction.
The deliverance came in a way altogether unexpected
by Jehoshaphat, no doubt; but faith never asks how
can, or how will, God fulfil His promise. It is enough

to know that He *has* promised; the method must be
left to Him.

"And Judah came to the mountain-watch in the
wilderness, and they looked toward the multitude, and
behold, they were dead bodies fallen to the earth, and
none had escaped. And Jehoshaphat and his people
came to plunder the spoil of them, and they found
among them in abundance, both riches with the dead
bodies, and precious things, and they stripped off for
themselves more than they could carry away; and they
were three days in plundering the spoil, it was so
much." And then, on the battlefield, they hold a
thanksgiving meeting. "And on the fourth day they
assembled themselves in the valley of Berachah, for
there they blessed Jehovah; therefore the name of that
place was called the valley of Berachah (blessing) unto
this day." "It is a broad, rich vale, watered with copious
springs, affording space for a large multitude"(Fausset).

The 48th psalm is supposed to have been sung in
the temple on their return to Jerusalem. "And they returned, all the men of Judah and Jerusalem, and Jehoshaphat at their head, to go again to Jerusalem
with joy; for Jehovah had made them to rejoice over
their enemies. And they came to Jerusalem with lutes
and harps and trumpets, to the house of Jehovah."

This miraculous deliverance of Judah had a salutary
effect on the nations about them. "And the terror of
God was on all the kingdoms of the lands, when they
had heard that Jehovah had fought against the enemies of Israel. And the realm of Jehoshaphat was
quiet; and his God gave him rest round about" (2
Chron. 20: 29, 30, N. Tr.).

Jehoshaphat's alliance with the king of Israel and the king of Edom for the invasion of Moab was probably after this. It would be unaccountable that a man of such piety and faith as he should be repeatedly betrayed into unholy confederacies did we not know what "the flesh" is—that it is no better in the saint than in the sinner, and is ever ready to betray the saint into wrongdoing unless he watches against it in the spirit of humility and self-distrust.* He almost repeats his former alliance with Ahab. It will come before us again, as we come to speak of king Jehoram, so we do not stop to dwell upon it here. These compromising entanglements appear to have been a special weakness with Jehoshaphat. He allied himself to Ahaziah, Ahab's son ("who did very wickedly"), to build ships to go to Tarshish. They were made at Ezion-Geber where Solomon had his navy built (1 Ki. 9 : 26). "And Eliezer the son of Dodavah, of Mareshah, prophesied against Jehoshaphat, saying, Because thou hast joined thyself to Ahaziah, Jehovah hath

---

* In both the Old and New Testaments, God's people are warned against these alliances of believers with unbelievers, of which Jehoshaphat's history is a sad and solemn example. God had particularly forbidden and warned Israel against idolatry and intermarriages with the nations around, knowing full well how easily their weak heart would follow in the evil ways of the nations. See Deut. 7 : 3–11 ; Exo. 20 : 4, 5, etc.

In like manner, but in a more spiritual way, are we Christians exhorted and warned against all "unequal yokes" with unbelievers. See 2 Cor. 6 : 11–18 ; 2 Tim. 2 : 20, 21 ; 1 Pet. 2 : 11, 12 ; 1 John 2 : 15–17, etc., etc.

We commend to the reader a pamphlet on this subject, "The Unequal Yoke" by C. H. M. At same publishers, price 6c. [Ed.]

broken thy works. And the ships were broken, and could not go to Tarshish" (2 Chron. 20: 37, N. Tr.). Psalm 48: 7 seems to allude to this. Thus he linked himself during his reign with three kings of the wicked house of Ahab, to his humiliation and sorrow; first with Ahab himself, and then with his sons Ahaziah and Joram, or Jehoram. No good came of any of these associations. The ships built in partnership were hardly launched before they were broken at Ezion-Geber—"*the devil's backbone*" * (1 Ki. 22 : 48). There is always something of the wiles or power of Satan in these unequal yokes. Child of God, beware of them!

Jehoshaphat reigned twenty-five years, and died at the age of sixty. His mother, Azubah, was the single Scripture namesake of Caleb's first wife (1 Chron. 2 : 18).

---

* So *Fausset*.

JEHORAM

(Exalted by Jehovah.)

(1 Kings 22 : 50 ; 2 Kings 8 : 16–24 ; 2 Chron. 21.)

"Give not thy . . . ways to that which destroyeth kings."—*Proverbs 31 : 3.*

OF the seven sons of Jehoshaphat, Jehoram was the eldest; and to him his father gave the kingdom, "because he was the first-born." It would seem, from 2 Kings 8 : 16, that he associated Jehoram with him on the throne during his lifetime. He probably foresaw and feared what was likely to occur after his death; and to avert, if possible, any such disaster, he endeavored to have the throne well secured to Jehoram before his decease. And to conciliate his remaining six sons, he "gave them great gifts of silver, and of gold, and of precious things, with fenced cities in Judah." They were not, probably, all children of one mother, as two of them bear exactly the same name—Azariah. This would make dissension among them all the more likely, and it is a warning to all to see Jehoshaphat ending his days with this threatening storm-cloud hanging over his house.

It was all the result of his ill-advised alliance with the ungodly house of Ahab, and what he sowed he, by dread anticipation at least, reaped. And his pos terity were made to reap it actually, in a most terrible way. "Now when Jehoram was risen up to the kingdom of his father, he strengthened himself, and slew all his brethren with the sword, and divers also of the princes of Israel." He had married the daughter of a "murderer" (2 Kings 6 : 32), and as a natural consequence he soon imbrued his own hands in blood. "Jehoram was thirty and two years old when he began to reign, and he reigned eight years in Jerusalem. And he walked in the ways of the kings of Israel, like as did the house of Ahab: for he had the daughter of Ahab to wife: and he wrought that which was evil in the eyes of the Lord."

Decadence of power at once set in, which the neighboring nations were not slow to perceive, and take advantage of. "In his days the Edomites revolted from under the dominion of Judah, and made themselves a king. Then Jehoram went forth with his princes, and all his chariots with him: and he rose up by night, and smote the Edomites which compassed him in, and the captains of the chariots." This happened at Zair (2 Kings 8 : 21), in Idumea, south of the Dead Sea. He barely escaped destruction, or capture, being surrounded by the enemy. He managed to extricate himself by a night surprise, but the expedition was a failure. "So the Edomites revolted from under the hand of Judah unto this day." The spirit of rebellion spread: "The same time also did Libnah revolt from under his hand; because he had forsaken the Lord God of his fathers."

His attitude toward idolatry was the exact reverse of that of his father. "He made high places in the

mountains of Judah, and caused the inhabitants of Jerusalem to commit fornication, and compelled Judah
thereto," or, "seduced Judah" (N. Tr.). He undid,
so far as lay in his power, all the good work of his
father Jehoshaphat. But how dearly he paid for his
wickedness! "And there came a writing to him from
Elijah the prophet (written prophetically before his
translation, evidently), saying, Thus saith the Lord
God of David thy father, Because thou hast not walked
in the ways of Jehoshaphat thy father, nor in the ways
of Asa king of Judah, but hast walked in the way of
the kings of Israel, and hast made Judah and the inhabitants of Jerusalem to go a whoring, like to the
whoredoms of the house of Ahab, and also hast slain
thy brethren of thy father's house, which were better
than thyself: behold, with a great plague will the Lord
smite thy people, and thy children, and thy wives, and
all thy goods: and thou shalt have great sickness by
disease of thy bowels, until thy bowels fall out by
reason of the sickness day by day."

Elijah's ministry and field of labor had been, it
would seem, exclusively among the ten tribes, the
kingdom of Israel. But the servant of God is used
here for a message to the king of Judah. And as it was
prophesied to him, so it came to pass. "The Lord
stirred up against Jehoram the spirit of the Philistines,
and of the Arabians, that were near the Ethiopians:
and they came up into Judah, and brake into it, and
carried away all the substance that was found in the
king's house, and his sons also, and his wives; so that
there was never a son left him, save Jehoahaz (called
Ahaziah, 2 Chron. 22 : 1), the youngest of his sons.

And after all this, (terrible as the stroke was) the Lord smote him in his bowels with an incurable disease. And it came to pass, that in process of time, after the end of two years, his bowels fell out by reason of his sickness: so he died of sore diseases. And his people made no burning for him, like the burning of his fathers." What a terrible recompense for his murders and idolatries! God made a signal example of him, that his successors might "see it and fear."

"Thirty and two years old was he when he began to reign, and he reigned in Jerusalem eight years, and departed without being desired [regretted]. Howbeit they buried him in the city of David, but not in the sepulchres of the kings." He is one of the most unlovely of all the kings of Judah. "Exalted by Jehohovah," he was for his wickedness thrust down to a dishonored grave. He took the kingdom when raised to its highest glory since the days of Solomon, and left it, after a reign of eight short years, with "Ichabod" (*the glory is departed*) written large upon it.

The proverb, "One sinner destroyeth much good" (Eccl. 9: 18), was sadly exemplified in this unhappy Jehoram's life. The lifetime's labor of some devoted man of God may be easily and quickly ruined, or marred, by some such "sinner." We see this illustrated in the case of Paul. After his departure, "grievous wolves" entered in among the flocks gathered by his toils and travail; also of their own selves men arose, "speaking perverse things, to draw away the disciples after them." And even before his martyrdom he wrote, weeping, of "the enemies of the cross of Christ," and was compelled to say, "All seek their

own, not the things which are Jesus Christ's."   Also,
"All they which be in Asia are turned away from me."
And one has only to compare the writings of the earliest Greek fathers (so-called) with the writings of the
apostle, to see how widespread and complete was the
departure from the truth of Christianity.   "Nevertheless [blessed word!] the foundation of God standeth
sure."   "And," the exhortation is, "let every one that
nameth the name of the Lord depart from iniquity"
(2 Tim. 2 : 19).   Oh, let not *me* be the "sinner" to
"destroy the work of God" (Rom. 14: 20).

AHAZIAH

(Sustained by Jehovah.)

(Also called, JEHOAHAZ, or AZARIAH.)

(2 Kings 8 : 24 ; 9 : 29 ; 2 Chron. 22 : 1-9.)

"For, lo, the kings were assembled, they passed by together."—*Psalm 48 : 4.*

AHAZIAH must have reigned as his father's viceroy during the last year of the latter's sickness. This is evident from a comparison of 2 Kings 8 : 25 with 9 : 29. He was the youngest and only remaining son of Jehoram (2 Chron. 21 : 17). "Two and twenty years old was Ahaziah when he began to reign." ("Forty and two" in 2 Chron. 22 : 2 is doubtless a transcriber's error. His father was only forty at his death.) "And he reigned one year in Jerusalem. And his mother's name was Athaliah, the daughter (or granddaughter) of Omri king of Israel. And he walked in the way of the house of Ahab, and did evil in the sight of the Lord, as did the house of Ahab; for he was the son-in-law of the house of Ahab." His mother, in some way or other, escaped the fate of the rest of Jehoram's wives (who were carried away captive at the time of the Philistine-Arabian invasion), and "was his counsellor to do wickedly." 2 Chron. 22 : 4 seems to give a slight hint that his father Jehoram repented during his last sufferings, and had broken away somewhat from the house of Ahab; "for they were his (Ahaziah's) counsellors after the death of his father, to his destruction." His father's death removed the check, and he at once united himself with his mother's relatives in their sins and warfare. "He walked also after their counsel, and went with Jehoram the the son of Ahab king of Israel to war against Hazael king of Syria at Ramoth-gilead."

This friendship cost him his life. "And the Syrians smote Joram (the king of Israel). And he returned to be healed in Jezreel because of the wounds which were given him in Ramah (or Ramoth), when he fought with Hazael king of Syria. And Azariah (Ahaziah) the son of Jehoram king of Judah went down to see Jehoram the son of Ahab at Jezreel, because he was sick. And the destruction of Ahaziah was of God by coming to Joram: for when he was come, he went out with Jehoram against Jehu the son of Nimshi, whom the Lord had anointed to cut off the house of Ahab." Ahaziah sees his uncle Jehoram slain in his chariot, and seeks in vain to make his escape from the hot-headed Jehu. "He fled by the way of the garden-house. And Jehu followed after him, and said, Smite him also in the chariot. And they did so at the going up to Gur, which is by Ibleam. And he fled to Megiddo, and died there. And his servants carried him in a chariot to Jerusalem, and buried him in his sepulchre with his fathers in the city of David." The account in Chronicles (we have been quoting from Kings) says, "he was hid in Samaria." There is no discrepancy here, for when he fled to the "garden-house" (Bethzan), he escaped to Samaria, where were his "brethren" and the princes of Judah.

Thence, followed by Jehu, he was pursued to the hill
Gur, and slain. Or "in Samaria" may mean simply
in the kingdom of Samaria. "And when they had
slain him, they buried him: Because, said they, he is
the son of Jehoshaphat, who sought the Lord with all
his heart." His being the grandson of Jehoshaphat
was all that saved his body from being eaten by unclean
dogs, like those of his great-aunt Jezebel and her son
Jehoram.

"So the house of Ahaziah had no power to keep
still the kingdom." And with these cheerless words
the record of the reign of Ahaziah closes. He was
the "seventh" from Solomon, and the first king of
Judah to die a violent death. His name is the first of
the royal line omitted in the genealogy of Matt. 1.
The first of the three names given him, Jehoahaz,—
"*whom Jehovah helps*,"—is markedly at variance with
his character. This may be the reason why he is
called by that name only once in Scripture (2 Chron.
21 : 19). He died at the early age of twenty-three.
It was no part of Jehu's commission to slay the king
of Judah; but he was found among those doomed to
destruction, and consequently shared their fate. And
God's call to His own, in that system of iniquity where
the spiritual Jezebel teaches and seduces His servants, is, "Come out of her, My people, that ye be not
partakers of her sins, *and that ye receive not of her
plagues*" (Rev. 18: 4). Oh that all His own might
even now lay this call to heart, and separate themselves from that which is fast shaping itself for its
ultimate apostasy and doom!

JEHOASH (or JOASH)

(Jehovah-gifted.)

(2 Kings 11, 12 ; 2 Chron. 22 : 10—24 : 27.)

Contemporary Prophet, ZECHARIAH, son of Jehoiada.

"It is He that giveth salvation unto kings : who delivereth David His servant from the hurtful sword."—
Psalm 144 : 10.

"AND when Athaliah the mother of Ahaziah saw that her son was dead, she arose and destroyed all the seed royal." Chronicles adds, " of the house of Judah" (we quote from Kings). "But Jehosheba, the daughter of king Joram, sister of Ahaziah, took Joash the son of Ahaziah, and stole him from among the king's sons which were slain; and they hid him, even him and his nurse, in the bedchamber from Athaliah, so that he was not slain."

"That wicked woman," is the character given this Athaliah by the Holy Ghost in 2 Chron. 24 : 7. She was just such a daughter as her infamous mother, "that woman Jezebel," was likely to produce. Her father was himself a murderer, and the family character was fully marked in her. She heartlessly slaughtered her own grandchildren in her lust for power. She would be *herself* ruler of the kingdom, even at the cost of the lives of helpless and innocent children. No character in history, sacred or secular, stands out blacker or more hideous than this daughter-in-law of the godly Jehoshaphat. Joash was only an infant at the time, and his mother (Zibiah of Beersheba), in all likelihood, dead—murdered, probably, by her fiendish mother-in-law. Jehosheba (*Jehovah's oath*, i. e., devoted to Him), the child's aunt, and wife of the high priest Jehoiada (*Jehovah known*), hid him, with his nurse, first in one of the palace bedchambers, and later in the temple (where she lived), among her own children, and perhaps as one of them. "And he was with them hid in the house of God six years: and Athaliah reigned over the land." It was God's mercy to the house of David, even as it had been declared at the time of the reign of Athaliah's husband Jehoram: "Howbeit the Lord would not destroy the house of David, because of the covenant that He had made with David, and as He promised to give a light to him and to his sons for ever" (2 Chron. 21 : 7).

Athaliah, no doubt, thought herself secure upon the throne of David. Six years she possessed the coveted power, and could say, "I sit a queen." She made the most of her opportunity to corrupt the kingdom with idolatry, and had a temple built to Baal. But in the seventh year her richly-merited retribution suddenly came upon her. "And in the seventh year Jehoiada sent and fetched the rulers over hundreds, with the captains and the guards, and brought them to him into the house of the Lord, and made a covenant with them, and took an oath of them in the house of the Lord, and showed them the king's son." "And they

went about in Judah, and gathered the Levites out of
all the cities of Judah, and the chief of the fathers of
Israel, and they came to Jerusalem.   And all the congregation made a covenant with the king in the house
of God.   And he (Jehoiada) said unto them, Behold,
the king's son shall reign, as the Lord hath said of the
sons of David."   Arrangements were then entered into
for the most unique coronation that was ever known.
Everything was ordered with great care and secrecy,
that suspicion should not be aroused.   Trusted men,
chiefly Levites, were stationed at important points
about the king's house and temple.   The sabbath day,
and the time for the changing of the courses of the
priests and Levites, may have been chosen so that the
unusually large number of people about the temple
would not excite suspicion in the minds of Athaliah
and her Baalite minions.   The Levites carefully guard-
ed the royal child, "every man with his weapons in
his hand," with strict orders to slay any one that
should attempt to approach him.   "And to the captains over hundreds did the priest give king David's
spears and shields, that were in the temple of the
Lord," and a strong guard was placed within the temple enclosure.   "Then they brought out the king's son,
and put upon him the crown, and gave him the testimony (a copy of the law, Deut. 17 : 18), and made him
king.   And Jehoiada and his sons anointed him, and
said, God save the king!"   It is a thrilling tale, and
nowhere given so well as in our time-honored Authorized Version.

"Now when Athaliah heard the noise of the people
running and praising the king, she came to the people

into the house of the Lord: and she looked, and, behold, the king stood at (or, on) his pillar (stage, or scaffold—*Gesenius*) at the entering in, and the princes and the trumpeters by the king: and all the people of the land rejoiced, and sounded with trumpets, also the singers with instruments of music, and such as taught to sing praise. Then Athaliah rent her clothes, and said, Treason! Treason!" "But Jehoiada the priest commanded the captains of the hundreds, the officers of the host, and said unto them, Have her forth of the ranges: and him that followeth her kill with the sword. For the priest had said, Let her not be slain in the house of the Lord. And they laid hands on her; and she went by the way by which the horses came into the king's house: and there she was slain. And Jehoiada made a covenant between the Lord and the king and the people, that they should be the Lord's people; between the king also and the people. And all the people of the land went into the house of Baal, and brake it down; his altars and his images brake they in pieces thorough-ly, and slew Mattan the priest of Baal before the altars. And the priest appointed officers over the house of the Lord. And he took the rulers over hundreds, and the captains, and the guard, and all the people of the land; and they brought down the king from the house of the Lord, and came by the way of the gate of the guard to the king's house. And he sat on the throne of the kings. And all the people of the land rejoiced, and the city was in quiet: and they slew Athaliah with the sword beside the king's house" (2 Kings 11).

Jehoiada and his wife had engaged in this danger-
ous business in faith, as is manifest by the words of
Jehoiada, "Behold the king's son shall reign, as the
Lord hath said of the sons of David." "The Lord
hath said" is quite enough for faith to move on or to
act whatever be the dangers, the difficulties and the
toils. And in that path all the wheels of Providence are
made to turn to bring about the successful end. God
gives the needful wisdom in it too, and so every step
and arrangement of this faithful man succeeds perfectly, all proving that whatever be the cunning and
craft of the devil in Athaliah, it must succumb to the
wisdom of God and of faith. The cause was of God ;
Joash was the only and rightful heir to the throne of
David, which by the promise of God was not to be
without an heir till that Heir should come who would
be "the sure mercies of David " and would need no
successor.

"Joash was seven years old when he began to
reign, and he reigned forty years in Jerusalem. His
mother's name also was Zibiah (*doe*, or *gazelle*) of
Beersheba. And Joash did that which was right in
the sight of the Lord all the days of Jehoiada the
priest. And Jehoiada took for him two wives; and
he begat sons and daughters." His uncle appears
to have exercised a wholesome influence over him.
The noting of his taking two wives for him is doubtless to manifest his godly concern for the succession
mentioned above.

"And it came to pass after this, that Joash was
minded to repair the house of the Lord. And he
gathered together the priests and Levites, and said

to them, Go out into the cities of Judah, and gather
of all Israel money to repair the house of your God
from year to year, and see that ye hasten the matter.
Howbeit the Levites hastened it not." Nothing was
done at the time. The spiritual condition of the
people made it difficult to accomplish anything.
"The people still sacrificed and burnt incense in
the high places," and would therefore feel little responsibility toward the temple at Jerusalem. The
lines in Pope's pantheistic "Universal Prayer,"

> "To Thee whose temple is all space,
>   Whose altar, earth, sea, skies!

would, no doubt, express pretty accurately their
thoughts in the matter. What little was contributed
was, it would seem, misappropriated towards the
maintainance of the priests and Levites. (See 2 Ki.
12; 7, 8, N. Tr.) This neglect continued until the
twenty.third year of Joash. Then "the king called
for Jehoiada the chief, and said unto him, Why hast
thou not required of the Levites to bring in, out of
Judah and out of Jerusalem, the collection, according
to the commandment of Moses the servant of the
Lord, and of the congregation of Israel, for the
tabernacle of witness?" (He had not neglected to
read the "testimony" delivered to him at his coronation, evidently). "For the sons of Athaliah, that
wicked woman, had broken up (devastated, N. Tr.)
the house of God; and also all the dedicated things
of the house of the Lord did they bestow upon
Baalim." True to what he had learned in the word
of God, he did not hesitate to admonish even the

high priest if he was negligent in carrying it out, for that Word is above all. And though he owed to his uncle a lasting debt of gratitude for the preservation of his infant life, he could, when occasion required, make request of him that he, as God's high priest, perform his duty in reference to the necessary repairs of that house over which he had been set by God. Would God he had continued in such a mind to the end of his reign.

"And at the king's commandment they made a chest, and set it without at the gate of the house of the Lord. And they made a proclamation through Judah and Jerusalem, to bring in to the Lord the collection that Moses the servant of God laid upon Israel in the wilderness." (See Ex. 30: 11–16.) "And all the princes and all the people rejoiced, and brought in, and cast into the chest, until they had made an end." It commended itself to the people's conscience, as what is of God usualy does, and they gave as the Lord loves to see His people give—cheerfully. "Now it came to pass, that at what time the chest was brought unto the king's office by the hand of the Levites, and when they saw that there was much money, the king's scribe and the high priest's officer came and emptied the chest, and took it, and carried it to his place again. Thus they did day by day, and gathered money in abundance. And the king and Jehoiada gave it to such as did the work of the service of the house of the Lord, and hired masons and carpenters to repair the house of the Lord, and also such as wrought iron and brass to mend the house of the Lord. So the workmen wrought, and the work was perfected by them, and they set the house of God in his state, and strengthened it." No exacting accounts were kept; there was no suspicion of dishonesty, or misappropriation; the most beautiful confidence prevailed, evidencing the work of God. When it is the work of God, the *heart* is engaged; selfish ends are absent; there is one common object; all this produces confidence: "Moreover they reckoned not with the men, in whose hand they delivered the money to be bestowed on the workmen: for they dealt faithfully."

More than sufficient was bestowed by the willing-hearted people, "And when they had finished it, they brought the rest of the money before the king and Jehoiada, whereof were made vessels for the house of the Lord, even vessels to minister, and to offer withal, and spoons, and vessels of gold and silver." Nor were the priests left unprovided for. "The money of trespass-offerings and the money of sin-offerings was not brought into the house of Jehovah; it was for the priests" (2 Ki. 12 : 16, N. Tr.)

"And they offered burnt-offerings in the house of the Lord continually all the days of Jehoiada. But Jehoiada waxed old, and was full of days when he died; a hundred and thirty years old was he when he died. And they buried him in the city of David among the kings (as well they might), because he had done good in Israel, both toward God, and toward His house." He had remembered the claims of the Holy One of Israel, and attended to them with vigor and fidelity. Nor could it be other than the energy of *faith* in a man nearly a hundred years old setting himself to overthrow such an enemy of God as Athaliah.

His extreme old age may account for his evident laxity in performing the king's command in regard to the repairing of the temple. He was born before the death of Solomon, and had seen much during his long life that peculiarly qualified him to become the protector and early guide of Jehoash. By him the kingdom was reestablished, and the cause of Jehovah revived during his last days on earth. He was a true king, in heart and mind, and it was meet that the aged patriarch's mitered head should be laid to rest among those who had worn the crown.

How long he had filled the office of high priest is not known. He succeeded Amariah, who was high priest under Jehoshaphat. What a contrast between him and those other two high priests, Annas and Caiaphas, of whom we read in the New Testament. He labored to maintain the succession; they labored to destroy the final Heir—"great David's greater Son." And when the time of rewards comes, what will be the unspeakable differences!

But now a cloud begins to appear that dims the brightness of the reign of Joash, and culminates in treachery and murder. "Now after the death of Jehoiada came the princes of Judah, and made obeisance to the king. Then the king harkened unto them. And they left the house of the Lord God of their fathers, and served groves and idols: and wrath came upon Judah and Jerusalem for this their trespass. Yet He sent prophets to them, to bring them again unto the Lord; and they testified against them: but

they would not give ear." The revival during Joash's
early reign had already lost its hold; it could not have
been of much depth when they could so quickly turn
aside to idols after Jehoiada's departure. But the
spirit of the good high priest was not dead; his worthy son Zechariah withstood and condemned their
backslidings. "And the Spirit of God came upon
Zechariah the son of Jehoiada the priest, which stood
above the people, and said unto them, Thus saith God,
Why transgress ye the commandments of the Lord,
that ye cannot prosper? because ye have forsaken the
Lord, He hath also forsaken you. And they conspired
against him, and stoned him with stones at the commandment of the king, in the court of the house of the
Lord." "At the commandment of the king"! Alas
for Joash's unfaithfulness to God, and base ingratitude
to the man who had been to him so great a benefactor! Zechariah was his cousin, and his foster-brother
too! "Thus Joash the king remembered not the kindness which Jehoiada his father had done to him, but
slew his son. And when he died, he said, The Lord
look upon it, and require it." This is, in all probability, the "Zacharias" referred to by our Lord, "whom ye
slew," He says, "between the temple and the altar."
He was the last *historical* Old Testament martyr, as
Abel had been the first. The prophet Urijah was
slain almost two hundred and fifty years after Zechariah, but it is not recorded in the historical canon of
Scripture; it is only mentioned incidentally in the
prophecy of Jeremiah (chap. 26 : 23). "Son of Barachias" (Matt. 23 : 35) presents no real difficulty. It may
have been a second name for Jehoiada (and would be a

very appropriate one too : "Barachias "—*blessed*); or, Barachias may have been one of Zechariah's earlier ancestors, as "son of" frequently means in Scripture. Luke, chap. 11 : 51, does not have "son of Barachias." But one of the first of the above explanations is preferable.* Anyway, he met his death at the hand of the very man for whom his mother and his father risked their lives. Other sons of Jehoiada were also slain by Joash (2 Chron. 24 : 25). "The Lord look upon it, and require it," the dying martyr said. Stephen, also stoned for his testimony, cried, when dying, "Lord, lay not this sin to their charge." Law, under which " every transgression and disobedience received a just recompense of reward," was the governing principle of the dispensation under which the martyr Zechariah died ; grace reigned in Stephen's day (as still in ours); therefore the difference in the dying martyrs' prayers. Both, though so unlike, were in perfect keeping with the dispensations under which they witnessed.

---

* But see Num. Bible (Matthew), page 219. "There seems no good reason for supposing any other than Zechariah the prophet to be meant, though Zechariah the son of Jehoiada is generally taken to be. But this leaves the 'son of Barachias' to be accounted for, when the 'son of Jehoiada' also would have better reminded them of the history. It seems also too far back (in Joash's time) for the purpose, when summing up the guilt of the people."

"As to Zechariah the prophet, he was the son of Berachiah, and grandson of Iddo ; and 'the Jewish Targum states that Zechariah the son of Iddo, a prophet and priest, was slain in the sanctuary.' "—See "The Irrationalism of Infidelity," by J. N. Darby, pp. 150–159.—[*Ed.*

"The Lord require it." And He did, and that right
speedily—for He does not disregard the dying prayers
of men like Zechariah. "And it came to pass at the
end of the year, that the host of Syria came up against
him: and they came to Judah and Jerusalem, and destroyed all the princes of the people from among the
people" (they were judged first for having been chiefly
guilty in persuading the king to forsake Jehovah,) "and
sent all the spoil of them unto the king of Damascus.
For the army of the Syrians came with a small company of men, and the Lord delivered a very great host
into their hand, because they had forsaken the Lord
God of their fathers. So they executed judgment
against Joash. And when they were departed from
him (for they left him in great diseases), his own servants conspired against him for the blood of the sons
of Jehoiada the priest, and slew him on his bed, and
he died: and they buried him in the city of David,
but they buried him not in the sepulchres of the
kings." 2 Kings 12 : 17, 18 records a previous invasion of Syrians under Hazael, when Joash bought him
off with gold and other treasures taken from the temple and the king's palace. It was then that they discovered the real weakness of the army of Joash (spite
of its being "a very great host"); hence only "a small
company of men" was sent out on the second expedition against him. "There is no king saved by the
multitude of a host," wrote that king (Ps. 33 : 16)
whose throne Joash so unworthily filled. And his
time to receive the due reward of his deeds was come,
and there was no power on earth that could have saved
him. The murdered Zechariah's name (*Jah hath re-*

membered) must have had a terrible significance to
him as he lay in " great diseases " on his bed in the
house of Millo, the citadel of Zion. And if he escaped
death at the hands of the Syrians by taking refuge in
the stronghold at the descent of Silla (2 Kings 12 : 20,
N. Tr.), it was only to be treacherously assassinated
by his servants, both of them sons of Gentile women
(2 Chron. 24 : 26), fruit of mixed marriages, condemned by the law. So disobedience brings its own
bitter reward, and what God's people sow they always,
in some way or other, reap. Joash abundantly deserved his inglorious and terrible end. It can be ever
said, when the judgments of God are seen to come
upon such as he, " Thou art righteous, O Lord, which
art, and wast, and shalt be, because Thou hast judged
thus. For they have shed the blood of saints and
prophets, and Thou hast given them blood to drink;
for they are worthy " (Rev. 16 : 5, 6).

AMAZIAH

(Strength of Jah.)

(2 Kings 14 : 1–20 ; 2 Chron. 25.)

Contemporary Prophets:
Several unnamed (two in 2 Chron. 25).

———

"A king ready to the battle."—*Job 15 : 24.*

———

"AMAZIAH was twenty and five years old when he began to reign, and he reigned twenty and nine years in Jerusalem. And his mother's name was Jehoaddan (*Jehovah-pleased*) of Jerusalem." He evidently reigned a year jointly with his father (comp. 2 Kings 13 : 10; 14 : 1 ; 2 Chron. 24 : 1) during the latter's last sickness, when the "great diseases" were upon him.

"And he did that which was right in the sight of the Lord, but not with a perfect heart." "Yet not like David his father," it is said ; "he did according to all things as Joash his father did." Just like this is the lack of heart-devotedness in the children of God. He allowed the "high places" to remain, and the people sacrificed and burned incense upon them.

"Now it came to pass, when the kingdom was established to him, that he slew his servants that had killed the king his father. But he slew not their chil-

dren, but did as it is written in the law, in the book of
Moses, where the Lord commanded, saying, The fathers shall not die for the children, neither shall the
children die for the fathers, but every man shall die
for his own sin." (See Deut. 24 : 16.) He made a good
beginning in thus adhering closely to the law. Happy
would it have been for him and for his kingdom had
he continued as he began. "As soon as the kingdom
was confirmed in his hand" appears to imply that the
state affairs were somewhat unsettled at his father's
death. What follows confirms this thought. "Moreover Amaziah gathered Judah together, and made
them captains over thousands, and captains over hundreds, according to the houses of their fathers, throughout all Judah and Benjamin." He began to reorgan-
ize the scattered army. "And he numbered them
from twenty years old and above, and found them three
hundred thousand choice men, able to go forth to war,
that could handle spear and shield."

An expedition against Edom was probably in his
mind in this organization of his forces. And trusting
more to "the multitude of a host" than to the Lord,
"he hired also a hundred thousand mighty men of valor
out of Israel for a hundred talents of silver." But God
does not want mercenaries in His battles—neither then,
nor now. So "there came a man of God to him, saying, O king, let not the army of Israel go with thee; for
the Lord is not with Israel, to wit, with all the children
of Ephraim. But if thou wilt go (i. e., with them), do it,
be strong for the battle : God shall make thee fall before the enemy : for," he adds, "God hath power to
help, and to cast down." He may retain them if he

wishes, but he has the consequences set before him.
God knew the corrupting influence this body of
Ephraimites would have upon the army of Judah.
" Shouldest thou help the ungodly ? " the prophet Jehu
asked Jehoshaphat. Here Amaziah reverses the order, and would have the ungodly help him. And, besides, " the children of Ephraim " were not particularly
famous for their courage. " The children of Ephraim,
being armed, and carrying bows, turned back in the
day of battle," was the inglorious record back of them
(Ps. 78 : 9). But Amaziah thinks of the advance
wages already paid to these hireling warriors : " But
what shall we do for the hundred talents which I have
given to the army (lit., troop, or band,) of Israel?
And the man of God answered, The Lord is able to
give thee much more than this." It is a fine word for
any child of God who may find himself in a position
compromising the truth, and who cannot see his way
out without serious pecuniary loss. " The Lord is
able to give thee much more than this "; and if He
does not more than make it up in temporal things, He
will repay it in what is infinitely better—in those spiritual things, which are eternal. And " to obey is better
than sacrifice," anyway and *always*.

Amaziah profited by the word, and separated the
mercenaries, and sent them home again. " Wherefore their anger was greatly kindled against Judah,
and they returned home in great (lit., fierce) anger."
This refusal of their assistance only makes manifest
their real character. They had long ago turned away
from Jehovah; what did they care now for His honor
or the good of Judah ? So they avenge their supposed

insult by falling upon defenceless cities on Judah's northern frontier; they plunder them, and slay mercilessly
three thousand of their own flesh and blood! Such
could not help in God's army then; neither can men
with selfish motives be helps in Christ's cause now.

"And Amaziah strengthened himself, and led forth
his people, and went to the valley of salt (south of the
Dead Sea), and smote of the children of Seir ten thousand. And other ten thousand left alive did the children of Judah carry away captive, and brought them
unto the top of the rock, and cast them down from
the top of the rock, that they all were broken in
pieces."

This seemingly cruel treatment of conquered enemies is related without comment. We know nothing of the attendant circumstances, nor the cause of
Judah's invasion. They lived in the cold, hard age of
law ("eye for eye, tooth for tooth, nail for nail"), and
we must not measure their conduct by the standard we
have received from Him who came "not to destroy
men's lives, but to save them." A hundred years ago
men were hung in enlightened "Christian" England
for stealing sheep. Voltaire seems never to have condemned the English for it. Yet what government, for
a like offence, would take a human life to-day? Amaziah's army may have believed themselves justified in
meting out such horrible punishment to the Edomites.
But we neither judge nor excuse them for their terrible
act. God has left it without comment. It was not
God's act, but Amaziah's. He "took Selah (Petra,
the rock, Edom's capital) by war." ("It lay in a hollow,
enclosed amidst cliffs, and accessible only by a ravine

through which the river winds across its site."—*Fausset*), "and called the name of it Joktheel (*the reward of
God*) unto this day." He seems to have looked upon
this captured city as God's repayment for the one hundred silver talents lost upon the worthless Ephraimites. And does not God ever repay His obedient people with abundant increase?

But success with Amaziah (as with most of us) puffs
him up. Inflated with his subjugation of the Edomites, he impudently challenged the king of Israel to
meet him in combat, saying, "Come, let us look one
another in the face." The offended Ephraimites had
indeed wantonly wronged some of his subjects; yet for
this the king of Israel was less responsible than Amaziah himself, who had hired them to enter his army.
He "took advice," we read, in doing this. Like his
father Joash, he was led into disaster by "the counsel
of the ungodly." But it was of God, for the punishment of his idolatry. For, before this, when "Amaziah was come from the slaughter of the Edomites,"
we read that "he brought the gods of the children of
Seir, and set them up to be his gods, and bowed down
himself before them, and burned incense unto them.
Wherefore the anger of the Lord was kindled against
Amaziah, and he sent unto him a prophet, which said
unto him, Why hast thou sought after the gods of the
people, which could not deliver their own people out
of thy hand?" A child might understand such rea-
soning. "And it came to pass, as he talked with him,
that the king said unto him, Art thou made of the
king's counsel? forbear; why shouldest thou be smitten? Then the prophet forbare, and said, I know

that God hath determined to destroy thee, because
thou hast done this, and hast not harkened unto my
counsel." So God let him take other counsel (since
he refused His own), that led to his ruin.

To Amaziah's rash challenge the king of Israel
makes a scornful reply by the language of a parable.
He says: "The *thistle* that was in Lebanon (Amaziah)
sent to the *cedar* that was in Lebanon (himself, Joash),
saying, Give thy daughter to my son to wife: and
there passed by a wild beast that was in Lebanon (Joash's army), and trode down the thistle." And he
adds, "Thou sayest [to thyself], Lo, thou hast smitten
the Edomites—and thy heart lifteth thee up to boast.
Abide now at home; why shouldest thou meddle to
thy hurt, that thou shouldest fall, even thou, and Judah with thee?" Good, sound advice, this. "But
Amaziah would not hear; for it came of God, that He
might deliver them into the hand of their enemies, because they sought after the gods of Edom. So Joash
the king of Israel went up; and they saw one another
in the face, both he and Amaziah king of Judah, at
Beth-shemesh, which belongeth to Judah. And Judah
was put to the worse before Israel, and they fled every
man to his tent. And Joash the king of Israel took
Amaziah king of Judah, the son of Joash, the son of
Jehoahaz, at Beth-shemesh, and brought him to Jerusalem, and brake down the wall of Jerusalem from the
gate of Ephraim to the corner gate, four hundred cu-
bits." This is the first time the walls of Jerusalem
had ever been injured. It was on the north—the only
side from which the city is easily accessible. Josephus
(IX., 9, § 9) states that Joash gained entrance into the

city by threatening to kill their captive king if the inhabitants refused to open the gates. The victorious
Joash now took all the gold and silver, and the holy
vessels, and all the treasures that were found in the
temple and the king's house; he took hostages also,
and returned to Samaria.

Amaziah lived more than fifteen years after his humiliating defeat and capture by the king of Israel.
He died by violence, like his father and grandfather
before him. "Now after the time that Amaziah did
turn away from following the Lord they made a conspiracy against him in Jerusalem; and he fled to Lachish: but they sent to Lachish after him, and slew him
there. And they brought him upon horses, and buried
him with his fathers in the city of Judah," or of David.
His "turning away from following the Lord" was
probably his final and complete apostasy from Jehovah God of Israel; not when he first bowed down to
the gods of Seir, which was the beginning of his downward course. Lachish was the first of the cities of
Judah to adopt the idolatries of the kingdom of Israel
("the beginning of the sin to the daughter of Zion:
for the transgressions of Israel were found in thee,"
Micah 1 : 13), and it was natural for the idolatrous
Amaziah to seek an asylum there. They brought his
body back to Jerusalem on horses, as they would a
beast. (Contrast Acts 7 : 16.) His name means
"strength of Jah"; but we read, "he strengthened
himself" (2 Chron. 25 : 11); his character of self-suffi-
ciency thus belying his name—a thing not uncommon
in our day, *especially among a people called " Christians.*"

He was assassinated at the age of fifty-four. His mother's name, "Jehovah-pleased," would indicate that she was a woman of piety; and it may be that it was due to her influence that he acted righteously during the earlier portion of his reign. The record of his reign has the same sad monotony of so many of the kings of Judah at this period—"his acts first and last"—the first, full of promise; and the last, declension, or apostasy. "Wherefore let him that thinketh *he* standeth take heed lest *he* fall."

UZZIAH

(*Strength of Jehovah.*)

(2 Kings 15 : 1–7 ; 2 Chron. 26.)

Contemporary Prophets:
ZECHARIAH, of 2 Chron. 26 : 5;
ISAIAH ; HOSEA ; AMOS.

"He (the Lord) shall cut off the spirit of princes : He
is terrible to the kings of the earth."—*Psalm 76 : 12.*

"THEN all the people of Judah took Uzziah, who
was sixteen years old, and made him king in
the room of his father Amaziah. He built
Eloth, and restored it to Judah, after that the king
slept with his fathers." He is called Azariah (*helped
by Jehovah*) elsewhere: the names were so nearly
equivalent in meaning as to be applied interchange-
ably to him. He seems to have come by the throne,
not in the way of ordinary succession, but by the direct
choice of the people. The princes had been destroyed
by the Syrians toward the close of his grandfather Joash's reign (2 Chron. 24 : 23), leaving the people a
free hand. "For the transgression of a land many
are the princes thereof," wrote Solomon, more than a
century before; and this weeding out was not altogether to be regretted: perhaps, nor entirely unnecessary. If the princes selfishly "seek their own" things,

they are incapable of judging aright; whilst a needy, suffering people instinctively turn to a deliverer. Their choice here of Azariah was a good one, as the sequel proved. His first recorded work, the building, enlargement, or fortification of Eloth (Elath), and its restoration to the crown of Judah, was an early pledge of the great industrial prosperity of his reign. It belonged to Edom, and was lost to Judah during the reign of Joram (2 Kings 8 : 20). It was a seaport on the Red Sea, near Ezion-geber (1 Kings 9 : 26), and must have made a most important mart for the extensive commerce in his administration. It was taken by Rezin king of Syria fifty years later, who expelled the Jews, and occupied it permanently. (See 2 Kings 16 : 6.)

"Sixteen years old was Uzziah when he began to reign, and he reigned fifty and two years in Jerusalem. His mother's name also was Jecoliah of Jerusalem." His was the longest *continuous* reign (Manasseh's, fifty-five years, was interrupted by his deposition and captivity by the king of Babylon) of any of the kings of Judah. His mother's name, *Jah will enable*, might indicate that she had pious expectations of her son, by the help of God. And in this she would not be disappointed, for " he," it is said, " did that which was right in the sight of the Lord, according to all that his father Amaziah did "; that is, during the earlier portion of his reign. "And he sought God in the days of Zechariah, who had understanding in the visions of God (in the seeing of God, marg.): and as long as he sought the Lord, God made him to prosper." "Understanding in the visions of God " is not equivalent to having prophetical visions from God. LXX., Syr.,

Targ. Arab., Kimchi, etc., read, "who was (his) in-
structor in the fear of God," which is probably the
general sense of the expression. Nothing more is
known of this prophet, but his record is on high; and
the coming "day" will declare what else, whether of
good or bad, was accomplished by him during his
earthly life. So shall it also, reader, in the case of
you and me.

From city building for the peaceful purpose of commerce, Uzziah turns to retributive warfare. "And he
went forth and warred against the Philistines, and
brake down the wall of Gath, and the wall of Jabneh,
and the wall of Ashdod, and built cities about (or, in
the country of) Ashdod. And God helped him against
the Philistines, and against the Arabians that dwelt in
Gur-baal, and the Mehunim." Thus he avenged the
Philistine invasion during the reign of Jehoram
(2 Chron. 21 : 16, 17), and punished their allies. It
says, "The *Lord* stirred up against Jehoram the spirit
of the Philistines, and of the Arabians," etc. This
did not excuse them for their wrong-doing. "*God*
helped Uzziah against the Philistines, and against the
Arabians." They were the unconscious instruments
used by God in the chastening of His people. Their
motive was entirely of another kind, and after eighty
years God metes out to them the punishment their
attack on the land of Judah deserved. This is an important principle which must be borne in mind in any
study of God's ways in government, with either men or
nations. (See Isa. 10 : 5–19.)

"And the Ammonites gave gifts to Uzziah : and his
name was spread abroad even to the entering in of

Egypt; for he strengthened himself exceedingly." He "built towers" in Jerusalem, and fortified them. He also "built towers in the desert" ("the steppe-lands west of the Dead Sea "), and cut out many cisterns; "for he had much cattle, both in the low country " (literally, "the Shepheleh," the low hills between the mountains and the Mediterranean), "and in the plains " (east of the Dead Sea). His wealth seems to have been chiefly in stock and agriculture. He had "husbandmen also, and vinedressers in the mountains, and in Carmel: for he loved husbandry." He was an earnest and successful agriculturist. He probably gave special attention to the tillage of the soil because of the prophecies of Hosea and Amos (his contemporaries) concerning the scarcity about to come. (See Hosea 2: 9; 4: 3; 9: 2; Amos 1: 2; 4: 6–9; 5: 16–19.)

He also gave attention to military matters, and thoroughly organized his army, "that made war with mighty power, to help the king against the enemy." He saw too that his army was thoroughly equipped, as we read: "And Uzziah prepared for them throughout the host shields, and spears, and helmets, and coats of mail, and bows, and even slinging-stones. And he made in Jerusalem machines invented by skilful men, to be upon the towers and upon the bulwarks, wherewith to shoot arrows and great stones.* And his name spread far abroad; for he was marvelously helped, till he became strong." (N. Tr.)   But alas,

---

* In these details, by which Uzziah's kingdom was strengthened and his people blessed and enlarged, God would call *our* attention, surely, to what will strengthen and bless His people *now :* first, the precious and abundant food of the land we

what is man! After all this well-doing, Uzziah's heart
is lifted up with pride. Then came his act of sacrilege—the dark blot upon the record of this otherwise
blameless man's life. "But"—alas, those "buts" in
so many life-records of God's saints!—"when he was
strong, his heart was lifted up to his destruction: for
he transgressed against the Lord his God, and went
into the temple of the Lord to burn incense upon the
altar of incense"—explicitly forbidden by the law.
(See Ex. 30 : 7, 8; Num. 16 : 40; 18 : 7.) "And Azariah the priest went in after him, and with him fourscore priests of the Lord, that were valiant men: and
they withstood Uzziah the king, and said unto him,
It appertaineth not unto thee, Uzziah, to burn incense
unto the Lord, but to the priests the sons of Aaron,
that are consecrated to burn incense: go out of the
sanctuary; for thou hast trespassed; neither shall it
be for thine honor from the Lord God. Then Uzziah
was wroth, and had a censer in his hand to burn incense: and while he was wroth with the priests, the
leprosy even rose up in his forehead before the priests
in the house of the Lord, from beside the incense altar.
And Azariah the chief priest, and all the priests, looked
upon him, and, behold, he was leprous in his forehead,
and they thrust him out from thence; yea, himself
hasted also to go out, because the Lord had smitten
him. And Uzziah the king was a leper unto the day

occupy—the precious fruits of His grace appropriated through
patient cultivation on our part, by which our souls are richly
fed and strengthened; then, that watchful care against inroads
of the enemy—uniting and strengthening God's people against
the assaults and wiles of Satan.—[Ed.

of his death, and dwelt in a several [separate] house, being a leper; for he was cut off from the house of the Lord." It was a fearful stroke from God. Death was the actual penalty enjoined by the law for his crime (Num. 18 : 7), and leprosy was really that—a living death, prolonged and intensified. "Let her not be *as one dead*, of whom the flesh is half consumed," was said of Miriam, who was smitten with a like judgment, and for a similar offence. God is holy, and must vindicate His word against every transgressor. He is no respecter of persons, and brings to light, sooner or later, every man's work and purposes of heart—not excepting His best servants. (See Num. 12 : 10–12; 1 Tim. 5 : 24, 25.)

The actuating motive in this audacious act of king Uzziah's is not made known. It has been suggested that he wished, like the Egyptian kings, to combine in himself both the office of king and high priest, so arrogating to himself the religious as well as the civil power. But whatever the immediate impelling motive, we know the primary *cause* of his profane deed. It was *pride*, the really "original sin," that hideous parent-sin of all succeeding sins, whether among angels, or among men (1 Tim. 3 : 6; Ezek. 28 : 2, 17). "He was marvelously helped till he was strong. But *when he was strong*, his heart was lifted up to his destruction." "Strength of Jehovah" was the meaning of his name; and happy would it have been for him had he realized that only in *His* strength is any really strong. "My strength," says He who is "the Almighty" (Rev. 1 : 8), "is made perfect in weakness." "When I am weak, then am I strong," wrote one who knew his own utter powerlessness and his Lord's sufficient strength. "Be strong *in the Lord*," he cautions his fellow-weaklings. Uzziah prospered; and because of his prosperity, his foolish heart was lifted up with pride: and in him was fulfilled his great ancestor's proverb, "The prosperity of fools shall destroy them": and another—"Pride goeth before destruction, and a haughty spirit before a fall" (Prov. 1: 32; 16: 18).

"Now the rest of the acts of Uzziah, first and last, did Isaiah the prophet, the son of Amoz, write. So Uzziah slept with his fathers, and they buried him with his fathers in the field of the burial which belonged to the kings; for they said, He is a leper: and Jotham his son reigned in his stead." They would not lay his leprous body in their "Westminster Abbey," but buried him in a field (in earth, perhaps) adjoining the sepulchres of their kings. He died about the time of the founding of Rome. It was "in the year that king Uzziah died" that Isaiah entered upon his full prophetic ministry. The moral condition of the nation during the close of Uzziah's reign is revealed in the first five chapters of his prophecy. He was also the historiographer of his reign. It is not known in just what year of Uzziah's reign he was smitten with leprosy. Nor is it certain just when the great earthquake occurred (Amos 1: 1; Zech. 14: 5). From Amos 1: 1, compared with other scripture chronological references, it is quite certain that it was not later than seventeen years after Uzziah's accession to the throne, and not when he was smitten with leprosy, as Josephus mistakenly affirms.

JOTHAM

(Jehovah–perfect.)

(2 Kings 15 : 32–38 ; 2 Chron. 27 : 1–4.)

Contemporary Prophets: ISAIAH; MICAH; HOSEA.

"Mercy and truth preserve the king : and his throne is upholden by mercy."—*Proverbs 20 : 28.*

"JOTHAM was twenty and five years old when he began to reign, and he reigned sixteen years in Jerusalem. His mother's name also was Jerushah, the daughter of Zadok." Jotham was regent over the kingdom after the judgment of God had fallen upon his father. "And Jotham his son was over the king's house, judging the people of the land" (2 Chron. 26 : 21). This would indicate that Uzziah was guilty of his impious trespass in the very latter part of his long reign, as Jotham was only a young man of twenty-five at his father's death, and he could not have been judging the people of the land many years before this. His mother's name, Jerushah (*possessed*), daughter of Zadok (*just*), would seem to imply that she was really the Lord's, and just before Him. She, like every true mother, would have considerable influence over her son, in the formation of his character. So we read, "And he did that which was right in the sight of the Lord, according to all that his father Uzziah did : *how. beit he entered not into the temple of the Lord.*" He

avoided the folly of his headstrong father, and did not
"rush in where angels fear to tread."

"And the people did yet corruptly." The prophecies of Isaiah and Micah contain much detail of the
manner of their wickedness, which was indeed great.
It probably increased rapidly toward the close of Uzziah's reign, though from the beginning of his rule
"the high places were not taken away: as yet the people did sacrifice and burnt incense on the high places"
(2 Kings 14 : 4). True, the sacrifices and incense were
offered to Jehovah; but Jerusalem, Scripture said, was
"the place where men ought to worship"; and this
departure, though considered unimportant, probably,
by many godly Israelites, only paved the way for
greater and more serious violations of the law. God's
people are only safe as they adhere carefully and
closely to the very letter of the word of God. The
slightest digressions are often the prelude of wide and
grave departures from obedience to God's will as revealed in His Word. The beginning of sin is, like
strife, "as when one letteth out water."

And "he built the high gate of the house of the
Lord, and on the wall of Ophel he built much." The
"high gate" led from the king's house to the temple
(see 2 Chron. 23 : 20), and Jotham's building it (re-
building, or repairing) is very significant. He wished
free access from his own house to that of the Lord.
He would strengthen the link between the two houses—
keep his line of communication open (to use a military
figure) with the source of his supplies of strength and
wisdom. This is one of the secrets of his prosperity
and power.

"Moreover he built cities in the mountains of Judah, and in the forests he built castles and towers." He built where most men would have thought it unnecessary, or too much trouble—in the "mountains" and "forests." He neglected no part of his kingdom, but sought to strengthen and fortify it everywhere. And as a result, he prospered. "He fought also with the king of the Ammonites, and prevailed against them. And the children of Ammon gave him the same year a hundred talents of silver, and ten thousand measures of wheat, and ten thousand of barley. So much did the children of Ammon pay unto him, both the second year and the third. So Jotham became mighty, *because he prepared his ways before the Lord his God.*" That high gate between the palace and the temple was better than a Chinese wall around his kingdom. It is in communion with God that all real prosperity and power is found.

"Now the rest of the acts of Jotham, and all his wars, and his ways, lo, they are written in the book of the kings of Israel and Judah." "*All* his wars" implies that during his sixteen years' reign he was actively engaged in conflict with enemies, subduing some, like the Ammonites, and repelling the invasions of others (Rezin king of Syria, and Pekah king of Israel). His "ways" too were written. God's saints are called to *walk*, as well as to war. "I have fought a good fight," said one; "I have finished my course," he also adds. This last was his "ways." Ours, like king Jotham's, "are written in the book." May we say then, like another Hebrew king, "I will take heed to my ways"! (Psa. 37 : 1). Jotham is the only one of all the Hebrew kings, from Saul down, against whom God has nothing to record. In this his character is in beautiful accord with his name, *Jehovah-perfect.* "All the world," we know, is "guilty before God." "All have sinned," God says. But in his *public* life, Jotham, like Daniel, was perfect, or blameless. " *We*"—Daniel's enemies say—"shall not find anything against this Daniel, except *we* find it against him concerning the law of his God." Yet this same Daniel says, "I was confessing my sin" (Dan. 6 : 5; 9 : 20). Man saw nothing to condemn : Daniel knew God's eye saw much. And, like the honest man that he was, he puts it on record with his own hand that he had sins to be confessed to God.

"And Jotham slept with his fathers, and they buried him in the city of David : and Ahaz his son reigned in his stead." Had Micah Jotham's death in mind when he wrote, "The godly [man] hath perished out of the land"? (Micah 7 : 2, New Tr.) From what follows in the chapter, down to the 7th verse, it would appear so. The violence, fraud, bribery, treachery, and other forms of wickedness described here, is just what prevailed after Jotham, under Ahaz' infamous rule. Jotham was indeed a godly man, and well might the righteous say on his death, "Help, Lord, for the godly man ceaseth!" or, "is gone."

The record of his reign is brief, but full of brightness. His "memory," like that of all "the just," "is blessed." He was the tenth of Judah's kings, and *God always claims His tithe;* and in Jotham, the "Jehovah-perfect," it was found.

AHAZ

(Possessor.)

(2 Kings 16; 2 Chron. 28.)

Contemporary Prophets:
ISAIAH; MICAH; HOSEA; ODED.

"It is an abomination to kings to commit wickedness: for the throne is established by righteousness."—*Proverbs 16 : 12.*

A HAZ was wicked as his father Jotham was righteous. "Ahaz was twenty years old when he began to reign, and he reigned sixteen years in Jerusalem: but he did not that which was right in the sight
of the Lord, like David his father: for he walked in
the ways of the kings of Israel, and made also molten
images for Baalim. Moreover he burnt incense in the
valley of the son of Hinnom, and burnt his children
in the fire, after the abominations of the heathen
whom the Lord had cast out before the children of Israel. He sacrificed also and burnt incense in the
high places" (not removed in Jotham's day, 2 Kings
15 : 35), "and on the hills, and under every green tree."
It seems strange that the best of men frequently have
the worst of sons. Ahaz' mother is not mentioned,
and it is possible that his father was unfortunate in
his choice of a wife. A king with the heavy responsibilities of government pressing constantly upon him
can have little time to give to the training of his chil-

dren: that important duty must fall largely on the mother. It was not every king of Judah that was blessed with such a mother as king Lemuel's (Prov. 31).

But whoever, or whatever, Ahaz' mother may have been, he was himself responsible for his idolatrous deeds, and God punished him accordingly. "Wherefore the Lord his God delivered him into the hand of the king of Syria; and they smote him, and carried away a great multitude of them captives, and brought them to Damascus. And he was also delivered into the hand of the king of Israel, who smote him with a great slaughter." These statements in no way clash with what is recorded in 2 Kings 16: 5—that these confederate kings "could not overcome him." They could not get into the city, nor reach the king personally, though they entered the land. "God delivered him," and "they smote him," means his people and kingdom. Elath was also lost to Judah at this time (2 Kings 16: 5). It was the purpose of "the two tails of these smoking firebrands" to dethrone king Ahaz, and set up in his stead "the son of Tabeal" (a Syrian, probably; it is not a Hebrew name). It was doubtless Satan's plot, if not man's, to destroy the Davidic dynasty; and God, for this reason, did not deliver Jerusalem into their hands. But the slaughter and slavery of the people at large throughout the kingdom was something almost unparalleled. See 2 Chron. 28: 6. This is why Isaiah took with him his son Shear-jashub (*the remnant shall return*), when he went forth to meet king Ahaz. There should be a remnant left to return to the land; and the virgin should bear a son, so there should not fail a king upon the throne of

David.   The dynasty could never be destroyed, for of
Immanuel's kingdom there shall be no end.   See
Isa. 7.

"Pekah the son of Remaliah slew in Judah a hundred and twenty thousand in one day, which were all
valiant men"—the flower of Ahaz' army—"because
they had forsaken the Lord God of their fathers."
And though the king himself escaped, God's rod
reached him through his son: "And Zichri, a mighty
man of Ephraim, slew Maaseiah the king's son."   He
also slew the "governor of the house," and "Elkanah
that was next to the king."   How, or where, we know
not.   God can find the guilty where and when He will.

"And the children of Israel carried away captive of
their brethren two hundred thousand, women, sons
and daughters, and took away also much spoil from
them, and brought the spoil to Samaria.   But a
prophet of the Lord was there, whose name was Oded:
and he went out before the host that came to Samaria,
and said unto them, Behold, because the Lord God of
your fathers was wroth with Judah, He hath delivered
them into your hand, and ye have slain them in a rage
that reacheth up unto heaven.   And now ye purpose to
keep under the children of Judah and Jerusalem for
bondmen and bondwomen unto you : but are there not
with you, even with you, sins against the Lord your
God?"—alas, how many and how great were Israel's
sins!   "Now hear me therefore, and deliver the captives again, which ye have taken captive of your brethren : for the fierce wrath of the Lord is upon you"—
and they were themselves, in a few short years, carried captive beyond Babylon.   "Then certain of the

heads of the children of Ephraim, Azariah the son of Johanan, Berechiah the son of Meshillemoth, and Jehizkiah the son of Shallum, and Amasa the son of Hadlai, stood up against them that came from the war, and said unto them, Ye shall not bring in the captives hither : for whereas we have offended against the Lord already, ye intend to add more to our sins and to our trespass : for our trespass is great, and there is fierce wrath against Israel."

Here is faithfulness and denunciation of sin where one might least expect it—in the city of Samaria, and from leaders, heads of the people. There were not ten righteous men in Sodom ; and Samaria, one might think, was not much better. But all there had not bowed the knee to Baal, and they speak for truth and right with boldness in the very face of a returning, victorious army. And their words have the desired effect ; for the wicked will sometimes give heed to the words of the righteous in a most wonderful way. " So the armed men left the captives and the spoil before the princes and all the congregation. And the men which were expressed by name rose up, and took the captives, and with the spoil clothed all that were naked among them, and arrayed them, and shod them, and gave them to eat and to drink, and anointed them, and carried all the feeble of them upon asses, and brought them to Jericho, the city of palm trees, to their brethren : then they returned to Samaria." Their conduct was morally beautiful, especially when looked at upon the dark background of the evil times and kingdom in which they lived. And the righteous Lord who loveth righteousness has seen to it that these men of tender heart and upright conscience should be "expressed by name." The incident is like a little gleam of light shining out of the rapidly deepening darkness, and the God of Israel has placed it on eternal record, and published it abroad, that men might know that He never forgets a kindness done to His people, even when they suffer, under His government, the just punishment of their sins.

"At that time did king Ahaz send unto the kings of Assyria to help him." Yes, it was "*at that time,*" when Israel, the last, was first, and Ahaz, on the throne of David, frantically invoking the aid of the Assyrian, became last. The Edomites, emboldened, doubtless, by the success of Rezin and Pekah, invaded the land and "carried away captives." The Philistines also invaded "the low country, and the south of Judah," and settled themselves in the captured cities. "For the Lord brought Judah low because of Ahaz king of Israel; for he made Judah naked [lawless, N. Tr.], and transgressed sore against the Lord."

The days were indeed dark: a cloud of gloom had settled over the once fair land and kingdom of David. Stroke succeeded stroke, and humiliation followed humiliation. But there was no national repentance, and the king (the responsible cause of it all) only hardened himself in rebellion and folly. The king of Assyria came, but, instead of really helping him, "distressed him." He took the treasure Ahaz "stripped" for him from the house of the Lord, and from his own house, and the houses of the princes. It was just as the prophet Isaiah had forewarned him: "The Lord shall bring upon thee, and upon thy people, and upon thy

father's house, days that have not come, from the days
that Ephraim departed from Judah; even the king of
Assyria" (Isa. 7 : 17). He trusted in man, made flesh
his arm, his heart departing from the Lord, and
brought upon himself and kingdom the consequent
curse and barrenness (Jer. 17 : 5). "And in the time
of his distress did he trespass yet more against the
Lord." How different was his great ancestor David!
"In my distress," he says, "I called upon the Lord,
and cried unto my God " (Ps. 18 : 6). Even his wicked
grandson Manasseh sought the Lord his God " when
he was in affliction." But Ahaz seemed determined
to fill up the measure of his sins, and, like the apos-
tates of Christendom during the outpouring of "the
vials of the wrath of God upon the earth," who, though
"they gnawed their tongues for pain," still "blasphemed the God of heaven," and repented not of their
deeds to give Him glory (Rev. 16). Each humiliating
disaster, instead of turning Ahaz to God, drove him
further into sin. It is plainly seen therefore why the
inspired chronicler should despisingly write, " This is
that king Ahaz! "

Oh, the blind delusion of demon-worship!—" He
sacrificed unto the gods of Damascus, *which smote him :*
and he said, Because the gods of the kings of Syria
help them, therefore will I sacrifice to them, that they
may help me. But they were the ruin of him, and of
all Israel." He says, in effect, "Jehovah does not
help me as the deities of the Syrian kings help them;
so it is better for me to forsake Him and worship gods
that will do me some good." So he " gathered together
the vessels of the house of God, and cut in pieces the

vessels of the house of God, and shut up the doors of the house of the Lord." His apostasy was now complete. "And he made him altars [for false gods] in every corner of Jerusalem. And in every several city of Judah he made high places to burn incense unto other gods, and provoked to anger the Lord God of his fathers." How far can they fall who, instead of being obedient to the word of God, are moved and governed by everything which has some present, apparent success!

How shameful is his obsequious appeal to the king of Assyria—"I am thy servant and thy son: come up, and save me out of the hand of the king of Syria"—and that greedy monarch, for the silver and gold sent him, went to Damascus and slew Rezin, its king. "And king Ahaz went to Damascus to meet Tiglath-pileser king of Assyria"—at his command perhaps, to do him honor personally—"and saw an altar that was at Damascus: and king Ahaz sent to Urijah the priest the fashion of the altar, and the pattern of it, according to all the workmanship thereof. And Urijah the priest built an altar according to all that king Ahaz had sent from Damascus: so Urijah the priest made it against king Ahaz came from Damascus. And when the king was come from Damascus, the king saw the altar: and the king approached to the altar, and offered thereon. And he burnt his burnt-offering and his meat-offering, and poured his drink-offering, and sprinkled the blood of his peace-offerings, upon the altar." The pattern of the altar caught his ritualistic eye, and he must needs imitate it—not unlike a class to-day who go to Rome for elties, and then set up at home cheap imitations in churches that were once called Protestant. The real Rome awes men (for Babylon is "the GREAT"), but her little imitators move us only to pity. King Ahaz finds in Urijah the high priest a willing tool to his idolatrous designs. Untrue to his name (*light of Jehovah*), he yields unscrupulous obedience to his sovereign's orders, instead of rebuking him for his abominable act. For his degrading subserviency, probably, his name is omitted from the sacerdotal list in 1 Chron. 6: 4–15, Better have lost life than honor—when it is that true and eternal honor " which comes from God."

On this altar of new design Ahaz offers every kind of offering excepting that which he needed most for himself—the *sin*-offering. The plain brazen altar ("which was before the house of the Lord") seems to have offended his esthetic eye; so it was relegated to a place of comparative obscurity on the north side of his own foreign substitute. He arrogantly commanded the high priest as to what, and how, and when, to offer on his altar. And the unworthy successor of Jehoiada and Zechariah slavishly obeyed to the letter. "Thus did Urijah the priest, according to all that king Ahaz commanded." He reversed the apostles' maxim, that we "ought to obey God rather than men." *He* was of another mind: his eye was on the honor that comes from man; theirs was on that which comes from God.

"And king Ahaz cut off the borders [Heb., panels] of the bases, and removed the laver from off them; and took down the sea from off the brazen oxen that were under it, and put it upon a pavement of stones." Probably to obtain the precious metals of which they

were made, these sacrilegious innovations were introduced. "And the covert for the sabbath"—(covered
way) to be used on the sabbath by the royal worshipers—"that they had built in the house [of God],
and the king's entry without, turned he from the house
of the Lord for the king of Assyria." It was the high-
gate that his father Jotham had so significantly rebuilt.
Ahaz appears to have profaned it to the use of Tiglath-
pileser when worshiping his false gods (at Ahaz' altar
perhaps) on his visit to Jerusalem. "And the brazen
altar," he said, "shall be for me to inquire by," or
"consider." He either meant that he should use it
for purposes of divination,—linking Jehovah's great
name with his base idolatries,—or he would "consider" what should ultimately be done with it. And we
Christians "have an altar," even Christ, our Creator-
Redeemer, whom profane unitarian Higher Critics and
others dare to debase and degrade before their de-
ceived disciples, removing Him from His place of absolute preeminence, (like Ahaz with God's altar,) putting Him beside others, like Zoroaster and Confucius,
for "odious" comparison! And already they "consider" what they shall finally do with Him—relegate
Him to a place even of inferiority to some of their
heathen Asiatic reformers! And what shall the end
be? We know: "Another shall come in his own
name," and him they "will receive" (John 5 : 43).
The "man of sin—the son of perdition"—is to arise;
and "because they received not the love of the truth,
that they might be saved, . . . God shall send them
strong delusion, that they should believe a lie," etc.
(2 Thess. 2 : 10, 11.)

"Now the rest of his acts and of all his ways, first and last, behold, they are written in the book of the kings of Judah and Israel." "His acts," and "his ways"! God too has "ways" and "acts." "He made known His ways unto Moses, His acts unto the children of Israel" (Ps. 103 : 7). His *ways* were the manifestations of His nature; His *acts* more the displays of His power. "All his ways," it is said of Ahaz. And what manifestations of his heart's wickedness did his life of thirty-six years bring out! It is little wonder that the inspiring Spirit led the chronicler to call him "king of *Israel*" (2 Chron. 28 : 19)—so like was he to the nineteen idolatrous rulers of the northern kingdom. Even his people who shared in his wickedness are called "Israel," instead of Judah (2 Chron. 28 : 23). But there must have been some sense of righteousness (or shame) left in them; for we read, "They buried him in the city, even in Jerusalem: but they brought him not into the sepulchres of the kings of Israel." Corrupt as they themselves were, they felt that their late king had so exceeded in wickedness that it was not meet to lay his body among those of his royal ancestors.

The Philistines, who had good cause to fear the kings of Judah, had a special prophecy written for them by Isaiah at this time, bidding them not to rejoice at king Ahaz' death: "In the year that king Ahaz died was this burden." See Isa. 14 : 28–32, paragraphed as in N. Tr. He appears to have been little influenced by the faithful ministry of the evangelist-prophet. He was apparently a man of esthetic tastes (as even the ungodliest of men may be), from his admiration of the Damascus altar; he was also interested in the sciences, it would seem, from his introduction into Jerusalem of the Chaldean sun-dial (2 Kings 20: 11). Nor was he of a persecuting spirit, apparently, for he did not, like his grandson Manasseh, shed innocent blood, nor put to death the prophets. He was possessed (Ahaz—*possessor*) of much that men admire and magnify to-day; but all this, without godliness, is of absolutely no worth. Impenitent to the last, apparently, he died as he had lived: "and Hezekiah his son reigned in his stead."

HEZEKIAH

(Strength of Jehovah.)

2 Kings chaps. 18–21 ; 2 Chron. 29–32 ; Isa. 38, 39.

Contemporary Prophets :
ISAIAH ; MICAH ; NAHUM ; HOSEA.

"The king by judgment establisheth the land: but he
that receiveth gifts overthroweth it."—*Proverbs 29 : 4.*

"HEZEKIAH began to reign when he was five
and twenty years old, and he reigned nine
and twenty years in Jerusalem." We are con-
fronted here with what has been considered one of the
greatest chronological difficulties of the Bible. In few
words, it is this : Ahaz, Hezekiah's father, began his
reign, Scripture says, when he was twenty years of
age, and he reigned sixteen years in Jerusalem. And
Hezekiah, it says, was twenty-five years old when he
ascended the throne. This seems to teach that Ahaz
was but eleven years old when Hezekiah his son was
born, which is altogether unlikely, if not impossible.
Josephus does not touch upon the difficulty ; he possibly felt there was none. Modern commentators have
suggested various solutions of the problem, none of
which is satisfactory. Fausset says "twenty" in
2 Kings 16 : 2 is "a transcriber's error" for "twenty-
five"; citing the LXX., Syriac and Arabic of 2 Chron.
28 : 1. But, in reply to this, one pertinently writes :
"We may observe, that it is never advisable to find

any fault with the text except where there is no other tolerable solution, which is not the case here." The LXX. and other versions reading "twenty-five" for "twenty" in 2 Chron. 28 : 1 prove nothing, except, it may be, a tampering with the original text in order to get rid of a seemingly inexplicable difficulty.

Two legitimate explanations offer themselves. 1st, It is quite possible a break of some years may have occurred in king Ahaz' reign, either when he went to Damascus to meet Tiglath-pileser (2 Ki. 16 : 10); or, which seems more likely, when the king of Assyria came himself to Jerusalem (2 Kings 16 : 18; 2 Chron. 28 : 20, 21), and "distressed him." It would not be at all unlike these Assyrian kings for Tiglath-pileser to temporarily depose the king of Judah during his sojourn in those parts. 2d, Scripture does not say that Hezekiah began to reign *immediately* after the death of his father. True, the usual form of words is used— "Ahaz slept with his fathers . . . and Hezekiah his son reigned in his stead" (2 Chron. 28 : 27). But similar words are used in 2 Kings 15 : 30 : "And Hoshea the son of Elah made a conspiracy against Pekah the son of Remaliah, and smote him, and slew him, *and reigned in his stead*," when, in point of fact, he did not actually begin to reign until at least nine years later, as Scripture chronologists are generally agreed. (Compare 2 Kings 16 : 1 and 17 : 1.) So a number of years, Scripture permits us to believe, may have elapsed between the death of Ahaz (owing to the unsettled state of his kingdom) and the accession of Hezekiah. This would entirely do away with any difficulty as to Ahaz' immature age at the birth of his first-born.

In support of the first explanation it must be borne in mind that it is nothing unusual in Scripture to take no note of interruptions or breaks in chronology (compare 1 Kings 6 : 1 and Acts 13 : 18–22 ; the first, 480 years ; the second, 573—a difference of ninety-three years, just the number of years of Israel's five servitudes of 8, 18, 20, 7, and 40, under Mesopotamia, Moab, Canaan, Midian, and Philistia, respectively. See Judges 3 : 8 ; 3 : 14; 4 : 3; 6 : 1; 13 : 1. The Ammonite oppression must be omitted, not being truly in the land, but "on the other side Jordan" (see Judges 10 : 8); just as several generations are frequently omitted in the genealogies. If it is urged against either of these solutions that it would interfere with the harmony of the table of dates in this volume, it is replied that there is absolutely no positive proof that the interregnum between the reigns of Pekah and Hoshea was of nine years' duration. The calculation is based wholly on the figures used in reference to Ahaz and Hezekiah. As to any interference with late Old Testament chronology as a whole, it needs only to be said that chronologists are by no means agreed here, as in other portions of the Old Testament. Nor are the Hebrew, Septuagint and Samaritan texts in harmony as to dates. God seems purposely to have left the matter of dates somewhat undecided; nor is it for us "to know the times or the seasons, which the Father hath put in His own power."

But we proceed with Hezekiah : "His mother's name was Abia, the daughter of Zechariah." Her father was perhaps one of the two faithful witnesses of Isa. 8 : 2. Or, she may have been a descendant of the Zechariah who guided Uzziah during the earlier portion of his reign; or even of the martyr Zechariah, slain by order of king Joash. Anyway, she must have been a true "mother in Israel" to have raised so godly a son, with such a wicked father's example before him. O ye mothers, what a responsibility is yours, and what a privilege as well, to have God, as it were, say to you, "Take this child, and nurse it *for Me*, and I will give thee thy wages." Abia had her "wages," surely, when she saw her son renew and reform the desolated kingdom of his father David. Frequently, in truth, the hand that rocks the cradle rules the empire, whether it be for weal or for woe.

"And he did that which was right in the sight of the Lord, according to all that David his father did." If, as has been remarked, Ahaz was an extraordinarily bad man to have come of so good a father, so here the reverse is true: Hezekiah was a remarkably good man, with so notably wicked a father. How truly, and widely, does the wise Preacher's reflection as to one's successors apply, whether it be in a kingdom or the narrower circle of the household, "Who knoweth whether he shall be a wise man or a fool?" (Eccl. 2 : 19.)

Hezekiah began to manifest immediately what manner of king he should be. "He in the first year of his reign, in the first month, opened the doors of the house of the Lord" (which Ahaz his father had shut up), "and repaired them. And he brought in the priests and the Levites, and gathered them together into the east street, and said unto them, Hear me, ye Levites; sanctify now yourselves, and sanctify the house of the

Lord God of your fathers, and carry forth the filthiness out of the holy place. For our fathers have trespassed, and done that which was evil in the eyes of the Lord our God, and have forsaken Him, and have turned away their faces from the habitation of the Lord, and turned their backs. Also they have shut up the doors of the porch, and put out the lamps, and have not burned incense nor offered burnt-offerings in the holy place unto the God of Israel. Wherefore the wrath of the Lord was upon Judah and Jerusalem, and He hath delivered them to trouble, to astonishment, and to hissing, as ye see with your eyes. For, lo, our fathers have fallen by the sword, and our sons and our daughters and our wives are in captivity for this. Now it is in my heart to make a covenant with the Lord God of Israel, that His fierce wrath may turn away from us. My sons, be not now negligent; for the Lord hath chosen you to stand before Him, to serve Him, and that ye should minister unto Him, and burn incense." He begins at the only right place—the sanctuary; and at the right time—immediately—without delay, in the *first* month of the *first* year; and it was the *first day* (2 Chron. 29 : 17)—New-year, in fact. Whatever reforms were needed elsewhere in the kingdom, this must have precedence of them all. Other things could not be really right if this were wrong. Revival, with God, is like His judgment; it must begin at His house. See Ezek. 9 : 6 ; 1 Pet. 4 : 17. " Let them make Me a sanctuary, that I may dwell among them," was Jehovah's gracious command to them at the very beginning of their existence as a nation. Solomon said in his prayer, " That Thine eyes may be open toward this house night and day, even toward the place of which Thou hast said, My name shall be there." The temple was to the kingdom as the heart to the body—when it ceased to pulsate with activity and life, the body politic, or nation, could not but languish, stagnate, and die. If God had chosen them as His own peculiar nation out of all the rest, He must have the central place among them; His authority and claims must be recognized if they wished to be prospered by Him. So is it in this day of Church dispensation.

"My sons," he calls the priests and Levites, in true fatherly love to them, as every king should have toward his people. "The father of the coming [millennial] age," is one of the titles of our Lord Christ, who, as God's model King, shall reign over the happy inhabitants of the millennial earth in the glorious day now not far off. See Isa. 9 : 6, N. Tr.

"Then the Levites arose; . . . and they gathered their brethren, and sanctified themselves, and came, according to the commandment of the king, by the words of the Lord, to cleanse the house of the Lord. And the priests went into the inner part of the house of the Lord to cleanse it, and brought out all the uncleanness that they found in the temple of the Lord into the court of the house of the Lord. And the Levites took it, to carry it out abroad into the brook Kidron." On the eighth day the work was finished, the Sabbath, probably; and on the sixteenth day "they made an end." They began at the inner sanctuary, and ended at the porch. God always works from within—not like man, from the outside. God looks on the heart, and is not, like man, satisfied with a fair external appearance.

"Moreover all the vessels, which king Ahaz in his reign did cast away in his transgressions," they re-sanctified, and set them before the altar of burnt-offering, which they had also cleansed, with the shewbread table. "Then Hezekiah the king rose up early, and gathered the rulers of the city, and went up to the house of the Lord." There they offered "a sin-offering for the kingdom, and for the sanctuary, and for Judah." Then an atonement was made *for all Israel:* "for the king commanded that the burnt-offering and the sin-offering should be made for all Israel." His fatherly heart went out toward all the tribes. He loved and thought of them all, even though the bulk of them were divided from him, and subjects of the murderous conspirator Hoshea. He set Levites in the temple "with cymbals, and psalteries, and with harps," and the priests stood with the trumpets. "And when the burnt-offering began, the song of the Lord began also with the trumpets, and with the instruments ordained by David king of Israel." It was a wonderful day for Jerusalem; the number of offerings brought by the people was so large that the priests could not flay them all, and had to be assisted by the Levites. "So," we read, "the service of the house of God was set in order. And Hezekiah rejoiced, and all the people, that God had prepared the people: for the thing was done suddenly."

And now comes what may be considered the crowning act of this excellent king's life. "And Hezekiah sent to all Israel and Judah, and wrote letters also to

Ephraim and Manasseh, that they should come to the
house of the Lord at Jerusalem, to keep the passover
unto the Lord God of Israel.   For the king had taken
counsel, and his princes, and all the congregation in
Jerusalem, to keep the passover in the second month.
For they could not keep it at that time, because the
priests had not sanctified themselves sufficiently, neither had the people gathered themselves together to
Jerusalem.   And the thing pleased the king and all
the congregation."   There was beautiful harmony between king and people.   All was done willingly by
every one.   It was not as with Abijah, who "*commanded* Judah to seek the Lord God of their fathers"
(2 Chron. 14: 4).   Instead of commanding, the king
consults with the people here.   "So *they*," not he, the
king only, "established a decree to make proclamation throughout all Israel, from Beer-sheba even to
Dan, that they should come to keep the passover unto
the Lord God of Israel at Jerusalem."   "Because,"
the New Translation reads, "they had not held it for
a long time, as it was written" (2 Chron. 30: 5).   This
may mean that before this the passover had been entirely neglected, or that it had been a long time since
it was kept in the second month, "as it was written,"
in Num. 9: 10, 11.

If the first suggested meaning be the true one, what
a condition the nation must have been in to have
discontinued "for a long time," this, the primary and
most significant of all their yearly feasts.*   This

---

* It is not likely that the Passover-feast, in which *Jehovah's*
claims were especially remembered, would be kept during
the reign of the apostate king Ahaz, at least. And has the

revival in the very beginning of Hezekiah's reign is all the more remarkable in that it immediately succeeded what was probably the darkest period the kingdom of Judah had ever known. "Man's extremity is God's opportunity," certainly; and it is very frequently, if not always, "darkest just before dawn."

Posts carry these circular letters of invitation "throughout all Judah and Israel," saying, "Ye children of Israel, turn again to the Lord God of Abraham, Isaac, and Israel, and He will return to the remnant of you, that are escaped out of the hand of the kings of Assyria. And be ye not like your fathers, and like your brethren, which trespassed against the Lord God of their fathers, who therefore gave them up to desolation, as ye see. Now be ye not stiff-necked, as your fathers were, but yield yourselves unto the Lord, and enter into His sanctuary, which He hath sanctified forever: and serve the Lord your God, that the fierceness of His wrath may turn away from you. For if ye turn again unto the Lord, your brethren and your children shall find compassion before them that led them captive,† so that they shall

---

characteristic Christian institution, "the Lord's supper," fared any better? In a large part of Christendom—that which arrogantly calls itself "*The* Church"—this precious remembrance of our Lord in His sufferings and death, has been prostituted to "the Mass," in which a little dough baked as a wafer is, by a Romish priest's magic words, turned into "the very flesh and blood of the Lord"; and this little wafer is worshiped as "the Host"!! [Ed.

† A large part of Israel (from the ten tribes) had already been carried away captive by the king of Assyria. (See 2 Kings chap. 17.) [Ed.

come again into this land: for the Lord your God is gracious and merciful, and will not turn away His face from you, if ye return unto Him." It was a beautiful message, holding out comfort and hope to the sorrowing remnant of Israel, who had seen so many of their loved ones led away in bondage to the land of the Assyrian.

"So the posts passed from city to city through the country of Ephraim and Manasseh even unto Zebulun: but they laughed them to scorn and mocked them. Nevertheless divers of Asher and Manasseh and of Zebulun humbled themselves, and came to Jerusalem. Also in Judah the hand of the Lord was to give them one heart to do the commandment of the king and of the princes, by the word of the Lord." Some, as we see, were glad of the exhortation (those who had suffered most from the Assyrian, probably); Ephraim, the "cake not turned," with others, impiously and impudently mocked, and made light of the messengers and their message. It is not the only occasion on which God's message received this opposite treatment. Seven hundred years later, and seven hundred miles away, at Mars Hill in Athens, Paul delivered a more solemn message from his God but with like result: "some mocked," while certain "clave unto him and believed" (Acts 17). And it is the same to-day. Hast thou, my reader, believed God's gospel message, and, like some of Asher and Manasseh and of Zebulun, "humbled" thyself, and come to Jesus?—*hast thou?*

"And there assembled at Jerusalem much people to keep the feast of unleavened bread in the second month, a very great congregation." They removed

the unlawful altars found in the city "and cast them
into the brook Kidron." They killed and ate the
passover according to the law, as nearly as could be
done under the circumstances. "For a multitude of
the people, even many of Ephraim and Manasseh,
Issachar, and Zebulun, had not cleansed themselves,
yet did they eat the passover otherwise than it was
written. But Hezekiah prayed for them, saying, The
good Lord pardon every one that prepareth his heart
to seek God, the Lord God of his fathers, though he
be not cleansed according to the purification of the
sanctuary." He makes intercession for the people in
the spirit of the future King who shall sit "a priest
upon His throne." (Zech. 6 : 13.) "And the Lord
hearkened to Hezekiah, and healed the people."

The feast was kept "with great gladness," with
praise to God day by day on "instruments of praise."
" And Hezekiah spake comfortably unto all the
Levites that taught the good knowledge of the Lord."
As in all true revivals, the Scriptures had their place.
And how much the poor recovered people needed the
instruction given them by these Levites. Everyone
rejoiced (as well they might) and it was unanimously
agreed "to keep other seven days." "So there was
great joy in Jerusalem : for since the time of Solomon
the son of David king of Jerusalem there was not the
like in Jerusalem. Then the priests the Levites arose
and blessed the people (see Numb. 6 : 23–26): and
their voice was heard, and their prayer came up to
His holy dwelling-place, even unto heaven."

And then appears the practical result of this wonderful fourteen days' general meeting. "Now when all

this was finished, all Israel that were present went out to the cities of Judah, and brake the images in pieces, and cut down the groves, and threw down the high places and the altars out of all Judah and Benjamin, in Ephraim also and Manasseh, until they had utterly destroyed them all. Then all the children of Israel returned every man to his possession, into their own cities." Hezekiah then restores to order the priestly and Levitical services of the temple, "as it is written in the law of the Lord" (2 Chron. 31 : 3). "Moreover he commanded the people that dwelt in Jerusalem to give the portion of the priests and the Levites, that they might be encouraged in the law of the Lord." There was an immediate and generous response to this thoughtful call of the king. "The children of Israel brought in abundance the first-fruits of corn, wine, and oil, and honey, and of all the increase of the field; and the tithe of all things brought they in abundantly." This awakening to their responsibilities towards those who ministered in holy things was not confined to the inhabitants of Jerusalem; it extended itself to all the kingdom. "And concerning the children of Israel and Judah, that dwelt in the cities of Judah, they also brought in the tithe of oxen and sheep, and the tithe of holy things." The offering continued from the third to the seventh month—all through their harvest and vintage—and were stored in heaps. "And when Hezekiah and the princes came and saw the heaps, they blessed the Lord and His people Israel." And it was meet that they should do so; for here in these material fruits of the land they beheld the fruit of God's Spirit in His people. When

the king questioned the priests and Levites concerning the heaps, the chief priest "answered him and
said, Since the people began to bring in the offerings
into the house of the Lord, we have had enough to
eat"—alas, that it should ever have been otherwise
with them—"and have left plenty: for the Lord hath
blessed His people; and that which is left is this
great store." Chambers were prepared in the temple,
by Hezekiah's command, to house this superabundant
store. And they "brought in the offerings and the
tithes and the dedicated things faithfully." Arrangements were made and officers appointed for the proper distribution of this store. Everything was done
in systematic order, according to the king's commandment. "And thus did Hezekiah throughout all Judah,
and wrought that which was good and right and truth
before the Lord his God. And in every work that he
began in the service of the house of God, and in the
law, and in the commandments, to seek his God, he
did it with all his heart"—the only way to do anything—"and prospered." He was like the happy
man of Psalm 1, of whom it is said, "Whatsoever he
doeth shall prosper." This was John's highest wish
for the beloved and hospitable Gaius (3 Jno. 2, N. Tr.)
And it is written of the best Beloved of all, "The
pleasure of the Lord shall prosper in His hand."

So, having set in order the spiritual matters of the
kingdom, Hezekiah turned to the more material things
in his dominion. "He smote the Philistines, even
unto Gaza, and the borders thereof, from the tower of
the watchman to the fenced city" (2 Ki. 18: 8). Then
was fulfilled that which was spoken by the prophet

Isaiah, in the year that king Ahaz died: "Rejoice not thou, Philistia, all of thee, because the rod that smote thee [Uzziah] is broken [in Ahaz' death]; for out of the serpent's root [as they regarded him] shall come forth a viper [Hezekiah], and his root shall be a fiery flying serpent," etc. (Isa. 14: 29, N. Tr.)

"And he rebelled against the king of Assyria, and served him not." It would seem that this attempt to throw off the yoke of Assyria was premature; or, per-haps, the good king went beyond his faith; for when Sennacherib invaded his kingdom, we are pained to read that he took all the fortified cities. And Hezekiah weakened and sent to him at Lachish his submission, saying, "I have offended; return from me: that which thou puttest on me will I bear." This was humiliat-ing, though he does not grovel, like his worthless father saying, "I am thy son." His desire was right, but he may, in his zeal for the prosperity and glory of his kingdom, have anticipated God's time. Because of their former sins, Israel had become subject to the Assyrian, whom God had called "the rod of His anger," and even though restored to righteousness under Hezekiah, God in His wise, yet gracious, government may have seen fit to allow them to suffer awhile for their past, that they might fully realize by bitter and humiliating experience what a serious thing it is for a people to turn from the living God to idols. So, poor Hezekiah (how we feel for the dear man!) pays the heavy fine imposed upon him—"three hun-dred talents of silver and thirty talents of gold." To obtain this enormous amount, he had to almost strip bare the recently restored house of God and his palace of their treasures and utensils of silver and gold. He even had to strip from the temple doors and its pillars the gold that his own loving hand had but recently laid there. How it must have hurt his great and righteous heart to thus denude God's dwelling place of its wealth of glory! And all because of his own hasty action, he might think.

This was in the fourteenth year of his reign (2 Ki. 18 : 13). Fausset says "fourteenth" is a copyist's error for "twenty-seventh." But we hear too much about these "copyist's errors." "Fourteenth" agrees with Isa. 36 : 1 ; and it is the only number that will harmonize with Isa. 38 : 5. It may be for lack of faith that men try hard to make Scripture square with profane history, or what purports to be history. Just because a date in the Bible does not come out even with Babylonian or Assyrian chronology, or disagrees with some untrustworthy heathen inscription, commentators cry " Transcriber's error " ; as if imperfectly deciphered monuments and clay tablets must correct the word of God! "Fourteen" agrees with other portions and dates contained in Scripture ; so, to faith, it is perfectly satisfactory, whatever Assyriologists, or commentators influenced by them, may say.

Sennacherib for some reason or other, did not depart from Hezekiah, as he had hoped. Perhaps it was impossible for Hezekiah to obtain the sum demanded by the king of Assyria; or that villainous plunderer, after receiving the required amount, may have changed his mind (if he ever really meant to let the king of Jerusalem buy him off), and determined, before he quitted the country, to possess himself of

Hezekiah's capital. His intention became known to Hezekiah, "and he took counsel with his princes and mighty men." They were agreed to resist his capture of the city, and extensive preparations were made for the threatened siege. When all had been done that man could do, Hezekiah gathered the people "together to him in the street of the gate of the city," and addressed them with words of faith and courage: "Be strong and courageous," he said, "be not afraid nor dismayed for the king of Assyria, nor for all the multitude that is with him: for there be more with us than with him. With him is an arm of flesh; but with us is the Lord our God to help us, and to fight our battles." Fine words, these, and very different from his saying a short time before to Sennacherib, "I have offended," etc. His faith, though faint, had not altogether failed; and here it rises to its full height, and, like the restored Simon Peter, he is able, by his words and example, to "strengthen his brethren." "And the people rested themselves upon the words of Hezekiah king of Judah."

"After this did Sennacherib king of Assyria send his servants to Jerusalem, . . . unto Hezekiah king of Judah, and unto all Judah that were at Jerusalem, saying," etc.: then follows a harangue that for insolence and craftiness has never been exceeded. "Rabshakeh" (a title, not a name), Sennacherib's commander-in-chief, was the speaker. He was an accomplished diplomat, evidently, and delivered his artful speech in "the Jews' language." He, with his fellow-officers, "stood by the conduit of the upper pool, which is in the highway of the fuller's field"—on an

eminence, probably. Hezekiah's cabinet ministers
interrupt him in his discourse, saying, "Speak, I pray
thee, to thy servants in the Syrian language; for we
understand it : and talk not with us in the Jews' language in the ears of the people that are on the wall."
They little knew the wily Rab-shakeh, who, gaining
an advantage by their fear, answers : "Hath my master sent me to thy master, and to thee, to speak these
words? hath he not sent me to the men which sit on
the wall? . . . Then Rab-shakeh stood and cried with
a loud voice in the *Jews'* language, and spake, saying,"
etc. He does his best to frighten the populace, "shut
up like a bird in a cage," as Sennacherib's own inscription states. He hoped to incite sedition in the
city, in order to get possession without laying siege to
it. But he labored in vain; "the people held their
peace, and answered him not a word : for the king's
commandment was, saying, Answer him not."

His speech produced distress, however, and the
king's officers came to Hezekiah "with their clothes
rent, and told him the words of Rab-shakeh." And
Hezekiah "rent his clothes, and covered himself with
sackcloth, and went into the house of the Lord." He
turns to the true source of comfort in the dark hour;
and also sent to Isaiah the prophet, saying, "Thus
saith Hezekiah, This day is a day of trouble, and of
rebuke, and blasphemy" (for Sennacherib's servants
had spoken against the Lord God, against the God of
Jerusalem, as against the gods of the people of the
earth, which were the work of men's hands); "for the
children are come to the birth, and there is not strength
to bring forth. It may be the Lord thy God will hear

all the words of Rab-shakeh, whom the king of Assyria his master hath sent to reproach the living God; and will reprove the words which the Lord thy God hath heard: wherefore lift up thy prayer for the remnant that are left."

The prophet's reply is brief and decisive: "And Isaiah said unto them, Thus shall ye say to your master, Thus saith the Lord, Be not afraid of the words which thou hast heard, with which the servants of the king of Assyria have blasphemed Me. Behold, I will send a blast upon him, and he shall hear a rumor, and shall return to his own land; and I will cause him to fall by the sword in his own land."

Sennacherib, anxious to leave the country, yet unwilling to let such a stronghold as Jerusalem remain untaken, despatched a letter to the king, hoping against hope to frighten him into capitulation. "And Hezekiah received the letter of the hand of the messengers, and read it: and Hezekiah went up into the house of the Lord, and spread it before the Lord." How beautiful his childlike trust in the God of Israel! And there in the temple he prays as only a saint in his hour of distress can pray. (Read 2 Kings 19: 15–19.) God answers him through a message from Isaiah, in which full deliverance is assured him. "Therefore," it concludes, "thus saith the Lord concerning the king of Assyria, He shall not come into this city, nor shoot an arrow there, nor come before it with shield, nor cast a bank against it. By the way that he came, by the same shall he return, and shall not come into this city, saith the Lord. For I will defend this city, to save it, for Mine own sake, and for My servant David's sake. And it came to pass that night, that the angel of the Lord went out, and smote in the camp of the Assyrians a hundred fourscore and five thousand: and when they [or, 'men'] arose early in the morning, behold, they were all dead corpses. So Sennacherib king of Assyria departed, and went and returned, and dwelt at Nineveh. And it came to pass, as he was worshiping in the house of Nisroch his god, that Adrammelech and Sharezer his sons smote him with the sword: and they escaped into the land of Armenia."

"So let all Thine enemies perish, O Lord ;
But let them that love Him be as the sun when he goeth forth in his might."

"Thus the Lord saved Hezekiah and the inhabitants of Jerusalem from the hand of Sennacherib the king of Assyria, and from the hand of all other, and guided [lit., protected] them on every side. And many brought gifts unto the Lord to Jerusalem, and presents to Hezekiah king of Judah: so that he was magnified in the sight of all nations from thenceforth."

"In those days was Hezekiah sick unto death." "Those days" must refer to the time of the Assyrian invasion, or immediately after Sennacherib came up, in the fourteenth year of Hezekiah's reign; as fifteen years, the prophet said, should be added to his life. As he reigned twenty-nine years, there is no difficulty whatever in fixing the exact time of his sickness. Men make difficulties for themselves (where there really are none) by giving heed to uncertain monumental records, instead of abiding by the simple and sure statements of Holy Scripture.

"And the prophet Isaiah the son of Amoz came to him, and said unto him, Thus saith the Lord, Set thy house in order; for thou shalt die, and not live." Isaiah "came to him," it says. He had not gone personally to him, but sent word by a messenger, at the time of Sennacherib's investment of the city. Some have thought from this, and from certain passages in his prophecy, that there was a coolness, or even estrangement, between the prophet and the king, over his rebellion against Assyria. More likely it was the prophet's age (he must have been near eighty) that prevented him from going to the king. We can understand too how, when Hezekiah lay at the point of death, he would make a special effort to see him face to face. He was sent with heavy tidings to the childless king; and little wonder it was that the announcement of his death distressed him. True to his habit and faith in God, Hezekiah turns to Him in distress; and almost before he called, God answered. The prophet had not yet reached the middle court when God said to him, "Turn again, and tell Hezekiah the captain of My people, Thus saith the Lord, the God of David thy father, I have heard thy prayer, I have seen thy tears: behold, I will heal thee: on the third day thou shalt go up to the house of the Lord. And I will add unto thy days fifteen years; and I will deliver thee and this city out of the hand of the king of Assyria; and I will defend this city for Mine own sake, and for My servant David's sake." His full recovery was on the "third day." It is the day of resurrection (see Hos. 6: 2); and on that day Judah received her king as it were, in figure, from the dead.

His cure was in answer to prayer, though means were used—" a lump of figs." It is often more humble, and more according to God, to use means than not to use them. If the incident is typical, and the king's recovery on the third day (answering to the passage in Hosea) foreshadows Israel's national restoration, or resurrection, as in Dan. 12 : 2, we would naturally connect the lump of figs with Matt. 21 : 19–21 and 24 : 32—figure of Israel, now under death and the curse of God, but yet to revive and bear fruit. This is not pressed, but only suggested. But as " God's commandment is exceeding broad," so is His blessed Word very full; and it is " not of any private (or separate) interpretation."

Hezekiah quite properly asks for a sign to assure himself of his recovery. His hypocritical father, in mock modesty, refused to ask for a sign. He used a pious phrase in his refusal, saying, " I will not tempt the Lord." But he was not asked to " tempt God." God Himself had told him to ask for a sign. Unbelief and self-will were at the bottom of his blank refusal, though covered under this pious phrase. And he was not the last of religious unbelievers to use the same expression, and for a like purpose. (See Isa. 7.)

God gives the anxious king a sign; and a wonderful sign it was. The shadow turned back on the dial of Ahaz ten degrees, in answer to the prophet's prayer. It was a miracle, whatever way we take it. God could have reversed the revolution of the earth, had He seen fit to do so—for he is a poor clockmaker even, who cannot turn the hands of his own workmanship backward; or He could have caused the phenomenon by the ordinary law of refraction, or even by volcanic pressure from beneath have altered the inclination of the dial's *gnomon* for the time being. In any case it was a miracle, whatever the rationalist or skeptical astronomer may say to the contrary.

The news of this miracle reached Chaldea, and a deputation was sent from Babylon "to inquire of the wonder that was done in the land." And it was in "the business" of these "ambassadors" that the recovered king was ensnared with pride. The "letter" and the "present" from the king of Babylon were too much for his latent vanity—native to us all. What Sennacherib's letter and deputation of offensive diplomats could not effect (for they drove him to his knees), the letter and friendly commission from Merodach-baladan accomplished—to his ruin almost, and that of his kingdom. How like the Christian and this world! Its *frown* is comparatively powerless; it is its subtle *favor* that we have most to fear. "Hezekiah rendered not again according to the benefit done unto him; for his heart was lifted up"—not, as with Jehoshaphat, "in the ways of the Lord" (see 2 Chron. 17 : 6): "therefore there was wrath upon him, and upon Judah and Jerusalem. Notwithstanding Hezekiah humbled himself for the pride of his heart, both he and the inhabitants of Jerusalem, so that the wrath of the Lord came not upon them in the days of Hezekiah." It was not *spiritual* pride, as with his great-grandfather Uzziah; but *worldly* pride—"the pride of life," we might say. It was *his* precious things, *his* armor, *his* treasures, *his* house, *his* dominion, etc., that he showed the ambassadors from Babylon. When the prophet came to reprove him, he significantly asked, "What have they seen in *thy* house?" "All that is in *my* house have they seen," Hezekiah answered; "there is nothing among *my* treasures that I have not showed them." Why did he not show these learned heathen *God's* house? "every whit" of which showeth "*His* glory" (Ps. 29 : 9, marg.). There he could have explained to them the meaning of the brazen altar, and the sacrifices offered thereon; and who can tell what the result might not have been in the souls of these idolaters? They were brought to Hezekiah's very doors by one of God's wonders in creation; why did he not embrace the opportunity of showing them of His higher wonders of redemption? But no; they were shown what displayed the glory of the poor pride-filled king. The "benefit done to him" was apparently forgotten. He did not ask, like his great father David, "What shall I render unto the Lord for all His benefits toward me?" and who also said, "*Forget not* all His benefits." And we Christians, in a very much higher sense, have been made "partakers of the benefit." May we, in return, render unto God the glory due unto His name.

"God left him," it is said of Hezekiah, "to try him, that he might know what was in his heart." (See Deut. 8 : 2.) He learned, to his shame and sorrow, that there was a vast amount of *ego* there. It was well to know it, that it might be judged and put away before he should be betrayed by it into deeper and more serious sin. But when he hears the judgment pronounced by the prophet on his posterity, he meekly submits, and says, "Good is the word of the Lord which thou hast spoken. He said moreover, For there shall be peace and truth in my days." Of this last, one aptly remarks: "Not the language of mere selfishness, but of one feeling that the national corruption must at last lead to the threatened judgment; and thanking God for the stroke being deferred yet for a time."

"And Hezekiah had exceeding much riches and honor." "God had given him substance very much." "And Hezekiah prospered in all his works." His scribes "copied out" a selection of Solomon's proverbs (Prov. 25 : 1). Isaiah and other chroniclers recorded "the rest of his acts and goodness" (Heb., good works).

"And Hezekiah slept with his fathers, and they buried him in the chiefest of the sepulchres of the sons of David: and all Judah and the inhabitants of Jerusalem did him honor at his death. And Manasseh his son reigned in his stead."

Of all the kings of Judah since the days of Solomon, Hezekiah is the "burning and shining light." It was left to him to break in pieces the brazen serpent made by Moses in the wilderness. It had become a snare to the nation; for up to Hezekiah's day they had burned incense unto it. "And he called it Nehushtan"—*a piece of brass* (2 Kings 18 : 4). His reforming predecessors had lacked either the discernment to see the element of idolatry in the superstitious reverence shown it, or lacked the holy courage to destroy it in the face of popular opposition, probably. It had been used by God in the wilderness as a type of Christ "made sin" for our salvation, but the nation had degraded it (and themselves) by regarding it with a semi-idolatrous spirit, like Rome and its pretended relics of "the true cross," "the holy sepulchre," and what not. Hezekiah, to his honor be it said, did not hesitate to remove this occasion of offence, calling it what it really was—a [mere] piece of brass.

"And the rest of the acts of Hezekiah, and all his might, and how he made a pool, and a conduit, and brought water into the city, are they not written in the book of the chronicles of the kings of Judah?"

MANASSEH

(Forgetting.)

(2 Kings 21 : 1–18. 2 Chron. 33 : 1–20.)

Contemporary Prophet, JOEL.

"The king sent and loosed him ; even the ruler of the people, and let him go free."—*Psalm 105 : 20.*

"MANASSEH was twelve years old when he began to reign, and he reigned fifty and five years in Jerusalem : but did that which was evil in the sight of the Lord, like unto the abominations of the heathen, whom the Lord had cast out before the children of Israel."

"Extremes meet" : here, it would seem, is one of the worst and most cruel of kings that ever reigned—succeeding Hezekiah, of whom it was said, "After him was none like him among all the kings of Judah, nor any that were before him" (2 Kings 18 : 5). Had this good king been able to foresee the wickedness of his unworthy son, he would doubtless have had no desire to recover from his sickness. Better by far die childless than beget a son such as Manasseh proved to be. We must not presume to judge God's honored servant, but it does appear as if he would have done better to have meekly submitted to God's will in his sickness. He could surely have left it with God to care for the succession, as he knew the covenant made

with David, "ordered in all things and sure," and
have spared the nation that he loved the tears and
blood (to say nothing of God's honor in the matter)
that his desired descendant brought them to.   Nothing
to his honor is recorded as done by him after his recovery from his sickness.   True, his healing was in
answer to prayer, and a wonderful miracle was done
in pledge of it.   But so it was with Israel when they
requested flesh to eat.   " God gave them their request;
but sent leanness into their soul" (Ps. 106: 15).   A
miracle was performed for them too (that of the quails),
in order that they might have what they persisted in
desiring.   But there was only One who ever and always said, "Not My will, but Thine, be done." (Comp.
Ps. 21: 4.)

Manasseh quickly, it would seem, undid the work of
his father's early reign—which was also done "suddenly."   "For he built again the high places which
Hezekiah his father had broken down, and he reared
up altars for Baalim, and made groves, and worshiped
all the host of heaven, and served them.   Also he
built altars [for idolatry] in the house of the Lord,
whereof the Lord had said, In Jerusalem shall My
name be for ever.   And he built altars for all the host
of heaven in the two courts of the house of the Lord.
And he caused his children to pass through the fire in
the valley of the son of Hinnom : also he observed times,
and used enchantments, and used witchcraft, and dealt
with a familiar spirit, and with wizards : he wrought
much evil in the sight of the Lord, to provoke Him to
anger.   And he set a carved image, the idol which he
had made, in the house of God."

It is a terrible portrait to paint of any man ; but of
a king of Judah, and a son of Hezekiah the Good, it
seems almost incredible. It makes the heart turn sick
almost, to read the list of his abominations. He
"made Judah and the inhabitants of Jerusalem to err,
and to do worse than the heathen, whom the Lord
had destroyed before the children of Israel." It was
the worst of all corruptions—the corruption of the
best. The higher the fall, the deeper the plunge.
Alas, in the Corinthian church too there was such sin
as was "not so much as named among the Gentiles."
"I was almost in all evil in the midst of the congregation and assembly," one said (Prov. 5 : 14). "Worse
than an unbeliever," wrote another (1 Tim. 5 : 8).
Language like this may sound strange to some—
strangely sad, indeed, that such things *can* be, and
have been. Look at Rome, and see it verified. One
within the pale of Rome has even said, "The annals
of the church are the annals of hell!" And what
must the surrounding nations have thought of these
"annals" of Judah—"worse than the heathen"? Of
Manasseh and Judah it could then truly be said, as
the apostle, by the Spirit, declared seven hundred
years later, "The name of God is blasphemed among
the Gentiles through you."

"And the Lord spake to Manasseh, and to his people : but they would not hearken." He spoke, as
usual, through His prophets (2 Kings 21 : 10). This
was their message : "Because Manasseh king of Judah
hath done these abominations, and hath done wickedly above all that the Amorites did [how terrible!],
which were before him, and hath made Judah also to

sin with his idols: therefore thus saith the Lord God of Israel, Behold, I am bringing such evil upon Jerusalem and Judah, that whosoever heareth of it, both his ears shall tingle. And I will stretch over Jerusalem the line of Samaria, and the plummet of the house of Ahab: and I will wipe Jerusalem as a man wipeth a dish, wiping it, and turning it upside down. And I will forsake the remnant of mine inheritance, and deliver them into the hand of their enemies; and they shall become a prey and a spoil to all their enemies; because they have done that which was evil in My sight, and have provoked Me to anger, since the day their fathers came forth out of Egypt, even unto this day."

It was an appalling, though absolutely just, arraignment, and should have brought the nation to repentance. Its threats, if nothing more, should have startled them from their sins. They knew the fate of Samaria—already fallen; and Jerusalem should receive like punishment. The house of Ahab had perished, and *their* kings should not escape a similar judgment. But the message was evidently lost upon them; they proved themselves a more perverse people than the "men of Nineveh" who one hundred and fifty years before had "repented at the preaching of Jonas."

What prophets God used at this time is not known. Isaiah was still alive, possibly, though very aged, and the tradition may be true which says he "was sawn asunder"—with a wooden saw. Josephus does not mention this, though he does say that Manasseh "barbarously slew all the righteous men that were among the Hebrews. Nor would he spare the prophets."

(Ant. x. : 3, § 1.) "Moreover," says the inspired historian, "Manasseh shed innocent blood very much, till he had filled Jerusalem from one end to another; besides his sin wherewith he made Judah to sin, in doing that which was evil in the sight of the Lord" (2 Kings 21 : 16). Wicked as his grandfather Ahaz had been, he did not, so far as we know, redden his hands with blood like this human monster Manasseh. But the reaping came at last, though harvest-time was late, perhaps, in the long-suffering patience of God. "Wherefore the Lord brought upon them the captains of the host of the king of Assyria, which took Manasseh among the thorns, and bound him with fetters, and carried him to Babylon." They refused to hear the *word*, so they were compelled to feel the *rod*. As befitted this monster of evil, Manasseh was brought in chains to Babylon.

Scripture gives no hint as to the time of this event, but it appears from Assyrian monuments to have been somewhere about the middle of his reign. It was the old and oft-demonstrated law of retribution working itself out: the occasion of the sin becoming the instrument of its punishment. Hezekiah sinned in the "matter of the ambassadors" from Babylon, and it is to Babylon that his son Manasseh goes as a captive.

"And when he was in affliction, he besought the Lord his God, and humbled himself greatly before the God of his fathers, and prayed unto Him : and He was entreated of him, and heard his supplication, and brought him again to Jerusalem into his kingdom. Then Manasseh knew that Jehovah He was God."

"He humbled himself *greatly*," as well he might, for
his guilt indeed was very great. "When he was in
affliction"—no doubt, he owned the justice of his punishment. "I know, O Lord," he could say, "that Thy
judgments are right, and that Thou in faithfulness
hast afflicted me" (Ps. 119 : 75).

We have no details of Manasseh's sufferings in his
Babylonian captivity. God takes no pleasure in the
punishment of His people, and very tenderly covers
with the veil of silence all that can be profitably kept
back. He heard Manasseh's bitter cry of repentance
and entreaty, and restored him to his kingdom. This
was grace indeed—"grace abounding."

On his return to Jerusalem he began to build and
fortify, "and put captains of war in all the fenced cities." But, what was better, "he took away the strange
gods, and the idol out of the house of the Lord, and
all the altars that he had built in the mount of the
house of the Lord, and in Jerusalem, and cast them
out of the city. And he repaired the altar of the Lord,
and sacrificed thereon peace-offerings and thank-offerings, and commanded Judah to serve the Lord God of
Israel." He undertook to undo, as far as possible,
his former works of wickedness. His name Manasseh
means *forgetting;* and Josephus says : "When he was
come to Jerusalem, he endeavored, if it were possible,
to *cast out of his memory* his former sins against God;
of which he now repented." But the innocent lives
that he had taken he could never restore, nor could he
ever wholly undo the evil of his former course. So
great had been his iniquity, and that of Judah with
him, that God never forgave it, nationally (2 Kings 23 :

26; 24: 4; Jer. 15: 4). *Personally*, through his confession and humiliation before God, Manasseh was forgiven; and it is good to see the great change in his after life, and that he did not forget his indebtedness to God for His matchless grace to him, as his "*thank-offerings*" on the restored altar indicate. He was the Old Testament "chief of sinners," a "pattern" at that time in whom God "showed forth all long-suffering," to any who should turn to Him in penitence and faith. Newton's lines, no doubt, would well express the spirit of his grateful thoughts :—

> "Amazing grace ! how sweet the sound,
> That saved a wretch like me !
> I once was lost, but now am found,
> Was blind, but now I see ! "

"Now the rest of the acts of Manasseh, and his prayer unto his God, and the words of the seers that spake to him in the name of the Lord God of Israel, behold, they are written in the book of the kings of Israel. His prayer also, and how God was entreated of him, and all his sins, and his trespass, and the places wherein he built high places, and set up groves and graven images, before he was humbled : behold, they are written among the sayings of the seers" (or, "*Hozia*," a prophet.—*Keil*). His mother's name was Hephzibah (*my delight is in her*). See Isa. 62 : 4. She may have been a pious woman, and so her name not have been inappropriate to her character; but if so, she had very little influence over her son—unlike the Eunice (*victorious*) of a later day, and many more besides.

"And Manasseh slept with his fathers, and was buried in the garden of his own house, in the garden of Uzza: and Amon his son reigned in his stead." His body found no place of rest among the kings, showing how the consequences of sin follow men even to the grave.

The so-called "Prayer of Manasseh" in the Apocrypha is a fiction, and was even declared so by so credulous a body as the Council of Trent.

> "KINGS ON THE THRONE;
> Yea, He doth establish them for ever,
> And they are exalted.
> And if they be bound in fetters,
> And be holden in cords of affliction;
> Then He showeth them their work,
> And their transgressions that they have exceeded.
> He openeth also their ear to discipline,
> And commandeth that they return from iniquity.
> If they obey and serve Him,
> They shall spend their days in prosperity,
> And their years in pleasures.
> But if they obey not,
> They shall perish by the sword,
> And they shall die without knowledge."
>
> —*Job 36 : 7–12.*

AMON

(Training, or *skilled.)*

(2 Kings 21 : 19–26 ; 2 Chron. 33 : 21–25.)

"Is it fit to say to a king, Thou art wicked? and to
princes, Ye are ungodly?"—*Job 34: 18.*

"AMON was twenty and two years old when he began to reign, and he reigned two years in Jerusalem. And his mother's name was Meshullemeth, the daughter of Haruz of Jotbah. And he did
that which was evil in the sight of the Lord, as his
father Manasseh did. And he walked in all the way
that his father walked in, and served the idols that his
father served, and worshiped them: and he forsook
the Lord God of his fathers, and walked not in the
way of the Lord."

He was probably born after his father's return from
Babylon, so must have had a godly training. The
expression, "he *forsook* the Lord," would seem to indicate that he had in his earlier days professed to worship Him. His mother's name, Meshullemeth (*recon-
ciliation,* or, *to be safe),* might have reference to his
having been born subsequently to her husband's recon-
ciliation to the Lord, or his safe return from his Babylonian captivity. This would increase Amon's responsibility,—having had such advantages,— and consequently enhance his guilt. Her father's name, Haruz

(*earnest*) of Jotbah (*pleasantness*) leads to the supposition that Amon's mother, like his grandmother, must have been a good woman. But all good women do not always prove to be good *mothers;* and it would be no strange or unusual thing if some of these Hebrew "heirs-apparent" to the throne were permitted to do pretty much as they pleased, and in this way prepared to act the part of self-willed transgressors and rebels against God, when the time came for them to take the kingdom. For "a child left to himself bringeth his mother to shame" (Prov. 29 : 15).

There is not one bright spot in this king's character to relieve the darkness of his life's brief record. He "humbled not himself before the Lord," it says, "as Manasseh his father humbled himself; but Amon trespassed more and more" (or, "multiplied trespass," marg.). So odious did he make himself, even to the backslidden people, that they rid themselves of his unwelcome presence by the hand of assassins. "And his servants conspired against him, and slew him in his own house." His subjects must have been reduced to desperate straits when they would thus violate God's expressed prohibition—"Touch not Mine anointed." Jeremiah and Zephaniah must have been youths about this time, and the former's reluctance to taking up the prophetic work to which he was called can well be understood when the true condition of affairs in Judah at that time is known. Both could see quite plainly what they might expect if faithful to their trust.

"But the people of the land slew all them that had conspired against king Amon; and the people of the land made Josiah his son king in his stead." "The people of the land," or country, may be in contra-distinction to the "inhabitants of Jerusalem." The centre of light and privilege is not always the seat of righteousness and "godly sincerity," but commonly the reverse, as here, apparently. The "provincial" is frequently more loyal and upright than the imperious citizen of the capital.

The record of the reign of Amon is most briefly told —in but sixteen verses. And well it should be so. There is enough for our admonition, after the lessons given in his father's history.

"And he was buried in his sepulchre in the garden of Uzza: and Josiah his son reigned in his stead." Uzza means *strength*; and death, the strong one, over-came this king of Judah, *trained*, or *skilled*, in wicked-ness, in his twenty-fourth year.

"He passed away, and, lo, he was not; yea, I sought him, but he could not be found."

JOSIAH

(*Supported by Jehovah.*)

(2 Kings chaps. 22, 23 ; 2 Chron. 34–35.)

Contemporary Prophet, JEREMIAH.

"A wise king scattereth the wicked, and bringeth the wheel over them."—*Proverbs 20 : 26.*

" JOSIAH was eight years old when he began to reign, and he reigned thirty and one years in Jerusalem. And his mother's name was Jedidah, the daughter of Adaiah of Boscath. And he did that which was right in the sight of the Lord, and walked in all the way of David his father, and turned not aside to the right hand or to the left."

At last, after more than three hundred years, the prophecy of "the man of God out of Judah" is fulfilled: "Behold, a child shall be born unto the house of David, Josiah by name; and upon thee [the idol altar at Bethel] shall he offer the priests of the high places that burn incense upon thee, and men's bones shall be burnt upon thee" (1 Kings 13 : 2). "For in the eighth year of his reign, while he was yet young [sixteen], he began to seek after the God of David his father: and in the twelfth year he began to purge Judah and Jerusalem from the high places, and the groves, and the carved images, and the molten images.

And they brake down the altars of Baalim in his presence; and the images [lit., *sun-pillars*], that were on high above them, he cut down; and the groves, and the carved images, and the molten images, he brake in pieces, and made dust of them, and strowed it upon the graves of them that had sacrificed unto them. And he burnt the bones of the priests upon their altars, and cleansed Judah and Jerusalem."

"God's purposes will ripen fast,"

is true, in a certain sense; yet in another sense

"The mills of God grind slow."

Scoffers long may have asked, "Where is the promise of this coming prince, this child of the house of David, named Josiah?" And as generation after generation passed, and no prince of that name appeared, even the righteous may have questioned in their minds and wondered if God had forgotten, or doubted if the prophecy were really true. Did Jedidah (*beloved*) know of this prophecy when she named her first-born? or the child's grandmother, Adaiah (*Jah has adorned*)? They were of the town of Boscath, a *swell* (of ground), and at last the time had come when he should *rise* of whom the prophet had spoken; and the prophecy was now fulfilled—as all God's word must be.

"And so did he in the cities of Manasseh, and Ephraim, and Simeon, even unto Naphtali, with their mattocks round about. And when he had broken down the altars and the groves, and had beaten the graven images into powder, and cut down all the idols throughout all the land of Israel, he returned to

Jerusalem." It took six years of labor to accomplish this; and "in the eighteenth year of his reign, when he had purged the land, and the house," he commissioned his officers of state "to repair the house of the Lord his God." Levites were sent throughout the land to collect the money necessary for this work. "And they put it in the hand of the workmen that had the oversight of the house of the Lord, and they gave it to the workmen that wrought in the house of the Lord, to repair and amend the house: even to the artificers and builders gave they it, to buy hewn stone, and timber for couplings [or joists], and to floor the houses which the kings of Judah had destroyed. And the men did the work faithfully." Manasseh, though restored personally, had not the energy—or influence, perhaps—to do this work. Everything must have been in a ruined state when the young Josiah began his work of restoration.*

And now a great discovery was made. A hid treasure (long lost, no doubt) was found, "better than of gold or rubies rare." "And when they brought out the money that was brought into the house of the Lord, Hilkiah the priest found a book of the law of the Lord given by Moses. And Hilkiah answered and said to Shaphan the scribe, I have found the book of the law in the house of the Lord. And Hilkiah delivered the book to Shaphan. And Shaphan carried

---

* The shameful idolatry that filled the land had to be cleared away before any claim to, or restoration of, Jehovah's worship could be made. Hence this must be accomplished ere Jehovah's temple is restored—which in Hezekiah's day was done *first* (2 Chron. 29 : 3).—[*Ed.*

the book to the king, and brought the king word back
again, saying, All that was committed to thy servants,
they do it. And they have gathered together the
money that was found in the house of the Lord, and
have delivered it into the hand of the overseers, and
to the hand of the workmen." He says nothing of the
new-found treasure as yet. It may not have been a
treasure in his eyes, perhaps. Like many at the present time, he was more occupied with "workmen" and
"money" than with God's book, which He has "magnified," not merely above all Christian work or mis-
sionary enterprise (though these have their place), but
"above all His name." Shaphan did not despise the
book, but he had not yet, like many a modern scribe,
realized the importance of that blessed volume. Then
—after "money," and "overseers," and "workmen,"
have all been mentioned—"then, Shaphan the scribe
told the king, saying, Hilkiah the priest hath given
me a book"—only *a* book! "And Shaphan read it
before the king."

"And it came to pass, when the king had heard the
words of the law, that he rent his clothes." He then
commanded the temple curators, and his servant Asa-
iah, saying, "Go, inquire of the Lord for me, and for
them that are left in Israel and in Judah, concerning
the words of the book that is found: for great is the
wrath of the Lord that is poured out upon us, because
our fathers have not kept the word of the Lord, to do
after all that is written in this book." It was, no
doubt, the Pentateuch—either the original, as written
by Moses, or the temple copy (Deut. 31 : 26), used in
days gone by at the coronation of their kings (.See

Deut. 17 : 18 ; 2 Chron. 23 : 11.) How long it had been lost is not known; probably since the beginning of Manasseh's reign at least.

"And Hilkiah, and they that the king had appointed, went to Huldah the prophetess, the wife of Shallum the son of Tokehath, the son of Hasrah, keeper of the wardrobe: now she dwelt in Jerusalem in the second quarter [of the town]; and they spoke with her to that effect" (2 Chron. 34 : 22, N. Tr.). Why they did not inquire of Jeremiah, or Zephaniah (who were contemporary with Josiah (Jer. 1 : 3 ; Zeph. 1 : 1), is uncertain. Anathoth, Jeremiah's birthplace, was only three miles from Jerusalem, and so within easy reach. Both these prophets, however, may have been too young at the time to be consulted as prophets by the nation. (See Jer. 1 : 2).

Huldah's answer was a most impressive one: "Thus saith the Lord God of Israel, Tell ye the man that sent you to me, Thus saith the Lord, Behold, I will bring evil upon this place, and upon the inhabitants thereof, even all the curses which are written in the book which they have read before the king of Judah: because they have forsaken Me . . . therefore My wrath shall be poured out upon this place, and shall not be quenched. And as for the king of Judah, who sent you to enquire of the Lord, so shall ye say unto him, Thus saith the Lord God of Israel, concerning the words which thou hast heard, because thy heart was tender, and thou didst humble thyself before God, when thou heardest His words against this place, and against the inhabitants thereof, and humbledst thyself before Me; . . I have even heard thee also, saith the

Lord. Behold, I will gather thee to thy fathers, and thou shalt be gathered to thy grave in peace, neither shall thine eyes see all the evil that I will bring upon this place, and upon the inhabitants of the same. So they brought the king word again."

In wrath God remembers mercy; and like his great-grandfather Hezekiah, Josiah is comforted with the assurance that there should be a postponement of these impending judgments during his day, because he, like Hezekiah, humbled himself. He at once gathered all the elders of the land together, and with them and the priests and Levites, "and all the people, great and small: and he [or, one] read in their ears all the words of the book of the covenant that was found in the house of the Lord."

"And the king stood on the dais and made a covenant before Jehovah, to walk after Jehovah, and to keep His commandments and His testimonies and His statutes with all his heart and with all his soul, to establish the words of this covenant that are written in this book. And all the people stood to the covenant" (2 Kings 23: 3, N. Tr.) On the young king's part this was all real, no doubt, but one has only to read the earlier part of Jeremiah's prophecy to see how hypocritical it was with the mass of the people. (See Jer. 3: 10, marg.) They had enthusiastically entered into covenants with the Lord before, and the outcome was always the same—breakdown, and wider departure from God than ever before.

The work of reformation is then extended: "And Josiah took away all the abominations out of all the countries that pertained to the children of Israel, and made all that were present in Israel to serve, even to serve the Lord their God. And all his days they departed not from following the Lord, the God of their fathers" (2 Chron. 34: 33).

"Moreover the altar that was at Bethel, and the high place which Jeroboam the son of Nebat, who made Israel to sin, had made, both that altar and the high place he brake down . . . And as Josiah turned himself, he spied the sepulchres that were there in the mount, and sent, and took the bones out of the sepulchres, and burned them upon the altar, and polluted it, according to the word of the Lord which the man of God proclaimed, who proclaimed these words [O altar, altar, thus saith the Lord; Behold a child shall be born unto the house of David, Josiah by name; and upon thee shall he offer the priests of the high places that burn incense upon thee, and men's bones shall be burnt upon thee. 1 Kings 13: 2.] Then he said, What title is that that I see? And the men of the city told him, It is the sepulchre of the man of God which came from Judah, and proclaimed these things that thou hast done against the altar of Bethel. And he said, Let him alone; let no man move his bones. So they let his bones alone, with the bones of the prophet that came out of Samaria."

It is not certain if this remarkable incident occurred before, or after, the finding of the copy of the law in the temple; (see Author's Introduction). It proves however that after the lapse of at least three centuries the prophecy of the Judean prophet was still fresh in the minds of men. God not only lets none of His words fall to the ground, but takes care also that in some way or other they are preserved in the memories of those concerned in them. The "title" on the man of God's tomb would help, no doubt, to keep the occurrence from being forgotten. How awed and encouraged Josiah the king must have felt, to know that he had been named and appointed by God for the work he was doing, so many generations before. How it would tend to impress upon him the force and meaning of such scriptures as the 139th psalm. And witnessing how literally the prophecy of the man of God was fulfilled, he and all his people, would be convinced that the prophecies of Huldah and Jeremiah against themselves would in like manner be exactly fulfilled.

Moved, no doubt, by what was written in the recovered book of the law regarding it, "Josiah kept a passover unto the Lord in Jerusalem." Careful preparations were made that everything might be done according to the written word of God. It was in the eighteenth year of his reign, so was probably celebrated immediately after the completion of the temple repairs and the finding of the book. (Comp. 2 Chron. 34 : 8, and 35 : 19). "And he set the priests in their charges, and encouraged them to the service of the house of the Lord. And said unto the Levites, that taught all Israel, which were holy unto the Lord, Put the holy ark in the house which Solomon the son of David king of Israel did build, it shall not be a burden upon your shoulders: serve now the Lord your God and His people Israel. And prepare yourselves by the houses of your fathers, after your courses, according to the writing of David king of Israel, and according to the writing of Solomon his son." It was all to be done *according to what was written.* Josiah evidently took great care as to this, and so became a beautiful example for all who long to please the Lord and desire to decline "neither to the right hand nor to the left," like this godly king, from following Him. Some in the kingdom might think him too much bound to the letter of these writings, but he would have God's approval, which was quite enough. No one can say where the wilful departure of a hair's breadth may not eventually lead. The safety of all is to keep as far away from the edge of the precipice as possible. "Then shall I not be ashamed, when I have respect unto all Thy commandments" (Ps. 119: 6).

Josiah tells the Levites to put the ark in its proper place in the temple, and not bear it any longer on their shoulders. It is the last *historical* reference to the ark in Scripture. It would almost appear, from Jer. 3: 16, that it had been made an object of ostentatious display, and was possibly borne by the Levites in procession through the streets of Jerusalem. It is never after heard of, and probably perished when the temple was burned by the Chaldees (2 Chron. 36: 19).

The king further commands the Levites: "Kill the passover," he says, "and sanctify yourselves, and prepare your brethren, that ye may do *according to the word of the Lord* by the hand of Moses." And such a passover it was!—"there was no passover like to that kept in Israel from the days of Samuel the prophet; neither did all the kings of Israel keep such a passover as Josiah kept, and the priests, and the Levites, and all Judah and Israel that were present, and the inhabitants of Jerusalem." It even exceeded the great passover under Hezekiah, which had not been equaled since "the time of Solomon son of David king of Israel" (2 Chron. 30 : 20). Josiah's surpassed that of all the kings, and found its compeer only in that of the prophet.

And now comes the closing act in this stirring drama of Josiah's life. "After all this, when Josiah had prepared the temple, Necho king of Egypt came up to fight against Charchemish by Euphrates : and Josiah went out against him. But he sent ambassadors to him, saying, What have I to do with thee, thou king of Judah ? I come not against thee this day, but against the house wherewith I have war : for God commanded me to make haste : forbear thee from meddling with God, who is with me, that He destroy thee not." It was a fair warning, and Josiah should certainly have heeded it. Necho came against Assyria, and had no quarrel with Josiah. He was a man of enterprise and energy. It was he who attempted to connect the Red Sea with the Nile by a canal. Phenician navigators, under his patronage, circumnavigated the continent of Africa. He came by sea on this expedition, and landed at Accho. So he was not even on Josiah's territory when that king culpably marched his forces against him.

"Nevertheless Josiah would not turn his face from him, but disguised himself, that he might fight with him, and harkened not unto the words of Necho from the mouth of God,* and came to fight in the valley of

---

* The word " from the mouth of God " may sometimes come through such as are not true servants of God. See John 11 : 49–51 : Num. 23 : 5 ; Josh. 13 : 22. [Ed.

Megiddo. And the archers shot at king Josiah; and the king said to his servants, Have me away; for I am sore wounded. His servants therefore took him out of that chariot, and put him in the second chariot that he had; and they brought him to Jerusalem, and he died, and was buried in one of the sepulchres of his fathers."

"Why shouldest thou meddle to thy hurt, that thou shouldest fall?" said the king of Israel to Amaziah, Josiah's ancestor, years before (2 Kings 14:10). Josiah should also have been familiar with the proverb, "copied by the men of Hezekiah," "He that passeth by, and meddleth with strife belonging not to him, is like one that taketh a dog by the ears" (Prov. 26:17). And another: "It is an honor for a man to cease from strife: but every fool will be meddling" (Prov. 20:3). It was not of faith, else why "disguise" himself? There is no record of any prayer before the battle, as in the case of so many of his godly ancestors; and this rash act of Josiah seems unaccountable. He may have suspected that Necho had some ulterior design upon his kingdom; but as the king of Egypt strongly disclaimed any such intention, Josiah's unprovoked attack upon him was wholly unjustified. And God, who is the God of peace and righteousness, would not preserve him, as he had Jehoshaphat. There is another light, too, in which Josiah's early end may be looked at. The people were utterly unworthy of such a godly ruler, and their wickedness, spite of external reformation, called loudly for judgment; so the righteous was taken away from the evil to come. Viewed from this standpoint, it was a mercy to the man himself; but to the nation, speaking after the manner of men, it was a dire calamity.

They evidently realized this, for we read, "All Judah and Jerusalem mourned for Josiah. And Jeremiah lamented for Josiah: and all the singing men and the singing women spake of Josiah in their lamentations to this day, and made them an ordinance in Israel: and, behold, they are written in the lamentations." These "lamentations" must not be confounded with Jeremiah's "Lamentations," written over (and therefore after) Jerusalem's fall. (Comp. Jer. 22 : 10– 13; Zech. 12 : 11.)

Josiah was the last good king to sit upon the throne of David, "till HE come whose right it is." And he was the last whose body found a resting-place among the kings, "the sepulchres of his fathers."

"The memory" of this "just" and energetic king is "blessed." When only twenty years of age he began the herculean task of cleansing his kingdom of its abominations. There were "vessels that were made for Baal," and "for all the host of heaven," to be brought forth out of the temple; there were "idolatrous priests whom the kings of Judah had ordained," to be "put down"—them that burned incense to "Baal, to the sun, and to the moon, and to the planets." "And he brake down the houses of the sodomites [men consecrated to vile purposes], that were by the house of the Lord, where the women [also consecrated to heathen deities] wove hangings [tents] for the groves." "Joshua the governor of the city" had high places at the entrance of his gate which Josiah fearlessly "broke down." He took away the "horses

that the kings of Judah had given to the sun, at the
entering in of the house of the Lord, by the chamber
of Nathan-melech the chamberlain, . . . and burned
the chariots of the sun with fire." "And the altars
that were on the top [or roof] of the upper chamber of
Ahaz, which the kings of Judah had made, and the
altars which Manasseh had made in the two courts of
the house of the Lord, did the king beat down " (or shat-
tered).   He seems to have had few sympathizers, or
supporters, in his reforms, and superintended some of
the work personally.   (See 2 Kings 23 : 16.)   He could
not be blamed if the mass of the people were hypocritical and unreal.   (See Zeph. 1 : 5).   Genuine repentance is not wrought by a king's command, but
he did all that lay in his power, and did not permit a
single visible vestige of idolatry to remain in his realm.
It is significant that when this last righteous king of Judah died, the whole land was outwardly cleansed of its
abominations.   And when his work was done, God
called him home, though an Egyptian arrow was His
messenger.   "And like unto him was there no king
before him, that turned to the Lord with all his heart,
and with all his soul, and with all his might, according to all the law of Moses; neither after him arose
there any like him " (2 Kings 23 : 25).

"Now the rest of the acts of Josiah, and his goodness, according to that which was written in the law
of the Lord, and his deeds, first and last, behold, they
are written in the book of the kings of Israel and
Judah."

JEHOAHAZ

(Jehovah-seized.)

(2 Kings 23 : 30–34 ; 2 Chron. 36 : 1–4.)

Contemporary Prophets:
JEREMIAH; HABAKKUK; ZEPHANIAH.

"The kings of the earth, and all the inhabitants of the world, would not have believed that the adversary and the enemy should have entered into the gates of Jerusalem." *Lamentations 4 : 12.*

"THEN the people of the land took Jehoahaz the son of Josiah, and made him king in his father's stead in Jerusalem. Jehoahaz was twenty and three years old when he began to reign, and he reigned three months in Jerusalem."

The regular succession to the throne of Judah ceased with the lamented Josiah. Jehoahaz was not the eldest son of the late king. Johanan and Jehoiakim were both older than he (1 Chron. 3 : 15). He was made king by popular choice: it was the preference of the multitude, not the appointment of God. "And his mother's name was Hamutal (*delight*), the daughter of Jeremiah of Libnah. And he did that which was evil in the sight of the Lord, according to all that his fathers had done." He and Zedekiah, the last of Judah's nineteen kings, were born of the same mother (2 Kings 24 : 18). He was about nine years

older than his brother Zedekiah, though in 1 Chron.
3 : 15 his name is placed last, because of his much
shorter reign, probably.   He is likened in Ezekiel 19:
1–4 to "a young lion, and it learned to catch the prey;
it devoured men."   This is the only hint given us as
to the character of his sin.   Josephus says of him that
he was "an impious man, and impure in his course of
life."   He was probably guilty of deeds of violence.
In Jer. 22 : 11 he is called, significantly, Shallum (*to
whom it is requited*) ; and by this name he is registered
in the royal Judean genealogy (1 Chron. 3 : 15).   His
name is omitted from among those of our Lord's ancestors in Matt. 1.   Necho, it is said, made his half-
brother Eliakim "king in the room of Josiah *his father*,"
which may imply that God did not recognize Jehoahaz,
the people's choice, as being in a true sense the
successor.

"And the king of Egypt put him down at Jerusalem, and condemned the land in a hundred talents of
silver and a talent of gold."   It is elsewhere stated
that he was taken to Riblah in the land of Hamath
and bound; which in no wise contradicts what is quoted above.   History informs us that after his victory
at Megiddo, Necho intended to march to the Euphrates; but, hearing of Jehoahaz' elevation to the throne
by popular acclamation, he sent a division of his army
to Jerusalem, which deposed him, and brought him
captive to Riblah, where Necho and his chief forces
were.   This he did, it is said, because he believed Jehoahaz leaned toward an alliance with Assyria against
him.

"And the king of Egypt made Eliakim his brother

king over Judah and Jerusalem, and turned his name to Jehoiakim. And Necho took Jehoahaz his brother, and carried him to Egypt." He never returned from Egypt. Jehoahaz (*Jehovah-seized*) had seized the throne that was not his by right, and in turn was seized by Necho, God's instrument, and carried to a land of exile, there to find a grave afar from the sepulchres of his fathers.

He was "anointed" at his coronation, but no extraordinary ceremony could make up for his defective title to the crown. Men have similar thoughts to-day; and as they feel they have no real title to a throne in heaven with Christ, they "are going about," increasing forms and elaborating ceremonies. Hence the rapid growth of Ritualism. "And the end is not yet."

JEHOIAKIM

(*Whom Jehovah will raise.*)

(2 Kings 23 : 34—24 : 6 ; 2 Chron. 36 : 5–8.)

Contemporary Prophets:
JEREMIAH; ZEPHANIAH; EZEKIEL.

"His confidence shall be rooted out of his tabernacle, and it shall bring him to the king of terrors."—*Job 18 : 14.*

" JEHOIAKIM was twenty and five years old when he began to reign, and he reigned eleven years in Jerusalem : and he did that which was evil in the sight of the Lord his God. Against him came up Nebuchadnezzar king of Babylon, and bound him in fetters, to carry him to Babylon. Nebuchadnezzar also carried [some] of the vessels of the house of the Lord to Babylon, and put them in his temple at Babylon."

Jehoiakim was of most unlovely character—treacherous, revengeful, and bloodthirsty. He was several years Jehoahaz' senior, and was not born of the same mother. "And his mother's name was Zebudah (*gainfulness*), the daughter of Pedaiah of Ramah." The mother's name boded no good for her son ; and so it came to be. He taxed the land to give the money according to the commandment of Pharaoh : " he exacted the silver and the gold of the people of the land, of every one according to his taxation, to give unto Pharaoh-Necho." Having been slighted by the people in their choice of his younger half-brother, he would make no effort to ease the people's burdens, but rather increase them. He was in no way under obligations to them; and having behind him the power of Egypt, he had little to fear from them. (See 2 Ki. 23 : 34, 35.) His wickedness is depicted figuratively in Ezek. 19 : 5–7. He too, like his deposed predecessor, "became a young lion, and learned to catch the prey, and devoured men. And he knew their desolate palaces, and he laid waste their cities; and the land was desolate, and the fulness thereof, by the noise of his roaring." His violence and rapacity are graphically represented here.

In the fifth year of his reign a fast was proclaimed among his subjects (the king seems to have had no part in it), and Baruch, Jeremiah's assistant, read in the ears of all the people the message of God to them from a book. Ready tools informed the king of what was being done, and he ordered the book brought and read before him. "Now the king sat in the winter house in the ninth month : and there was a fire on the hearth burning before him. And it came to pass, that when Jehudi had read three or four leaves, he cut it with the penknife [Heb., scribe's knife], and cast it into the fire that was on the hearth, until all the roll was consumed in the fire that was on the hearth. Yet they were not afraid, nor rent their garments, neither the king, nor any of his servants that heard all these words." It was an act of daring impiety, especially for a Jew, who was taught to look upon all sacred writing with greatest reverence. But Jehoiakim was fast hardening himself past all feeling, and no qualms

of conscience are perceptible over his sacrilegious act.
Jeremiah sent him a personal and verbal message,
than which king never heard more awful. "And thou
shalt say to Jehoiakim king of Judah, Thus saith the
Lord, Thou hast burned this roll, saying, Why hast
thou written therein, saying, The king of Babylon shall
certainly come and destroy this land, and shall cause
to cease from thence man and beast? Therefore thus
saith the Lord of Jehoiakim king of Judah, He shall
have none to sit upon the throne of David : and his
dead body shall be cast out in the day to the heat,
and in the night to the frost. And I will punish him
and his seed and his servants for their iniquity." See
Jer. 36.

He also attempted to put Urijah the prophet to death
because he prophesied against Jerusalem and the land.
The prophet fled to Egypt, whence Jehoiakim sent
and fetched him, and "slew him with the sword, and
cast his dead body into the graves of the common
people"—his bitter hatred of God and His truth vent-
ing itself even on the body of His slaughtered servant,
denying it the right of burial among the sepulchres of
the prophets. See Jer. 26 : 20–24. In just retribution God repaid him in kind for his murder and insult.
"Therefore thus saith the Lord concerning Jehoiakim
the son of Josiah king of Judah : They shall not lament for him, saying, Ah my brother! or, Ah my sister!" (as in family mourning) : "they shall *not* lament
for him, saying, Ah lord! or, Ah his glory!" (public
mourning.) "He shall be buried with the burial of
an ass, drawn and cast forth beyond the gates of Jerusalem" (Jer. 22 : 18, 19). And so it happened unto

him : Nebuchadnezzar defeated and drove out of Asia
Jehoiakim's master, Necho. (See 2 Kings 24 : 7.) "In
his days Nebuchadnezzar king of Babylon came up,
and Jehoiakim became his servant three years : then
he turned and rebelled against him." And though
Nebuchadnezzar could not immediately punish him,
his punishment came from another quarter. "The
Lord sent against him bands of the Chaldees, and
bands of the Syrians, and bands of the Moabites, and
bands of the children of Ammon, and sent them
against Judah to destroy it, according to the word of the
Lord which He spake by His servants the prophets."

Now as to his end : Scripture (historically) is silent.
2 Chron. 36 : 6 states that Nebuchadnezzar "bound
him in fetters, to carry him to Babylon." It does
not say he *was* taken there. He may have been re-
leased after promising subjection to his conqueror.
But even if it could be proven that he was actually
carried to Babylon, it would in no wise contradict
what is recorded in 2 Kings 24 : 6 ("So Jehoiakim
slept with his fathers"); for he might easily have returned to Jerusalem, as other Jewish captives at a later
date did. And though there is no historical record
in Scripture concerning his death, this is nothing to
show that the prophecies of Jeremiah concerning his
end were not fulfilled to the letter. We do not really
need the history of it, for prophecy in Scripture is
only pre-written history—its advance sheets, we might
say. It is enough to know what God had foretold
concerning it; the fulfilment is certain. Josephus
states that Nebuchadnezzar finally came and slew Jehoiakim, "whom he commanded to be thrown before

the walls, without any burial" (Ant. x. 6 § 4). "So
Jehoiakim slept with his fathers" simply expresses his
death; it is a distinct expression in Scripture from
"*buried* with his fathers," as a comparison of 2 Kings
15 : 38 and 16 : 20 will readily show. So the king
who denied the prophet's body honorable burial was
himself "buried with the burial of an ass." He muti-
lated and burnt God's book; and his body was in turn
"drawn"* (torn) and burnt unburied in the scorch-
ing sun.

His wicked life was a sad contrast to that of his
righteous father. "Did not thy father eat and drink"
(lived plainly), "and do justice and judgment, and
then it was well with him?" asked Jeremiah; "He
judged the cause of the poor and needy; then it was
well with him: was not this to know Me? saith the
Lord" (Jer. 22 : 15, 16). Necho changed his name,
but could not change his nature.

"Now the rest of the acts of Jehoiakim, and his
abominations which he did, and that which was found
in him, behold, they are written in the book of the
kings of Israel and Judah: and Jehoiakin his son
reigned in his stead."

His name, like that of his brother, is omitted from
the royal genealogy of Matt. 1. "His uncleanness
and iniquity" are mentioned in the Apocrypha (1 Es-
dras 1 : 42). During his reign (when Nebuchadnezzar
took the kingdom) "the times of the Gentiles" began.
And until they be "fulfilled," Jerusalem "shall be
trodden under foot," even as it is this day.

---

* Heb. *saw-khab'*, translated "tear" in Jer. 15 : 3.

JEHOIACHIN

(Jehovah will establish.)

(2 Kings 24 : 8–17.)

Contemporary Prophets :
JEREMIAH; ZEPHANIAH; EZEKIEL.

" He looseth the bond of kings, and girdeth their loins
with a girdle."—*Job 12 : 18.*

" JEHOIACHIN was eighteen years old when he
began to reign, and he reigned in Jerusalem
three months. And his mother's name was Nehushta, the daughter of Elnathan of Jerusalem. And
he did that which was evil in the sight of the Lord,
according to all that his father had done" (2 Kings
24 : 8, 9). 2 Chron. 36 : 9 makes him eight years old
at the beginning of his reign, instead of eighteen, as
here : so in LXX. and Vulg. But some Hebrew MSS.,
Syriac, and Arabic, read "eighteen" in Chronicles ; so
"eight" must be an error of transcription. All the
internal evidence is in favor of eighteen. See Jer. 22 :
28–30; Ezek. 19 : 7.

His character was no different from that of his two
predecessors. It is the same sad, unvarying record :
"He did that which was evil." How the godly must
have longed for that "King" mentioned by Isaiah,
who should "reign in righteousness"! They little

knew, or even suspected, perhaps, all that their nation
would have to suffer, and the long, weary centuries—
aye, millenniums—that would have to wear themselves
away before that day of "righteousness and peace"
should come. But there was something about even
this wicked king that could give them hope—his name,
Jehovah will establish. They might not know the time;
the *fact* they were assured of. And so they could
"with patience wait for it."

Nehushta, his mother's name, means *copper*. It refers to anything of copper, whether a copper coin, or
a copper mirror or *fetters :* and both she and her son,
with all his family and retinue, were carried captive to
Babylon. "And Nebuchadnezzar king of Babylon
came against the city, and his servants did besiege it.
And Jehoiachin the king of Judah went out to the king
of Babylon, he, and his mother, and his servants, and
his princes, and his officers: and the king of Babylon
took him in the eighth year of his [Nebuchadnezzar's]
reign. And he carried out thence all the treasures
of the house of the Lord, and the treasures of the
king's house, and cut in pieces all the vessels of gold
which Solomon king of Israel had made in the temple
of the Lord, as the Lord had said. And he carried
away all Jerusalem, and all the princes, and all the
mighty men of valor, even ten thousand captives, and
all the craftsmen and smiths : none remained, save the
poorest sort of the people of the land. And he carried
away Jehoiachin to Babylon, and the king's mother,
and the king's wives" (*wives*, confirming the reading
eighteen against *eight*), "and his officers, and the
mighty of the land, those carried he into captivity from

Jerusalem to Babylon." This was all "*as the Lord said,*" through His prophet Jeremiah (Jer. 20 : 5). Heaven and earth will pass away and perish, but not one word of God.

The temple was despoiled of its remaining treasures. A few years before the king of Babylon had carried away the solid and smaller vessels (2 Chron. 36 : 7). On this occasion he (lit.) "*cut* the gold off." the larger plated vessels—the ark, the altar of incense, the show-bread table, etc. There is no contradiction here, or any where in Scripture, for "the Scripture cannot be broken." The king's mother would be the queen *mother* mentioned in Jer. 13 : 18.

The Babylonian captivity dates from Jehoiachin's reign. He never returned from his captivity. There he spent thirty-six years in prison until the death of Nebuchadnezzar in his eighty-third, or eighty-fourth year, after a reign of forty-three years. His son Evil-merodach succeeded him on the throne. This son had once been himself shut up in prison by his father, where he probably made the acquaintance of the royal Hebrew captive. He was not like the ungrateful butler who, when out of prison, "forgat Joseph"; he remembered his old prison companion. "And it came to pass in the seven and thirtieth year of the captivity of Jehoiachin king of Judah, in the twelfth month, in the five and twentieth day of the month, that Evil-merodach king of Babylon, in the first year of his reign, lifted up the head of Jehoiachin king of Judah, and brought him forth out of prison, and spake kindly unto him, and set his throne above the throne of the kings that were with him in Babylon; and changed his prison garments: and he did continually eat bread before him all the days of his life. And for his diet there was a continual diet given him of the king of Babylon, every day a portion until the day of his death, all the days of his life" (Jer. 52 : 31–34).

He was not the first king of David's house to be held a prisoner there. Some time before, his father's great-grandfather, Manasseh, was brought a prisoner, and there in his affliction he sought and found the Lord. Whether Jehoiachin ever did so, we cannot say. His name (as "Jechonias") is the last of the kings of Judah, mentioned in the list of Matthew, chap. 1. The next is "Jesus who is called Christ," anointed King, not of Israel or the Jews only, but of the nations also (Rev. 15 : 3, marg.)

Jeremiah said of Jehoiakim, (Jehoiachin's father) "He shall have none to sit upon the throne of David" (Jer. 36 : 30). The word "sit" here means to "*firmly* sit," or "dwell"; and Jehoiachin's short three months' reign was not that surely. And Zedekiah, Jehoiachin's successor, was Jehoiakim's *brother*, not his son.

Though, like his father, "he did evil *in the sight of the Lord*," Jehoiachin appears to have been a favorite with the populace. "Is this man Coniah* a despised broken idol?" (or, "vase") ironically inquired the prophet. But he immediately adds, "Is he a vessel wherein is no pleasure?"—which is really what he was in God's eyes. "Wherefore are they cast out, he and his seed, and are cast into a land which they knew not? O earth, earth, earth, hear the word of the

---

* In 1 Chron. 3 : 17 Jehoiachin is given as Jeconiah, of which "Coniah" is an abbreviation.

Lord: Thus saith the Lord, Write ye this man childless, a man that shall not prosper in his days: for no
man of his seed shall prosper, sitting upon the throne
of David, and ruling any more in Judah" (Jer. 22 : 28–
30). "Childless" here does not mean without descendants (for the prophecy itself mentions "his seed")
but "no direct lineal heir to the throne" (Fausset).
Matt. 1 : 12 shows conclusively that he had descendants ("Jechonias begat Salathiel"), as does also 1
Chron. 3 : 17 ("The sons of Jeconiah; Assir," etc.).
The prophecy probably refers to his uncle's succeeding him to the throne instead of his son Assir—his
first-born, probably; or it may have been a prophecy
of Assir's premature death; and this may be why Assir
is not mentioned in the genealogy in Matthew. Anyway, God made no mistake. He speaks, and it is
done; He commands, and it stands fast. "And the
word of our God shall stand forever."

ZEDEKIAH

(Righteousness of Jehovah.)

(2 Kings 24 : 17—25 : 21 ; 2 Chron. 36 : 11–21.)

Contemporary Prophets:
JEREMIAH; EZEKIEL; DANIEL; OBADIAH.

"Her king and her princes are among the Gentiles:
the law is no more : her prophets also find no vision from
the Lord."—*Lamentations 2 : 9.*

" AND the king of Babylon made Mattaniah his father's brother king in his [Jehoiachin's] stead,
and changed his name to Zedekiah.   Zedekiah
was twenty and one years old when he began to reign,
and he reigned eleven years in Jerusalem.   And his
mother's name was Hamutal, the daughter of Jeremiah
of Libnah.   And he did that which was evil in the
sight of the Lord, according to all that Jehoiakim had
done.   For through the anger of the Lord it came to
pass in Jerusalem and Judah, until he had cast them
out from His presence, that Zedekiah rebelled against
the king of Babylon."

Zedekiah was Josiah's youngest son, and full brother
of Jehoahaz.   He was, at his father's death, only ten
years old.   Nebuchadnezzar changed his name (as a
token of his vassalage) but did not put upon him the
name of some heathen deity, as in the case of Daniel
and the three Hebrew children.   He " had made him
swear by God," and his new name, *Righteousness of
Jehovah*, may have been given him to remind him of
his oath; or, it may have had some connection, even

in the heathen king's mind, with Jehovah's righteousness in taking from this wicked people (called by His
name) their political independence, and subjecting
them to his dominion.

"Zedekiah rebelled against the king of Babylon."
He had no real faith in Jehovah, Israel's covenant-
keeping God, and therefore did not scruple to break
his covenant with Nebuchadnezzar. But how dearly
he paid for this violation of his oath !   "And it came
to pass, in the ninth year of his reign, . . . that Nebuchadnezzar king of Babylon came, he, and all his
host, against Jerusalem, ... and the city was
besieged unto the eleventh year of king Zedekiah.
And on the ninth day of the fourth month the famine
prevailed in the city, and there was no bread for the
people of the land.   And the city was broken up, and
all the men of war fled by night by the way of the
gate between two walls, which is by the king's garden :
(now the Chaldees were against the city round about)
and the king went the way toward the plain.   And
the army of the Chaldees pursued after the king, and
overtook him in the plains of Jericho : and all his
army were scattered from him.   So they took the king,
and brought him up to the king of Babylon to Riblah;
and they gave judgment upon him.   And they slew
the sons of Zedekiah before his eyes, and put out the
eyes of Zedekiah, and bound him with fetters of brass,
and carried him to Babylon."

The occasion of this rebellion was Zedekiah's hope
of assistance from the king of Egypt. (See Ezek. 17 :
11–21.)   He also vainly attempted to form an alliance
with the surrounding nations, for the purpose of rid-

ding himself, and them, of the yoke of the Babylonish king. (See Jer. 27 : 1–11.)* Pharaoh-hophra attempted to relieve Zedekiah during the siege, but was driven back into Egypt by Nebuchadnezzar's army, who then returned and reinvested Jerusalem. (See Jer. 37 : 5–10.) It was a terrible siege, lasting eighteen months; famine and pestilence prevailed. Mothers boiled and ate their own children (Lam. 4 : 10). At midnight (Josephus) the Chaldees gained entrance into the city, and the fugitive king was captured. He was brought, with his sons, to Nebuchadnezzar at Riblah, "on the high road between Palestine and Babylon, where the Babylonian kings remained in directing the operations of their armies in Palestine and Phenicia" (Fausset).

Here his terrible punishment was meted out to him for his perfidy in violating his solemn compact with his master. After seeing his own children slain before him, his own eyes were "dug" out of their sockets, and he was bound "with double chains of bronze" (2 Kings. 25 : 7, lit.), and led off to Babylon. So the two seemingly contradictory prophecies of Jeremiah (32 : 4) and Ezekiel (12 : 13) were literally fulfilled. At Babylon he was cast into prison "till the day of his death" (Jer. 52 : 11). "Until I visit him" (Jer. 32 : 5), might imply that he was finally set at liberty, but "till the day of his death" precludes any such construction. It is more agreeable to take the expression to mean that God in mercy would visit him with repentance and a true knowledge of Himself as He did to Manas-

---

*In Jer. 27 : 1 read, "Zedekiah" for "Jehoiakim"; so Syr., Arab.; and one of Kennicott's MSS. Comp. vers. 3, 12, and chap. 28 : 1. "Jehoiakim" is a copyist's error, evidently.

seh before him. How often God has used the stern
hand of his government to break down the pride and
rebellion of the heart, and through such "visitation"
secure to the penitent soul the truest of all liberty—deliverance from the bondage of sin. So would his soul
be set free, though his body remain in bondage.

> "Stone walls do not a prison make,
>   Nor iron bars a cage,
> If I have freedom in God's love,
>   And in my soul am free.

Josephus (Ant. x. 8 § 8) says Nebuchadnezzar "kept
Zedekiah in prison until he died; and then buried him
magnificently." This agrees with Jer. 34:5: "Thou
shalt die in peace: and with the burnings of thy fathers, the former kings which were before thee."

Zedekiah has been justly characterized as "weak
vacillating, and treacherous." His weakness and subserviency to his princes mark him as a man wholly un-
fit to wear a crown, or sit upon a throne: "Behold he
[Jeremiah] is in your hand," he says to them, "for the
king is not he that can do anything against you" (Jer.
38 : 5). He was hypocritical also. He feigned a desire for the prophet's prayers, saying, "Pray now unto
the Lord our God for us" (Jer. 37 : 3). He pretended
too, at times, to have confidence in the prophecies of
Jeremiah ("Enquire, I pray thee, of the Lord for us,"
Jer. 21 : 2), which when delivered, he refused to heed,
or believe. "He did that which was evil in the sight
of the Lord his God, and humbled not himself before
Jeremiah the prophet speaking from the mouth of the
Lord"(2 Chron. 36 : 12). He was not so openly wicked
as his three predecessors, perhaps, and not willingly

given to persecution.   This is probably why Josephus judging after the standards of men, speaks of "his gentle and righteous disposition."   But the Lord seeth not as man seeth, neither are His thoughts man's thoughts. He says, "He stiffened his neck, and hardened his heart from turning unto the Lord God of Israel."   So God took him away in His anger.

The temple was burned to the ground; and only a miserable remnant of the nation was left in the land ("the poor") "to be vine-dressers, and husbandmen" (2 Ki. 25:12).   Rebellion arose even among these, and for fear of the Chaldees they fled to the land of Egypt, only to miserably perish there, as Jeremiah had faithfully, and with tears, warned them.

For seventy years the land "lay desolate"; after which a remannt was permitted to return, that, six hundred years later, "wise men" might come from that very land of the East, enquiring where they might find Him that was "born King of the Jews."

Until that day the godly remnant of His heritage could only pray, in the language of David—the type of that coming King—

"Oh, let the wrong of the wicked come to an end,
And establish Thou the righteous [Man] "(Psa.7:9).

"Even so, come, LORD JESUS"!

Note.   Further details in connection with these last four kings of Judah may be found in "Notes on Jeremiah," by E. A. Ironside—a most excellent exposition.

THE KINGS OF ISRAEL.

DYNASTIES OF THE KINGS OF ISRAEL.

1 Jeroboam; Nadab.

2 Baasha; Elah.

3 Zimri.

4 Omri; Ahab; Ahaziah; Joram.

5 { Jehu; Jehoahaz; Jehoash;
     Jeroboam II.; Zachariah.

6 Shallum.

7 Menahem; Pekaiah.

8 Pekah.

9 Hoshea.

JEROBOAM

(Whose people is many.)

1 Kings 11 : 26–40 ; 12–14 : 20; 2 Chron. 10 ; 13 : 1–20.

Contemporary Prophets:
AHIJAH ;
The Man of God out of Judah ; The Old Prophet of Bethel.

"The memory of the just is blessed : but the name of the wicked shall rot."—*Proverbs 10 : 7.*

JEROBOAM is an example of what is not at all uncommon in the East—a man exalted from a comparatively low station in private or public life to the highest, or one of the highest, positions in the land. We have scripture instances of this ; as Joseph, Moses, etc.; and secular history mentions not a few. Let us see how Jeroboam's elevation came about: "And Jeroboam the son of Nebat, an Ephrathite of Zereda, Solomon's servant, whose mother's name was Zeruah, a widow woman, even he lifted up his hand against the king. And this was the cause that he lifted up his hand against the king: Solomon built Millo [LXX., 'the citadel'], and repaired the breaches of the city of David his father. And the man Jeroboam was a mighty man of valor : and Solomon seeing the young man that he was industrious, he made him ruler over all the charge [or, levy] of the house of Joseph" (i. e., Ephraim and Manasseh).

This naturally gave him a place of importance in the eyes of his fellow-countrymen, and prepared the way for what was soon to follow. They evidently resented this enforcement of labor. "Thy father," they afterwards said to Rehoboam, "made our yoke grievous." They spoke of it, too, as a "heavy" yoke (1 Kings 12 : 4). There is no certain evidence that this was really so. What was being done by their labor was for the glory and security of the kingdom, whose prosperity all were supposed to profit by. See 1 Kings 4 : 25. It is possible, however, that they were set to work on what served only for self-gratification; for when men depart from the right way, as Solomon did, they soon become oppressive. This would furnish some justification for their discontent, which Jeroboam, it is quite certain, would take no pains to allay. He probably had discernment sufficient to see to what final event circumstances were gradually shaping themselves, and had his own personal ambitions in mind, as shall be presently seen.

"And it came to pass at that time when Jeroboam went out of Jerusalem, that the prophet Ahijah the Shilonite found him in the way ; and he had clad himself with a new garment; and they two were alone in the field. And Ahijah caught the new garment that was on him, and rent it in twelve pieces: and he said to Jeroboam, Take thee ten pieces : for thus saith the Lord, the God of Israel, Behold, I will rend the kingdom out of the hand of Solomon, and will give ten tribes to thee: (but he shall have one tribe for My servant David's sake, and for Jerusalem's sake, the city which I have chosen out of all the tribes of Israel:) because that they have forsaken Me, and have worshiped Ashtoreth the goddess of the Zidonians, Chemosh the god of the Moabites, and Milcom the god of the children of Ammon, and have not walked in My ways, to do that which is right in Mine eyes, and to keep My statutes and My judgments, as did David his father. Howbeit I will not take the whole kingdom out of his hand: but I will make him prince all the days of his life for David My servant's sake, whom I chose, because he kept My commandments and My statutes: but I will take the kingdom out of his son's hand, and will give it unto thee, even ten tribes. And unto his son will I give one tribe, that David My servant may have a light alway before Me in Jerusalem, the city which I have chosen Me to put My name there. And I will take thee, and thou shalt reign according to all that thy soul desireth, and shalt be king over Israel. And it shall be, if thou wilt harken unto all that I command thee, and wilt walk in My ways, and do that is right in My sight, to keep My statutes and My commandments, as David My servant did; that I will be with thee, and build thee a sure house, as I built for David, and will give Israel unto thee. And I will for this afflict the seed of David, but not forever." It was a solemn word, to which Jeroboam ought to have given earnest heed. Had he done so, he would never have come to his own melancholy end, nor would his dynasty have been so suddenly and violently terminated—ere the second generation had barely begun.

Whether intelligence of Ahijah's prophecy reached the ears of Solomon, or the elated Jeroboam betrayed

the secret by some overt act of rashness or insubordi-
nation, we are not told; but we read, "Solomon sought
therefore to kill Jeroboam. And Jeroboam arose, and
fled into Egypt, unto Shishak king of Egypt, and was
in Egypt until the death of Solomon." "He lifted up
his hand against the king," it says. Some abortive
attempt on his part to raise rebellion, it may have
been, to hasten the fulfilment of the prophecy concerning him. Comp. 2 Sam. 20 : 21. How unlike David,
the man after God's own heart, who, though even
anointed and chosen by the prophet Samuel to super-
cede Saul, would not injure a hair of the condemned
king's head, or raise a finger to bring the kingdom to
himself! David was a man of faith; and faith—that
precious "gift of God"!—ever waits on God—waits
for His time and way to fulfil His promises.

But Jeroboam knew nothing of faith. He had aspired secretly after power over his brethren (as the expression, "*according to all that thy soul desireth*," clearly
shows), and probably sought the accomplishment
of Ahijah's prophecy with pride's feverish haste, for
which he was compelled to seek an asylum in Egypt,
under the protection of Shishak, who had but recently
overthrown the late dynasty with which Solomon had
unlawfully allied himself by marriage. Ahijah had
distinctly said that Solomon should be "prince all the
days of his life," and it was only out of his *son's* hand
that the kingdom should be taken and transferred to
Jeroboam. But, like a wilful, impatient child, he could
not wait, and must needs take the case out of God's
hand and undertake for himself.

How long Jeroboam remained in Egypt is not

known; but we read that on the death of Solomon he returned, and was present at Rehoboam's coronation, when the rebellion was consummated. "And Rehoboam went to Shechem: for all Israel were come to Shechem to make him king. And it came to pass, when Jeroboam the son of Nebat, who was yet in Egypt, heard of it, . . . that they sent and called him. And Jeroboam and all the congregation of Israel came, and spake unto Rehoboam, saying," etc. The time was ripe. Solomon's incompetent son and successor, instead of heeding his father's wholesome proverb, "A soft answer turneth away wrath: but grievous words stir up anger," displayed his lack of wisdom and fitness to govern a liberty-loving people; and, as a consequence, he precipitated the separation of the already alienated northern tribes, to the weakening and almost ruin of a kingdom that had but recently extended from the Nile to the Euphrates, a distance of more than four hundred and fifty miles, and acknowledged by the surrounding nations as one of the most powerful empires of the earth.

The details of that memorable schism need not be entered into here, having been already gone over in the "Kings of Judah." (See REHOBOAM.) We have dwelt on the cause from the human, or circumstantial, side chiefly; the divine side is also given: "Wherefore the king (Rehoboam) harkened not unto the people; for the cause was from the Lord, that He might perform His saying, which the Lord spake by Ahijah the Shilonite unto Jeroboam the son of Nebat."

Jeroboam now becomes the spokesman of the disaffected tribes in the presentation of their petition, whose rejection snapped the already overstrained link that bound the tribes together. Though only presenting the people's petition, it is nevertheless probable that Jeroboam was not idle, but, like an artful politician, busy behind the scenes, till the coveted crown became his: "And it came to pass, when all Israel heard that Jeroboam was come again, that they sent and called him unto the congregation, and made him king over all Israel." He made historic Shechem his capital, and fortified it. He also made Penuel (*the face of God*—which should have reminded him of God's past dealings with the scheming Jacob) an important strategic point. Of Shechem one writes: "The situation is lovely; the valley runs west, with a soil of rich, black vegetable mould, watered by fountains, sending forth numerous streams, flowing west: orchards of fruit, olive groves, gardens of vegetables, and verdure on all sides, delight the eye"—the very spot for a man bent on self-pleasing, and aspiring to a life of luxury.

But the newly-crowned king quickly manifested that he did not hold his kingdom in faith as a trust from God. "And Jeroboam said in his heart, Now shall the kingdom return to the house of David" (the all-seeing Eye tells us what was going on in his heart, mark, which had never been anything but "an evil heart of unbelief"): and, he continues, "if this people go up to do sacrifice in the house of the Lord at Jerusalem, then shall the heart of this people turn again unto their lord, even unto Rehoboam king of Judah, and they shall kill me, and go again to Rehoboam king of Judah." "As a man thinketh in his heart, so is he." This man has neither trust in God, nor confidence in his fellows. He was like a former king (Saul), who, departing from God, began to be suspicious of everybody about him. Jeroboam evidently felt that he had no real hold upon the people's affections, and that his tenure of the crown was very precarious. He therefore wickedly devised a plan (which, alas, proved all too successful) to prevent a return of the tribes to their former allegiance to the house of David. "Whereupon the king took counsel, and made two calves of gold, and said unto them, It is too much for you to go up to Jerusalem: behold thy gods, O Israel, which brought thee up out of the land of Egypt. And he set the one in Bethel, and the other put he in Dan." The old limits of the land were "from Dan to Beersheba." Bethel lay near the southern border of Jeroboam's kingdom, and about twelve miles north of Jerusalem; while Dan was in the far north, at the sources of the Jordan. Thus by placing the calves at these extreme limits of his dominion, with the pretext of giving to all an easy access to a place of worship, the uneasy king hoped to prevent their return to Judah's God and kingdom. His kingdom, unlike Judah, with its temple at Jerusalem, had no divine centre. It was, in fact, a circumference without a centre, and its worship a matter of convenience and expediency.

"And this thing became a sin: for the people went to worship before the one, even unto Dan" (Bethel was taken from Jeroboam by Abijah. See 2 Chron. 13 : 19). "And he made a house of high places, and made priests of the lowest of the people, which were not of the sons of Levi." This was a direct violation of the law of God in reference to the priesthood.   See Num. 18 : 1–7.   And he did not stop there; regarding the legitimate priests and the Levites with special sus- picion evidently, and rejected their services.   " For Jeroboam and his sons," we read, "had cast them off from executing the priest's office unto the Lord : and he ordained him priests for the high places, and for the devils, and for the calves which he had made " (2 Chron. 11 : 14, 15).   Abijah, in his speech before the battle with Jeroboam, says to him and his follow- ers, " Have ye not cast out the priests of the Lord, the sons of Aaron, and the Levites, and have made you priests after the manner of the nations of other lands? so that whosoever cometh to consecrate himself with a young bullock and seven rams, the same may be a priest of them that are no gods."   Rome, since the Reformation, has been fond of comparing that glorious and undoubted work of God to Israel's secession un- der Jeroboam, and likening this voluntary consecration of unauthorized persons to the ordination of Protes- tant ministers.   While the utter falsity of the applica- tion of the former illustration is at once apparent, there is doubtless some truth in the latter.   But the force of the figure recoils upon themselves, for the ranks of their own priesthood are recruited entirely by volun- teer candidates from all classes and conditions of men. The mistake of Protestantism is the confounding of priesthood with ministry (two entirely different things in Scripture); Rome's error is the assumption of all priestly functions by a humanly-consecrated few, to the exclusion of every member of the Church, every one of which is a priest, according to the testimony of

Scripture. See 1 Peter 2 : 5, 9, etc. This is not a continuation, nor yet an amplification, of the Jewish priesthood, but one of an entirely different order—"a *royal*
priesthood." Christ is the "great High Priest," of
whom Aaron was the type; and every true believer a
priest of the same spiritual family, typified by Aaron's
sons. Heb. 5 : 4 has its direct application to the *high*
priesthood only, though the *principle* may be applied
to ministry; but to Christian priesthood proper the
verse has no application whatever, for a believer is a
priest, not by special call, but solely in virtue of his
link with Christ by faith.

Lessons from Jeroboam's act as to the priesthood
can surely be learned by both Romanism and Protestantism, but the right of a *class* among God's people
to the exclusive exercise of priestly functions is certainly not one of them. On the contrary, his action
illustrates just what they themselves have done—shut-
ting out the body of those who are truly the children
of God, and therefore truly priests, and consecrating
to the office men who have never been born of God,
and have no right or qualification whatever therefore
to the privilege.

Viewed even as a stroke of policy, this ejection of
the Lord's priests and the Levites was a blunder.
They went over in a body, almost, to Jeroboam's rival,
and thereby "strengthened the kingdom of Judah."
By being over-anxious to preserve his power, he lost
what was, no doubt, the choice part of his kingdom.
Similar to this was the banishment of the Huguenots
from France—the most intelligent, enterprising and
God-fearing portion of its citizens—an act from which

that country has never yet fully recovered, and, perhaps, never will. So, too, of the persecution of the Reformed in the Netherlands, and elsewhere on the Continent. And England, of all her "stalwart sons," possessed none more stanch and true than those who, for conscience' sake, forsook the land they loved, and sought an asylum among the desolate wildernesses of America.

Other unlawful innovations were introduced by Jeroboam. "And Jeroboam ordained a feast in the eighth month, on the fifteenth day of the month, like unto the feast that is in Judah, and he offered upon the altar [in imitation of Solomon]. So did he in Bethel, sacrificing unto the calves that he had made: and he placed in Bethel the priests of the high places which he had made. So he offered upon the altar which he had made in Bethel the fifteenth day of the eighth month, even in the month which he had devised of his own heart; and ordained a feast unto the children of Israel: and he offered upon the altar, and burnt incense." This "feast," of Jeroboam's, was in imitation of the feast of tabernacles, which God had commanded to be observed in the *seventh* month: the eighth was the month which Jeroboam "had *devised of his own heart*"—always "deceitful" and "desperately wicked." And how many practices and customs in Christendom have been "devised" of men's own hearts which have no foundation in Scripture! For many seem to imagine that it is quite permissible in spiritual things to do "every man that which is right in his own eyes," instead of "Thus saith the Lord." God condemned Israel for doing that which, He says,

"I commanded them not, neither came it into My heart" (Jer. 7 : 31 ; also, 19 : 5 ; 32 : 35). It is the thoughts of *God's* heart, not mine, that I am to heed and put into practice. These He has revealed in His Word, and it is our happiness and wisdom to heed *that*, and not "commandments" and "doctrines of men."

"And, behold, there came a man of God out of Judah by the word of the Lord unto Bethel: and Jeroboam stood by the altar to burn incense." If Jeroboam would not have Jehovah's *priests*, God sends His *prophet* into his land. "And he cried against the altar in the word of the Lord, and said, O altar, altar, thus saith the Lord: Behold, a child shall be born unto the house of David, Josiah by name; and upon thee shall he offer the priests of the high places that burn incense upon thee, and men's bones shall be burnt upon thee. And he gave a sign the same day, saying, This is the sign which the Lord hath spoken ; Behold, the altar shall be rent, and the ashes that are upon it shall be poured out." It was a bold message, but delivered in faithfulness. It was directed, not against the king, but the priests, though the king seemed to feel the force of its application to himself. "And it came to pass, when king Jeroboam heard the saying of the man of God, which had cried against the altar in Bethel, that he put forth his hand from the altar, saying, Lay hold on him. And his hand, which he put forth against him, dried up, so that he could not pull it in again to him. The altar also was rent, and the ashes poured out from the altar, according to the sign which the man of God had given by the word of the Lord." Jeroboam had forgotten, or ignored, the reproof administered by God to kings almost a thousand years before; "Touch not Mine anointed, and do My prophets no harm" (Ps. 105 : 14, 15). He was quickly reminded of his error, and entreated pardon. "And the king answered and said unto the man of God, Entreat now the face of the Lord thy God, and pray for me, that my hand may be restored me again." But it was his *heart* that had need of healing, rather than his hand. In this he was like the mass of men to-day, who look more to the hand and its deeds than the heart of sin that prompted the evil acts. The penitent publican smote upon his *breast*, as if to express that there, from within, came all the transgression, iniquity, and sin.

Jeroboam, however, is in a measure humbled, and his appeal for the prophet's intercession is regarded: "And the man of God besought the Lord, and the king's hand was restored him again, and became as it was before." Then he who would have persecuted a while ago, now would entertain and give a reward for his healing. "And the king said unto the man of God, Come home with me, and refresh thyself, and I will give thee a reward." But, like Daniel, who nobly answered king Belshazzar, "Let thy gifts be to thyself, and give thy rewards to another" (Dan. 5 : 17), so also "the man of God" refuses here to be patronized (oh, mark it, all ye servants of the living God), saying, "If thou wilt give me half thy house, I will not go in with thee, neither will I eat bread nor drink water in this place: for so it was charged me by the word of the Lord, saying, Eat no bread, nor drink water, nor turn again by the same way that thou camest. So he went another way, and returned not by the way that he came to Bethel."

It is not our purpose to follow the history of "the man of God," who was seduced to his death by the lie of the apostate old prophet of Bethel, but the narrative is full of wholesome instruction for us all, to adhere *strictly* to the word of God, and not be seduced from the simple path of obedience by the sophistries of men, professed "prophets" though they be; yea, be it an angel from heaven even, "let him be accursed" that perverts or contradicts the word of God. Reader, ponder well 1 Kings 13 : 11–32 ; for, like all things "written aforetime," it was "written for our instruction," "upon whom the ends of the ages are come," with all their attendant difficulties and dangers.

Jeroboam derived no lasting profit from the prophet's faithful testimony, or the mercy shown him in the restoration of his withered hand, for we read, "After this thing [the prophet's death?] Jeroboam returned not from his evil way, but made again of the lowest of the people priests of the high places : whosoever would, he consecrated him, and he became one of the priests of the high places. And this thing became sin unto the house of Jeroboam, even to cut it off, and to destroy it from off the face of the earth " (1 Kings 13 : 33, 34).

The threatened destruction of Jeroboam's house now begins. "At that time Abijah the son of Jeroboam fell sick. And Jeroboam said to his wife, Arise, I pray thee, and disguise thyself, that thou be not known to be the wife of Jeroboam ; and get thee to Shiloh : behold, there is Ahijah the prophet, which

told me that I should be king over this people.   And
take with thee ten loaves, and cracknels, and a cruse
of honey, and go to him : he shall tell thee what shall
become of the child."   Jeroboam's troubled spirit does
not turn to the old prophet of Bethel, or to others like
him in Israel, but turns, in his distress, to Jehovah's
prophet—a not uncommon thing with sinners, and a
striking witness of the power of conscience, as well as
a testimony to the influence of a righteous man in the
midst of abounding evil.   Ashamed, probably, to have
it known among his subjects that he preferred to con-
sult a prophet of Jehovah before those of his own idolatrous system, he sends his wife in disguise ; or, as
Shiloh, with Bethel, and other neighboring towns, had
been taken by Abijah king of Judah (see 2 Chron. 13 :
19), it would then be in the realm of his enemy.   Or,
could it be that, conscious of guilt, and afraid of bad
news, he hoped to deceive the prophet ?

" And Jeroboam's wife did so, and went to Shiloh, and
came to the house of Ahijah.   But Ahijah could not
see ; for his eyes were set by reason of his age.   And
the Lord said unto Ahijah, Behold, the wife of Jeroboam cometh to ask a thing of thee for her son ; for
he is sick : thus and thus shalt thou say unto her : for
it shall be, when she cometh in, that she shall feign
herself to be another woman.   And it was so, when
Ahijah heard the sound of her feet, as she came in at
the door, that he said, Come in, thou wife of Jeroboam ; why feignest thou thyself to be another ?
for I am sent to thee with heavy tidings "—alas,
poor mother !—" Go, tell Jeroboam, Thus saith the
Lord God of Israel, Forasmuch as I exalted thee from

among the people, and made thee prince over My people Israel, and rent the kingdom away from the house of David, and gave it thee : and yet thou hast not been as My servant David, who kept My commandments, and who followed Me with all his heart, to do that only which was right in Mine eyes ; but thou hast done evil above all that were before thee : for thou hast gone and made thee other gods, and molten images, to provoke Me to anger, and hast cast Me behind thy back "—fearful indictment !—" therefore, behold, I will bring evil upon the house of Jeroboam, and will cut off from Jeroboam every male, and him that is shut up and left in Israel, and will take away the remnant of the house of Jeroboam, as a man taketh away dung, till it be all gone. Him that dieth of Jeroboam in the city shall the dogs eat ; and him that dieth in the field shall the fowls of the air eat : for the Lord hath spoken it. Arise thou therefore, get thee to thine own house : and when thy feet enter into the city, the child shall die. And all Israel shall mourn for him, and bury him : for he only of Jeroboam shall come to the grave, because in him there is found some good thing toward the Lord God of Israel in the house of Jeroboam."

"Heavy tidings" these were indeed to a mother's heart! She was possibly a good woman, to have a son in whom God saw "some good thing toward the Lord." Sad indeed must have been her journey back to the city, and her dwelling, on entering which her son would die ! "And Jeroboam's wife arose, and departed, and came to Tirzah : and when she came to the threshold of the door, the child died ; and they buried him ; and all Israel mourned for him, accord-

ing to the word of the Lord, which He spake by the
hand of His servant Ahijah the prophet." Dear child,
Abijah (*Jehovah is my Father*) was his name; and his
heavenly Father called him home. It was an instance
of "the righteous" being "taken away from the evil
to come." And, it is written, "He shall enter into
peace: they shall rest in their beds, each one walking
in his uprightness" (Isa. 57 : 1, 2). We shall expect
to meet and greet thee, Jehovah's little child, in that
bright morning when for those who "have part in the
first resurrection" there shall be no more "evil to
come."

Jeroboam's battle with king Abijah, and his crushing defeat, have been entered into elsewhere (see ABI-
JAH), so need not be repeated here. Both the battle
and his child's death must have occurred toward the
close of his reign. See 2 Chron. 13 : 1. Thus disaster and sorrow would combine to help hasten his end;
and we read, "Neither did Jeroboam recover strength
again in the days of Abijah: and the Lord struck him,
and he died." God chastened him through two Abi-
jahs; one, of his own house; and the other, of the
house of David—terribly significant to him who had
cast that same Jehovah "behind his back."

"And the rest of the acts of Jeroboam, how he
warred, and how he reigned, behold, they are written
in the book of the chronicles of the kings of Israel."
This is that Jeroboam who "drave Israel from following the Lord, and made them sin a great sin" (2
Kings 17 : 21). God has placed the stamp of eternal
infamy on his name.

NADAB

(Willing.)

1 Kings 15 : 25–31.

"The house of the wicked shall be overthrown : but the tabernacle of the upright shall flourish."—*Proverbs 14: 11.*

"AND Nadab the son of Jeroboam began to reign over Israel in the second year of Asa king of Judah, and reigned over Israel two years. And he did evil in the sight of the Lord, and walked in the way of his father, and in his sin wherewith he made Israel to sin."

The sons of Jeroboam, together with their father, had ejected God's ordained priesthood, and had "cast them off from executing the priest's office unto the Lord" (2 Chron. 11 : 14). So Nadab followed in his father's ways; but God did not permit him to continue long in his wickedness. "And Baasha the son of Ahijah, of the house of Issachar, conspired against him; and Baasha smote him at Gibbethon, which belonged to the Philistines; for Nadab and all Israel laid siege to Gibbethon." Gibbethon was a town in Dan, allotted to the Levites of the family of Korah (Josh. 19 : 44; 21 : 23). It bordered on the land of the Philistines, and was probably seized by them on the emigration of the Levites to Judah. It means, *lofty place;* and it was while seeking to recover it to the crown, that Nadab was treacherously slain. But it was in fulfilment of the prophecy of Ahijah, "The Lord shall raise Him up a king over Israel, who shall cut off the house of Jeroboam that day: but what? even now."

"In the third year of Asa king of Judah did Baasha slay him, and reigned in his stead." Once on the throne, he began to execute the judgment of Jehovah against the remaining members of the house of Jeroboam, according to the aged Ahijah's word. "And it came to pass, when he reigned, that he smote all the house of Jeroboam; he left not to Jeroboam any that breathed, until he had destroyed him, according unto the saying of the Lord, which He spake by His servant Ahijah the Shilonite: because of the sins of Jeroboam which he sinned, and which he made Israel sin, by his provocation wherewith he provoked the Lord God of Israel to anger."

So ended the first of the nine dynasties that for two hundred and fifty years ruled (or misruled) the kingdom of Israel. Nadab's name means *willing;* and he appears to have been too willing to continue in, and perpetuate, the sin of his iniquitous father. He is not once mentioned in the book of Chronicles, nor is there any record in that book of his father's lifting up his hand against king Solomon, as in the Kings. See Author's Introduction. The inspired record of his uninteresting reign ends with the usual formula used in Kings: "Now the rest of the acts of Nadab, and all that he did, are they not written in the book of the chronicles of the kings of Israel?"

BAASHA

(" He who seeks," or " lays waste.")

1 Kings 15 : 27–16 : 7 ; 2 Chron. 16 : 1–6.

Contemporary Prophet :
JEHU son of HANANI.

"The Lord hath made all things for Himself : yea,
even the wicked for the day of evil."—*Proverbs 16 : 4.*

"IN the third year of Asa king of Judah began Baasha the son of Ahijah to reign over all Israel in
Tirzah, twenty and four years." With the beginning of a new dynasty, and the sad history of that
which had been before him, one might hope that Baasha would have taken a different course, and turned
to Jehovah. Alas, we read : "And he did evil in the
sight of the Lord, and *walked in the way of Jeroboam*,
and in his sin wherewith he made Israel to sin."

He was of Issachar, and had the tribal characteristic—
an eye for what appeared " pleasant "(Gen.49 : 15). So
he made beautiful Tirzah (which some derive from *rat-
zah*, " pleasant"; see Song of Sol. 6 : 4) the royal resi-
dence during his reign. Whatever he may have known
of God's *purpose* in the cutting off of Jeroboam's house,
his *motive* was not one of righteousness (like Jehu's,
later), for he was no better than those he murdered,
and continued to walk in their sin.

"Then the word of the Lord came to Jehu the son of Hanani against Baasha, saying, Forasmuch as I exalted thee out of the dust, and made thee prince over My people Israel; and thou hast walked in the way of Jeroboam, and hast made My people Israel to sin, to provoke Me to anger with their sins; behold, I will take away the posterity of Baasha, and the posterity of his house"—a terrible thought to an Israelite!—"and will make thy house like the house of Jeroboam the son of Nebat. Him that dieth of Baasha in the city shall the dogs eat; and him that dieth of his in the fields shall the fowls of the air eat." His doom, and that of all his house, is here solemnly pronounced. "Out of the dust" implies his lowly origin. How often do revolutionists imagine that because the obnoxious ruler is of noble birth, or royal lineage, the remedy is to put in the place of power one of their own class and rank! And how soon are they made to learn that "a servant when he ruleth" is the very worst type of tyrant known! No, it is not a question of natural birth, whether high or low, but of *new* birth and "ruling in the fear of God" which gives to any favored land such sovereigns as "Victoria the Good." Baasha was of plebeian stock, yet his name, *he who lays waste*, tells only too accurately what kind of a ruler he proved himself to be.

There was war between Baasha and Asa king of Judah all their days. He made a league with Benhadad king of Syria, and built, or fortified, Ramah on his southern border, to prevent, if possible, the influx of his subjects to Judah, whither they were attracted by the prosperity enjoyed under Asa. (See ASA.)

"Now the rest of the acts of Baasha, and what he did, and his might, are they not written in the book of the chronicles of the kings of Israel? So Baasha slept with his fathers, and was buried in Tirzah : and Elah his son reigned in his stead." And then a supplementary verse is added, to emphasize the fact that it was because of his idolatries and murder of the house of Jeroboam that God judged him and his family : "And also by the hand of the prophet Jehu the son of Hanani came the word of the Lord against Baasha, and against his house, even for all the evil that he did in the sight of the Lord, in provoking Him to anger with the work of his hands [his idols], in being like the house of Jeroboam; and because he killed him." God, who looks upon the heart, sees him but as an assassin for the accomplishment of his ambitious designs, slaying king Nadab and the entire house of Jeroboam.

ELAH

(An oak.)

1 Kings 16 : 8–14.

"Behold, the righteous shall be recompensed in the earth : much more the wicked and the sinner."—*Proverbs 11 : 31.*

"IN the twenty and sixth year of Asa king of Judah began Elah the son of Baasha to reign over Israel in Tirzah, two years. And his servant Zimri, captain of half his chariots, conspired against him, as he was in Tirzah, drinking himself drunk in the house of Arza, steward of his house in Tirzah. And Zimri went in and smote him, and killed him, in the twenty and seventh year of Asa king of Judah, and reigned in his stead."

Of the house of Jeroboam God had said : "I will take away the remnant of the house of Jeroboam as a man taketh away dung, till it all be gone "—so would it be with Baasha who had removed the remnant of Jeroboam's house by murder. "Drinking himself drunk" was Elah's occupation at the time of his assassination. Dissipation does not appear to have been the special sin of the kings of Israel and Judah generally (nor has it ever been characteristic of the Jewish race), as was the case with so many of their Gentile neighbors— witness Ben-hadad with his thirty-two confederate kings "drinking himself drunk in the pavilions"; 1 Kings 20 : 16).

Of Elah, Josephus (viii. 12, § 4) says he was slain

while his army was away at the siege of Gibbethon, begun in his father Baasha's day. His murder was perpetrated in the house of his steward Arza (*earthliness*), who was probably as given to self-indulgence as his master. Contrast the steward Obadiah, 1 Kings 18 : 3.

His murderer Zimri at once began to massacre "all the house of Baasha," sparing none, "neither of his kinsfolks, nor of his friends." It was complete extermination, even as God had ordained it should be. "Thus did Zimri destroy all the house of Baasha, according to the word of the Lord, which He spake against Baasha by Jehu the prophet, for all the sins of Baasha, and the sins of Elah his son, by which they . . . made Israel to sin, in provoking the Lord God of Israel to anger with their vanities" (idolatries).

Thus the house of Baasha, like that of Jeroboam before him, became extinct—the greatest calamity, to Jewish minds, that could overtake a man.

In less than fifty years the first two dynasties of Israel's kings had come to an end and every member of their families been exterminated. God meant to make their doom an example to those who should thereafter live ungodly. They stand as beacons, in these records, to warn all rulers and subjects off the rocks on which they struck to their everlasting ruin. "Who is wise, and he shall understand these things? prudent, and he shall know them? for the ways of the Lord are right, and the just shall walk in them: but the transgressors shall fall therein" (Hos. 14: 9). The usual formula ends the record of Elah's worthless life (1 Kings 16 : 14).

ZIMRI

(*Musical.*)

(1 Kings 16 : 9–20.)

———

"Whoso walketh uprightly shall be saved : but he that is perverse in his ways shall fall at once."—*Proverbs 28 : 18.*

———

"IN the twenty and seventh year of Asa king of Judah did Zimri reign seven days in Tirzah. And the people were encamped against Gibbethon, which belonged to the Philistines. And the people that were encamped heard say, Zimri hath conspired, and hath also slain the king: wherefore all Israel made Omri, the captain of the host, king over Israel that day in the camp."

"The triumphing of the wicked is short." It was sharply exemplified in the case of Zimri—just one week. He appears to have had no support from the people, who knew his character and desired not his rule. News of his assumption of the crown had no sooner reached the army at Gibbethon than they rejected his claims by proclaiming their commander-in-chief, Omri, king.

"And Omri went up from Gibbethon, and all Israel with him, and they besieged Tirzah. And it came to pass, when Zimri saw that the city was taken, that he went into the palace of the king's house, and burnt the king's house over him with fire, and died, for his sins which he sinned in doing evil in the sight of the Lord, in walking in the way of Jeroboam, and in his sin which he did, to make Israel to sin." Murderers are generally desperate characters ; and when it is beyond their power any more to destroy the lives of others, they, like wretched Zimri, frequently destroy their own. Satan "was a murderer from the beginning," and he knows how to goad them on to their destruction— body and soul. He knows the suicide's destiny after death. Judas, the traitor-suicide, we read, went "to his own place"—where "the unbelieving, and the abominable, and murderers," etc., have their place— in "the lake of fire."

Zimri's perfidy became a byword in Israel. The infamous Jezebel could refer to him and say, "Had Zimri peace, who slew his master?" "Treason is punished by treason," one has said, "and the slayer is slain." In Zimri was fulfilled the true proverb, "A man that doeth violence to the blood of any person shall flee to the pit; let no man stay him" (Prov. 28: 17). Let Zimri's end warn intentional regicides and traitors.

OMRI

(*Heaping.*)

1 Kings 16 : 15–28.

Contemporary Prophet : ELIJAH (?)

"The curse of the Lord is in the house of the wicked : but He blesseth the habitation of the just."—*Proverbs 3 : 33.*

CIVIL WAR, that most deplorable of all forms of armed conflict, followed Omri's assumption of the throne of Israel. "Then were the people of Israel divided into two parts : half of the people followed Tibni the son of Ginath, to make him king; and half followed Omri. But the people that followed Omri prevailed against the people that followed Tibni the son of Ginath : so Tibni died, and Omri reigned." "All Israel made Omri, the captain of the host, king over Israel that day *in the camp*," it says—that is, the *army* that was encamped against Gibbethon ; but a part of the tribes championed the cause of Tibni. Omri would be thus, during the four years' contest, in the position of military dictator. And with the soldiery at his back, he could hardly fail to prevail in the end against his adversary, whose death probably put an end to the conflict. Then Omri as king begins a new dynasty.

"In the thirty and first year of Asa king of Judah began Omri to reign over Israel, twelve years : six years reigned he in Tirzah. And he bought the hill

Samaria of Shemer for two talents of silver, and built
on the hill, and called the name of the city which he
built, after the name of Shemer, owner of the hill, Samaria" ("*Shomeron,*" Heb.). In the siege of Tirzah,
Omri may have seen its undesirableness as a capital,
from a military standpoint; or the pride of founding a
new capital may have led him to choose the hill of
Shemer. It lay about six miles to the northwest of
Shechem, the old capital; and the situation, according
to Josephus, combined strength, fertility, and beauty.
The hill was six hundred feet above the surrounding
country, and "the view," one writes, "is charming."
But more attractive to the Christian heart, is the site of
the old capital, Shechem, where our Lord,"wearied with
His journey, sat thus on the well." And there, in the
ears of "Jacob's erring daughter," He told of the free-
giving God, and of that living water, of which, if a
man drink, he shall never more thirst.

"But Omri wrought evil in the eyes of the Lord,
and did worse than all that were before him. For he
walked in all the way of Jeroboam the son of Nebat,
and in his sin wherewith he made Israel to sin, to provoke the Lord God of Israel to anger with their vanities" (idolatries). He seems to have formulated laws,
making Jeroboam's calf-worship, or other forms of
idolatry, obilgatory throughout his realm, which remained in force till the end of the kingdom, more than
two hundred years later. "For the statutes [a firmly-
established system.—*Fausset*] of Omri are kept, and
all the works of the house of Ahab" [Baal-worship]
(Micah 6 : 16). Such yokes men willingly bear, and
even cling to, so prone is the human heart to idolatry.

Omri was founder of the fourth and most powerful of the Israelitish dynasties—combining ability with the establishment of the basest idolatry. He formed an alliance with Ben-hadad I. king of Syria, who had streets made for, or assigned to, him in Samaria. See 1 Kings 20: 34. Samaria is called on the Assyrian monuments "Beth Omri" (*house of Omri*), in agreement with 1 Kings 16: 24. On the black obelisk, however, Jehu is mistakenly called "son of Omri." His name appears on the Dibon stone, on which Mesha states that Omri subjected and oppressed Moab till he, Mesha, delivered them out of his hand.

"Now the rest of the acts of Omri which he did, and his might that he showed, are they not written in the book of the chronicles of the kings of Israel?" He used this "might" of his, not to Israel's deliverance, but for the furtherance and establishment of idolatry, to Israel's ruin. His name was common to three tribes, Benjamin, Judah, and Issachar (see 1 Chron. 7: 8; 9: 4; 27: 18); so it is not certain out of which Omri came—though probably from Issachar (like Baasha). The murderous Athaliah, his granddaughter, is usually linked with his name in Scripture. See 2 Kings 8: 26; 2 Chron. 22: 2, etc.

"So Omri slept with his fathers, and was buried in Samaria. And Ahab his son reigned in his stead." His name means *heaping;* and by his iniquity he helped to heap up wrath against his dynasty, executed finally, thirty-six years later, on his great-grandson Joram, to the total extinction of the guilty house.

AHAB

(Brother of [his] father.)

1 Kings 16 : 29–17 : 1 ; 18 : 1–22 : 40 ; 2 Chron. 18.

Contemporary Prophets:
ELIJAH;
Micah son of Imlah.

"When the wicked are multiplied, transgression increaseth ; but the righteous shall see their fall."—*Proverbs 29 : 16.*

" AND in the thirty and eighth year of Asa king of Judah began Ahab the son of Omri to reign over Israel : and Ahab the son of Omri reigned over Israel in Samaria twenty and two years. And Ahab the son of Omri did evil in the sight of the Lord above all that were before him. And it came to pass, as if it had been a light thing for him to walk in the sins of Jeroboam the son of Nebat, that he took to wife Jezebel the daughter of Ethbaal king of the Zidonians, and went and served Baal, and worshiped him. And he reared up an altar for Baal in the house of Baal, which he had built in Samaria." Ahab was not the first to introduce Baal-worship in Israel : it had been known among them since their entrance into the land, but under his rule and the powerful influence of Jezebel, his wife, it became the established form of idolatry, as calf-worship was made under Jeroboam.

Baal was the sun-god of the ancient inhabitants of the land (as of the Phenicians), and his worship was accompanied by the most obscene rites and impurities.

Dius and Menander, Tyrian historians, mention an Eithobalus of Ahab's time, who was priest of Ashtoreth (female consort of Baal), who having murdered Pheles, became king of Tyre. See Josephus, *c. apion*, i. 18. This was, in all probability, Jezebel's father. Her zeal for the spread and maintenance of the worship of Baal and Ashtoreth, or Astarte, is therefore easily accounted for; hence, also, her inveterate hatred of the holy worship of Jehovah, and her murderous designs against His prophets. Her name means *chaste*—Satan's counterfeit or ridicule, as it were, of purity. Was it the hope of strengthening his kingdom, or her seductions, with the attractions of her painted face, that led Ahab into this alliance? Behind it all, we may be sure, Satan was seeking by this new move to utterly corrupt and destroy God's people and His truth from the earth. "And Ahab made a grove"—*Asherah*—an image, or pavilion, to Astarte—"and Ahab did more to provoke the Lord God of Israel to anger than all the kings of Israel that were before him.

"In his days did Hiel the Bethelite build Jericho: he laid the foundation thereof in Abiram (*father of height*) his first-born, and set up the gates thereof in his youngest son Segub (*aloft*), according to the word of the Lord, which he spake by Joshua the son of Nun." Jericho properly belonged to Judah, and Hiel, instead of remaining at Bethel, within his sovereign's realm, presumed to fortify (for this is what "build" means here) the city for his master Ahab, that he might, it would seem, command the ford of Jordan; for which trespass and disregard of God's word (see Josh. 6 : 26) the threatened judgment fell upon his first- and last-born sons. His name Hiel means, *God liveth ;* and he, presumptuous man! discovered to his sorrow that Jehovah was the living God, whose word will stand, and none can transgress it with impunity. Every transgressor, and all "the sons of disobedience," will find that He is always true to His word. "Hath He said, and shall He not do it? or hath He spoken, and shall He not make it good?" (Num. 23 : 19). His word concerning Jericho, "spoken" to Joshua five hundred years before, was made good upon the house of Hiel.

But God, who did not wink at Ahab's or the nation's wickedness, would yet seek to turn them back from their folly by sore discipline, and sent to them His servant Elijah. "And Elijah the Tishbite, who was of the inhabitants of Gilead, said unto Ahab, As the Lord God of Israel liveth, before whom I stand, there shall not be dew nor rain these years, but according to my word." Jehovah, not Baal, was Israel's God, in spite of Jezebel's seemingly successful attempt to foist her Canaanitish gods upon them; and Ahab should be made to know it. God uses a millennial form of discipline to teach him this. See Zech. 14: 17. And for three and one half years the land lay under the divine interdict of drought and famine. This drought appears to have extended even to Gentile lands; for it is mentioned in the annals of the Greek historian Menander. See Josephus, Ant. viii. 13, § 2.

"And it came to pass after many days, that the word of the Lord came to Elijah in the third year, saying, Go, show thyself unto Ahab; and I will send rain upon the earth. And Elijah went to show himself unto Ahab. And there was a sore famine in Samaria. And Ahab called Obadiah, which was the governor (steward, N. Tr.) of his house. (Now Obadiah feared the Lord greatly; for it was so, when Jezebel cut off the prophets of the Lord, that Obadiah took a hundred prophets, and hid them by fifty in a cave, and fed them with bread and water.) And Ahab said unto Obadiah, Go into the land, unto all fountains of water, and unto all brooks: peradventure we may find grass to save the horses and mules alive, that we lose not all the beasts. So they divided the land between them to pass throughout it: Ahab went one way by himself, and Obadiah went another way by himself." Ahab, as some one has said, cared more for the beasts of his stables than for his poor, starving subjects.

One wonders how a man like Obadiah (*worshiper of Jehovah*) came to hold office under such an abandoned idolater as Ahab. But there were "saints" in Nero's palace, whose salutations were considered worthy of apostolic mention; and godliness, as has been quaintly said, "is a hardy plant, that can live amidst the frosts of persecution and the relaxing warmth of a corrupt court, and not merely in the conservatory of a pious family."

Elijah, "as Obadiah was in the way," suddenly appeared before him, and gave him a terse message for his master: "Go, tell thy lord," he says, "Behold, Elijah is here." The poor lord-high-chamberlain, knowing well, no doubt, the murderous character of his master, trembles for his life. "What have I sinned," he says, "that thou wouldest deliver thy servant into the hand of Ahab, to slay me? As the Lord thy God liveth, there is no nation or kingdom, whither my lord hath not sent to seek thee: and when they said, He is not there; he took an oath of the kingdom and nation, that they found thee not. And now thou sayest, Go, tell thy lord, Behold, Elijah is here. And it shall come to pass, as soon as I am gone from thee, that the Spirit of the Lord shall carry thee whither I know not; and so when I come and tell Ahab, and he cannot find thee, he shall slay me." He evidently knew, dear man, that the husband of Jezebel set but slight value on any of his subjects' lives, and in his present temper would not hesitate, on the least provocation or suspicion, to slay him without mercy.

Assured by the prophet that Ahab should find him, as he said, Obadiah delivered his message. "And Ahab went to meet Elijah. And it came to pass, when Ahab saw Elijah, that Ahab said unto him, Art thou he that troubleth Israel?" What impudence! "And he answered, I have not troubled Israel; but thou, and thy father's house, in that ye have forsaken the commandments of the Lord, and thou hast followed Baalim" (or, the Baals).

The prophet then proposed to test publicly on mount Carmel whether Jehovah or Baal were God. To this the king accedes. "So Ahab sent unto all the children of Israel, and gathered the prophets together unto mount Carmel." The test was accordingly made, to the utter discomfiture of the Baal prophets. "Jehovah, He is God! Jehovah, He is God!" all the people cried; and at Elijah's command the four hundred and fifty prophets of Baal are led down to the brook Kishon, and slain there. See 1 Kings 18.

The people again acknowledging Jehovah as God, and the prophets of Baal destroyed, the purpose of the drought was accomplished. "And Elijah said unto Ahab,.Get thee up, eat and drink ; for there is a sound of abundance of rain."

Here the prophet's intercessory prayer is given us, to which James calls our attention : "Elijah was a man subject to like passions as we are, and he prayed earnestly that it might not rain: and it rained not on the earth . . and he prayed again, and the heavens gave rain." (Jas. 5 : 17, 18). A cloud, "like a man's hand" at first, soon fills the whole sky: the prayer is answered, and in the power of the Spirit of faith Elijah sends the word by his servant, " Go up, say unto Ahab, Prepare thy chariot, and get thee down, that the rain stop thee not. And it came to pass in the mean while, that the heaven was black with clouds and wind, and there was a great rain. And Ahab rode, and went to Jezreel."

Jezebel's indomitable will is now stirred to passion. Enraged, she threatens with an oath to make Elijah's life like that of her slaughtered favorites, and he in fear flees from the kingdom. She was evidently the real ruler in Israel, for Ahab, so far as Scripture informs us, did not make even the mildest kind of protest against her murderous threat.

Ahab's weakness is further made manifest by his servile answer to the besieging king of Syria: "And Ben-hadad the king of Syria gathered all his host together: and there were thirty and two kings with him, and horses, and chariots: and he went up and besieged Samaria, and warred against it. And he sent messengers to Ahab king of Israel into the city, and said unto him, Thus saith Ben-hadad, Thy silver and thy gold is mine; thy wives also and thy children, even the goodliest, are mine. And the king of Israel answered and said, My lord, O king, according to thy saying, I am thine, and all that I have." And when the messengers returned with more insolent demands, the king would probably have submitted to the humiliating conditions proposed, had not his more spirited and patriotic subjects advised otherwise, saying, "Harken not unto him, nor consent." A wicked man is never really anything but a *weak* man. It is only "the righteous" who is, as saith the proverb, "bold as a lion." When Ahab does refuse the king of Syria his unsoldierly demand, he says, half apologetically, "This thing I may not do." He does not use the bold, intensive "*will* not" of the three Hebrew children under more helpless circumstances, and to a more powerful king (Dan. 3: 18). Angered at even this meekly-put refusal, "Ben-hadad sent unto him, and said, The gods do so unto me, and more also, if the dust of Samaria shall suffice for handfuls for all the people that follow me." Then, more nobly, poor Ahab answers: "Tell him, Let not him that girdeth on his harness boast himself as he that putteth it off." Provoked at this reply, Ben-hadad, under the influence of drink, gave the mad order for instant attack upon the city.

But God's time for the humiliation of insolent Benhadad had come: "And, behold, there came a prophet unto Ahab king of Israel, saying, Thus saith the Lord, Hast thou seen all this great multitude? behold, I will deliver it into thy hand this day; and thou shalt know that I am the Lord. And Ahab said, By whom? And he said, Thus saith the Lord, Even by the young men (servants, Heb.) of the princes of the provinces. Then he said, Who shall order the battle? And he answered, Thou." God would humiliate Ben-hadad, not by any show of strength, as by the seven thousand soldiers left to Ahab, but by the *servants* of the princes of the provinces, who numbered two hundred and thirty-two. "And they went out at noon. But Ben-hadad was drinking himself drunk in the pavilions, he and the kings"—the thirty and two kings that helped him.

"And the young men of the princes of the provinces went out first; and Ben-hadad sent out, and they told him, saying, There are men come out of Samaria. And he said, Whether they be come out for peace, take them alive; or whether they be come out for war, take them alive. So these young men of the princes of the provinces came out of the city, and the army which followed them. And they slew every one his man: and the Syrians fled; and Israel pursued them: and Ben-hadad the king of Syria escaped on a horse with the horsemen. And the king of Israel went out, and smote the horses and chariots, and slew the Syrians with a great slaughter."

The expression "The king of Israel went out," coming, as it does, after the account of the going forth and victory of the young men and the small army, seems to imply that though, according to the prophet's word, he should order (or command) the battle, he remained cautiously behind, until the rout of the besiegers had begun: then, when danger is past, he comes forth from his place of security within the city walls, and assists in slaughtering an already defeated foe. God gave his army victory, that he might have another proof, in addition to that already offered on mount Carmel—so condescending and gracious is He—that He was Jehovah, the unchanging One. He would in this way too encourage and foster any little faith that might, as a result of the recent demonstration on mount Carmel, have sprung up in the hearts of the nearly apostate nation. Trust in Him He calls "precious faith" (2 Peter 1 : 1), so highly does He value it. In how many ways does God seek to gain and hold the confidence of men, for their everlasting good and glory! Reader, "hast *thou* faith?"

"And the prophet came to the king of Israel, and said unto him, Go, strengthen thyself, and mark, and see what thou doest: for at the return of the year the king of Syria will come up against thee." What patient, marvelous grace is God's! His goodness would lead men to repentance. So He sends His prophet, even to Ahab, to warn him of what the Syrians will do. "And it came to pass at the return of the year, that Ben-hadad numbered the Syrians, and went up to Aphek, to fight against Israel." This Aphek lay about six miles east of the sea of Galilee, on the direct road between the land of Israel and Damascus, and was a common battlefield of the Syrian kings. See 2 Kings 13 : 17. "And the children of Israel were numbered, and were all present, and went against them: and the children of Israel pitched before them like two little flocks of kids; but the Syrians filled the country. And there came a man of God, and spake unto the king of Israel, and said, Thus saith the Lord, *Because the Syrians have said*, The Lord is God of the hills, but He is not God of the valleys, *therefore* will I deliver all this great multitude into thy hand, and *ye shall know that I am Jehovah*"—another demonstration that Jehovah was the God of Israel.

For a whole week the two hostile armies lay en- camped one over against the other—Israel's poor little army "like two little flocks of kids," but with God on its side—and when they join battle on the sev- enth day, the "two little flocks of kids" destroy a host of a hundred thousand men. And the remnant of the defeated army, numbering twenty-seven thou- sand, that escaped being slaughtered by those whose land they had without provocation invaded, fled into the city of Aphek, where a wall fell upon them. Means were nothing with Israel's God, Jehovah, who is called "the God of battles"; He can save by many or by few; and what a mere handful (a few thou- sand) does not destroy of a vast army, He can shake down a wall upon the rest, and thus complete its deserved destruction.

This was the *third* occasion, within a short space of time, on which God would convince the king of Israel, and his people, that He was what His prophets pro- claimed Him to be—Jehovah, the God of Israel. He insists that, among men, "in the mouth of two or three witnesses," every word shall be established; and He will not Himself use an easier rule in His dealings with the sons of men. Ahab had this threefold testimony given him, but, alas, he entirely failed to profit by it. He is ensnared by Ben-hadad's guile, after God had placed him in his power; he not only let him live, but said, "He is my *brother*." It was the beginning of his final downfall.

A prophet now, by skilful artifice, brings before Ahab what he had done. Having induced a fellow-prophet to smite him, so that in smiting he wounded him, he then disguised himself, and hailed the king as he was passing by. "And he said, Thy servant went out into the midst of the battle; and, behold, a man turned aside, and brought a man unto me, and said, Keep this man : if by any means he be missing, then shall thy life be for his life, or else thou shalt pay a talent of silver. And as thy servant was busy here and there, he was gone." Ahab probably thought he had appealed to him as a suppliant, in reference to his forfeited life, or the ruinous fine; and he, like David before, pronounces his own sentence : "And the king of Israel said unto him, So shall thy judgment be ; thyself hast decided it. And he (the prophet) hasted, and took the ashes away from his face; and the king of Israel discerned him that he was of the prophets. And he said unto him, Thus saith the Lord, Because thou hast let go out of thy hand a man whom I appointed to utter destruction, therefore thy life shall go for his life, and thy people for his people. And the king of Israel went to his house heavy and displeased [sullen and vexed, N. Tr.], and came to Samaria." He made the same fatal mistake that king Saul made when he spared Agag. His calling the enemy of Israel "my brother," and taking him up into his chariot, may have sounded well and looked liberal to men like himself, who would applaud his conduct as magnanimous; but in God's eyes it was unpardonable disobedience, for which he and the nation would be made to suffer. Men might praise him, but of what worth are human plaudits to the man whose conduct God condemns? Ahab was not the last of that generation who love "the praise of men more than the praise of God" (John 12 : 43).

From that time Ahab appears to be given up of God: first, to covetousness and murder, and then to make war with and be slain by that nation whose blaspheming king he had called "my brother," and permitted to escape.

The first, his coveting of Naboth's vineyard, and the false accusation and murder of that righteous man, form one of the most painful and soul-stirring chapters in human history, whether secular or inspired. "And it came to pass after these things, that Naboth the Jezreelite had a vineyard, which was in Jezreel, hard by the palace of Ahab king of Samaria. And Ahab spake unto Naboth, saying, Give me thy vineyard, that I may have it for a garden of herbs, because it is near unto my house : and I will give thee for it a better vineyard than it; or, if it seem good to thee, I will give thee the worth of it in money." This Ahab, who could "brother" and spare a wicked Gentile king whom divine justice had doomed to destruction, can now, for the sake of gardening and enlarging the grounds about his palace, set about to murder a true brother. Though king, his offer to his neighbor Naboth is fearlessly refused. "And Naboth said to Ahab, The Lord forbid it me, that I should give the inheritance of my fathers unto thee." This was not obstinacy on Naboth's part, as some have supposed; nor yet a stubborn refusal to surrender his legal rights to do his king a favor. He was contending, not for his own rights (which scarcely becomes one who owes his all to God's free grace), but for God's, and those of his successors. "The land shall not be sold forever," God had said. Merciful provision was made in the law for a man who might have become reduced to extreme poverty. He was permitted to sell the land, but only to the year of jubilee, when it was to revert back to the original owner, or his heirs. Naboth could not plead poverty, so had no excuse to sell his vineyard, even to the king. There was also a law relating to property within a city's walls, which, if sold, must be redeemed within a year, or remain the possession of the purchaser forever. See Lev. 25. If Naboth's vineyard, adjoining Ahab's palace, lay within the city walls, it would, if sold, pass for all time out of the hands of Naboth's heirs.* Be that as it may, his firm refusal to sell out to his royal neighbor was a matter of conscience. Araunah's sale of his threshing-floor to David, and Omri's purchase of the hill of Samaria, cannot be called parallel cases. In the first instance Araunah, though a Jebusite (a Gentile), seemed fully to enter into David's purpose, and have fellowship with it. It was there-

---

Dwelling houses only were subject to this law (see Levit. 25: 29), and a vineyard could hardly be within city walls. 2 Kings 9: 21 and 31 indicate it was without the city. [Ed.

fore surrendering and offering his property to the
Lord Himself. In the second, the moral condition of
the nation was such that Shemer, an Israelite, was
probably unconcerned as to what God had said concerning the disposal of His land. Naboth was right,
both toward God and toward his family ties, whatever his critics may be disposed to say to the contrary;
but his resolute adherence to the right cost him both
his good name and his life.

"And Ahab came into his house heavy and displeased because of the word which Naboth the Jezreelite had spoken to him : for he had said, I will not give
thee the inheritance of my fathers. And he laid him
down upon his bed, and turned away his face, and
would eat no bread." His petulant conduct ill became a man—much less a king; it was rather that of
a spoiled child, peevish and in ill humor, because
crossed in his desire by one of his subjects. "But
Jezebel his wife came to him, and said unto him, Why
is thy spirit so sad, that thou eatest no bread?" Informed as to the cause of his dejection, her daring
spirit finds a ready way out of Ahab's difficulty.
"And Jezebel his wife said unto him, Dost thou now
govern the kingdom of Israel?" Alas, was it not *she*
that governed it really, with more daring ungodliness
than Ahab, her puppet husband? "Arise," says she,
"and eat bread, and let thy heart be merry. I will
give thee the vineyard of Naboth the Jezreelite."
Herself the daughter of a Gentile king, she was thoroughly schooled in court methods of disposing of re-
fractory subjects. She had not learned, as David, in
God's school, that kings should be the *shepherds* of

the people. Might made right in the kingdoms of the
nations, and she should show to her Hebrew husband
how quickly Naboth's objections to the king's demands could be overcome, in spite of anything, or
everything, written in the Mosaic code. "So she
wrote letters in Ahab's name, and sealed them with
his seal, and sent the letters unto the elders and to
the nobles that were in his city, dwelling with Naboth.
And she wrote in the letters, saying, Proclaim a fast,
and set Naboth on high among the people: and set
two men, sons of Belial, before him, to bear witness
against him, saying, Thou didst blaspheme God and
the king. And then carry him out, and stone him,
that he may die." How base could such men be, to
lend themselves as willing tools to her perfidious designs, and carry out her instructions to the letter!
Yet, public conscience might rebel at open murder;
and some appearance of justice had to be given her
act therefore. The moral effect on the nation of what
had happened on mount Carmel had, besides, probably not passed away; and this nefarious patron of
Baal had to proceed with a measure of caution, in her
wickedness. "And the men of his city, even the elders
and the nobles who were the inhabitants in his city,
did as Jezebel had sent unto them, and as it was written in the letters which she had sent unto them." Naboth was accordingly accused, taken out of the city,
and there stoned to death. "Then they sent to Jezebel, saying, Naboth is stoned, and is dead." All had
succeeded but too well. "And it came to pass, when
Jezebel heard that Naboth was stoned, and was dead,
that Jezebel said to Ahab, Arise, take possession of

the vineyard of Naboth the Jezreelite, which he refused
to give thee for money: for Naboth is not alive, but
dead. And it came to pass, when Ahab heard that
Naboth was dead, that Ahab rose up to go down to
the vineyard of Naboth the Jezreelite, to take possession of it."

Jezebel had had her will, but oh, the dreadfulness
of using God's institution to carry out the will of the
flesh! She knew the penalty for blasphemy against
Jehovah was death (Lev. 24: 16). She would find
associates to prove Naboth guilty of this, and thus
avenge herself upon the man who had dared to say
No to the desire of power. But, according to Jewish
doctors, if found guilty of blasphemy alone, his property would fall to his heirs the same as if he had died
under ordinary, or natural, circumstances. To secure
the vineyard, a further charge, of treason, therefore
must be trumped up against him; as in such a case
the estate of the condemned man went to the royal
exchequer. So Naboth was accused of blasphemy
both against "God and the king." See Ex. 22: 28.
And when the dark deed was done, the instigator of it
could coolly send to her husband, saying, "Naboth is
not alive, but dead."

But Naboth's God was not dead; He was still the
God "that liveth and seeth," as Ahab was soon to
know. "And the word of the Lord came to Elijah
the Tishbite, saying, Arise, go down to meet Ahab
king of Israel, which is in Samaria: behold, he is in
the vineyard of Naboth, whither he is gone down to
possess it. And thou shalt speak unto him, saying,
Thus saith the Lord, Hast thou killed, and also taken

possession? And thou shalt speak unto him, saying,
Thus saith the Lord, In the place where dogs licked the
blood of Naboth shall dogs lick *thy* blood, even thine."

Like most wicked men when reproved, Ahab looked
upon the fearless messenger of God as an enemy.
"Hast thou found me, O mine enemy?" he asks.
"Is it thou, the troubler of Israel?" he had asked the
faithful prophet on a former occasion (1 Kings 18:
17, N. Tr.). Here, when he can no longer link the
nation with himself in his guilt, he acknowledges the
personal character of the prophet's ministry, and calls
him his (not the nation's) enemy. "And he answered,
I have found thee: because thou hast sold thyself to
work evil in the sight of the Lord. Behold, I will
bring evil upon thee, and will take away thy posterity,
and will cut off from Ahab every male, and him that
is shut up and left in Israel, and will make thy house
like the house of Jeroboam the son of Nebat, and like
the house of Baasha the son of Ahijah, for the provocation wherewith thou hast provoked Me to anger, and
made Israel to sin." Judgment upon Jezebel also is then
pronounced. "And it came to pass, when Ahab heard
those words, that he rent his clothes, and put sackcloth upon his flesh, and fasted, and lay in sackcloth,
and went softly." Ahab is really affected, though su-
perficially, no doubt, by the prophet's declaration; and
God, who ever approves even the slightest indication
of repentance in transgressors, says to Elijah, "Seest
thou how Ahab humbleth himself before Me? because
he humbleth himself before Me, I will not bring the
evil in his days: but in his son's days will I bring the
evil upon his house."

We have now the closing incident in the life of this king of Israel, who "did sell himself to work wickedness in the sight of the Lord, whom Jezebel his wife stirred up."

"And they continued three years without war between Syria and Israel." In the third year, Jehoshaphat king of Judah (now linked to the house of Ahab by the marriage of his son and heir-apparent to the throne, to Athaliah, Ahab's daughter) came down on a friendly visit to the Israelitish capital. Ahab saw in the presence of so powerful an ally a splendid opportunity to use him to the extension of his kingdom. So he says to his servants, "Know ye not that Ramoth in Gilead is ours, and we be still, and take it not out of the hand of the king of Syria?" Ramoth-gilead was an important fortress, directly east of Samaria, and about twenty miles back from the Jordan. It was occupied during Solomon's magnificent reign by Ben-Geber, one of his twelve commissariat officers (1 Kings 4 : 13). Ben-hadad I. had taken it from Omri, according to Josephus (Ant. viii., 15 § 4). On Ahab's proposing to jointly recover this place to their family (now one, alas), Jehoshaphat at once acceded, saying, "I am as thou art," etc. (See JEHOSHAPHAT.) The four hundred court prophets all declared the success of the expedition a foregone conclusion. "Go up," they said, unanimously ; "for the Lord shall deliver it into the hand of the king." (2 Chron. 18 : 5 has "God," instead of "the Lord," as here : see Author's Introduction.) Ahab's ally did not appear entirely satisfied with such offhand, emphatic prophecies of good fortune ; he had evidently some misgivings of conscience, and was suspicious of this crowd of state-paid "peace-and-safety" preachers. So he cautiously asked if there was not another of Jehovah's prophets within call, of whom they might further inquire. "There is yet one man," answered Ahab, "Micaiah the son of Imlah, by whom we may inquire of the Lord: but I hate him; for he doth not prophesy good concerning me, but evil." And the good-natured king of Judah, ever willing to put the best construction possible on others' deeds, or words, replied, "Let not the king say so." "Hasten hither Micaiah the son of Imlah," Ahab commanded his officer; and the unpopular prophet was unceremoniously brought into the presence of the consulting kings. The two ill-matched kings sat each on his throne, arrayed in his robes of state, in an open space at the entrance of the gate of Samaria. Before them were gathered all the pseudo-prophets, prophesying their lies before their royal master and his uneasy confederate. One of the deceivers, striving after dramatic effect, had made iron horns, saying, "Thus saith the Lord, With these shalt thou push the Syrians, until thou have consumed them." "Go up to Ramoth-gilead, and prosper," they all with one voice said: "for the Lord shall deliver it into the king's hand."

Now Jehovah's prophet is brought, and in ironical agreement with what the time-serving four hundred had been saying, he also says, "Go, and prosper!" Ahab was quick to understand his irony, and adjured him (put him under oath) in Jehovah's name, to tell him nothing but that which was true. "And he said, I saw all Israel scattered upon the hills, as sheep that

have not a shepherd: and the Lord said, These have
no master: let them return every man to his house in
peace." "Did I not tell thee that he would prophesy
no good concerning me, but evil?" said Ahab to Jehoshaphat, on hearing this solemn announcement.
Jehovah's prophet now sets before them his vision of
a scene in heaven: the lying spirit in the mouth of
Ahab's prophets to allure him to his death. But this
is more than Ahab can bear, and he orders at once
that Micaiah be thrust into prison, and to be fed with
the bread and water of affliction, till he returned from
his expedition in peace. "And Micaiah said, If thou
return at all in peace, the Lord hath not spoken by
me. And he said, Harken, O people, every one of
you."

Could all this take place in the presence of Jehoshaphat, and he not protest? We know not. Scripture
is silent here. But, alas, what may not even a child
of God stoop to, away from God, in evil company!

The two kings now proceed to Ramoth-gilead, and
Ahab's treachery and cowardice again appear. He
artfully disguises himself, while inducing the unsus-
pecting Jehoshaphat to appear in battle in his royal
robes. Base and contemptible trickery!

He protects his own person at the probable sacrifice
of his generous friend. But "the unjust knoweth no
shame," and living for self destroys all nobleness of
character. The unhappy monarch had also been
under Jezebel's influence too long to have any uprightness remaining in him. Besides, he probably
feared Micaiah's prophecy more than he believed his
own prophets. Alas, his merited end had come. The

Syrians crowded close upon poor Jehoshaphat for a time; but God delivered him, and they perceived their mistake. "And a certain man drew a bow at a venture, and smote the king of Israel between the joints of the harness [or, armor]: wherefore he said unto the driver of his chariot, Turn thy hand, and carry me out of the host: for I am wounded." And at even, at the time of the going down of the sun, he died; "and the blood ran out of the wound into the midst of the chariot." The day was lost to Israel, and the humiliated army returned leaderless from the ill-fated campaign.

" So the king died, and was brought to Samaria : and they buried the king in Samaria. And one washed the chariot in the pool of Samaria; and the dogs licked up his blood; and they washed his armour; according to the word of the Lord which He spake." God's arrow found him, in spite of his disguise; and his colleague, though for a time a conspicuous target for every archer in the Syrian army, escaped. How true the couplet,

" Not a single shaft can hit,
  Till our all-wise God sees fit."

None who make God their trust need ever fear "the arrow that flieth by day " (Ps. 91 : 5).

" Now the rest of the acts of Ahab, and all that he did, and the ivory house which he made, and all the cities that he built, are they not written in the book of the chronicles of the kings of Israel?" He was evidently a man of luxurious tastes, which appears to have been also characteristic of his successors. (See

Amos. 3 : 15). His moral character, as given in the parenthetic passage of 1 Kings 21 : 25, 26, is a fearfully black one. " But (or surely) there was none like unto Ahab, which did sell himself to work wickedness in the sight of the Lord, whom Jezebel his wife stirred up (urged on, Heb.) And he did very abominably in following idols, according to all things as did the Amorites, whom the Lord cast out before the children of Israel." He was a true *brother* (or *friend*) of his father Omri, in his excessive wickedness.

The Moabite stone mentions Omri's son; his name also appears on the Assyrian Black Obelisk as " Ahab of Jezreel."

"So Ahab slept with his fathers; and Ahaziah his son reigned in his stead."

AHAZIAH

(*Whom Jehovah holds.*)

1 Kings 22 : 40, 49, 51 ; 2 Kings 1.

Contemporary Prophet, ELIJAH.

"The fear of the Lord prolongeth days : but the years
of the wicked shall be shortened."—*Proverbs 10 : 27.*

"AHAZIAH the son of Ahab began to reign over
Israel in Samaria the seventeenth year of
Jehoshaphat king of Judah, and reigned two
years over Israel.   And he did evil in the sight of the
Lord, and walked in the way of his father, and in the
way of his mother, and in the way of Jeroboam the
son of Nebat, who made Israel to sin.   For he served
Baal, and worshiped him, and provoked to anger the
Lord God of Israel, according to all that his father
had done."   It is a dark catalogue of iniquity, yet
only what might be expected of the offspring of such
a couple as Ahab and Jezebel.   So matched in wickedness were his parents that nothing short of a miracle
of grace could have made him anything better than
the description given of him here.

"And Ahaziah fell down through a lattice in his
upper chamber, that was in Samaria, and was sick :
and he sent messengers, and said unto them, Go,
enquire of Baal-zebub [*lord of flies*] the god of Ekron,

whether I shall recover of this disease." Ekron was the northernmost of the five chief Philistine cities, and contained the shrine and oracle of the vile abomination called Baal-zebub (the Beelzebub of the New Testament). Men love the gods that are most like unto themselves, so it is not surprising to see Ahaziah sending to this miserable Philistine god. But the sick king's messengers never reached the oracle. The God of Israel Himself, sending His prophet to intercept the king's messengers, answered His question. "But the angel of the Lord said to Elijah the Tishbite, Arise, go up to meet the messengers of the king of Samaria, and say unto them: Is it not because there is not a God in Israel, that ye go to enquire of Baal-zebub the god of Ekron? Now, therefore, thus saith the Lord, Thou shalt not come down from that bed on which thou art gone up, but shalt surely die."

The messengers returned to their royal master, and related what had taken place. "There came a man to meet us," they say, "and said unto us," etc. "What manner of man was he which came up to meet you, and told you these words?" the king enquired. "And they answered him, He was a hairy man, and girt with a girdle of leather about his loins. And he said, It is Elijah the Tishbite." In his perverse folly, Ahaziah orders him at once to be apprehended. But now the strong hand of Jehovah must be felt by the perverse king and his haughty captains: twice over the captains with their fifties are consumed by fire from heaven. But, as the third captain humbly pleads for his own life and of his fifty men sent forth to arrest Jehovah's prophet, the angel of the Lord bids Elijah, "Go down with him: be not afraid of him. And he arose, and went down with him unto the king." There, in the presence of the king, Jehovah's judgment is unflinchingly repeated to himself.

"So he died according to the word of the Lord which Elijah had spoken. And Jehoram reigned in his stead in the second year of Jehoram the son of Jehoshaphat king of Judah; because he had no son." This Jehoram was another son of Ahab (2 Kings 3: 1) and therefore brother of Ahaziah.

"Now the rest of the acts of Ahaziah which he did, are they not written in the book of the chronicles of the kings of Israel?" Yes, and they, with the wicked acts recorded here, are written in God's books above; not "of the chronicles of the kings of Israel " merely, but of the deeds and doings of every man's life, whether it be good or evil. Solemn facts for us all!

JORAM (or JEHORAM)

(Exalted by Jehovah.)

2 Kings 1 : 17 ; 3 : 1–27 ; 6 : 8—7 : 20; 9 : 1–26.

Contemporary Prophet, ELISHA.

"The wicked are overthrown, and are not : but the
house of the righteous shall stand."—*Proverbs 12 : 7.*

"NOW Jehoram the son of Ahab began to reign
over Israel in Samaria the eighteenth year of
Jehoshaphat king of Judah, and reigned twelve
years.   And he wrought evil in the sight of the Lord ;
but not like his father, and like his mother"—in contrast with his late brother Ahaziah, see 1 Kings 22 :
52—"for he put away the image of Baal that his
father had made.   Nevertheless he cleaved unto the
sins of Jeroboam the son of Nebat, which made Israel
to sin ; he departed not therefrom."   There is no discrepancy between "the eighteenth year of Jehoshaphat," here, and "the second year of Jehoram the son
of Jehoshaphat," as in 2 Kings 1 : 17.   Jehoshaphat
made his son joint-king a number of years before
his death, (see 2 Kings 8 : 16, *marg.*) which readily
accounts for the seeming contradictions in the above
noted passages.

"Then Moab rebelled against Israel after the death of Ahab." "And Mesha king of Moab was a sheep master, and rendered unto the king of Israel a hundred thousand lambs, and a hundred thousand rams, with the wool. But it came to pass, when Ahab was dead, that the king of Moab rebelled against the king of Israel" (2 Kings 3 : 4, 5). The defeat of the allied forces of Israel and Judah at Ramoth-Gilead, probably, emboldened him to take this step. Moab had been tributary to Israel ever since their subjugation by David, more than two hundred years before (see 2 Sam. 8 : 2). On the division of the kingdom, they appear to have paid their accustomed tribute to Jeroboam, as his kingdom embraced the two and a half tribes east of Jordan, whose territory extended to the kingdom of Moab. This revolt of Mesha is mentioned on the Moabite, or Dibon, stone. (See also Isa. 16 : 1.) The loss of this enormous annual income must have been keenly felt by Israel, and the attempt to secure its resumption occasioned this unhappy war in which Jehoshaphat, the king of Judah, again guiltily allied himself to Jehoram.

"And king Jehoram went out of Samaria the same time [of Mesha's rebellion—see AHAZIAH], and numbered all Israel. And he went and sent to Jehoshaphat the king of Judah, saying, The king of Moab hath rebelled against me: wilt thou go with me against Moab to battle? And he said, I will go up: I am as thou art, my people as thy people, and my horses as thy horses." It is a sadly compromising declaration to come from the lips of a king of the house and lineage of David. But it was the result of his joining affinity with the house of Ahab by his son Jehoram's marriage to the infamous Athaliah. So not only do "evil communications corrupt good manners," but that delicate sense of truthful consistency, so evidently lacking in Jehoshaphat here.

"And he said, Which way shall we go up? And he answered, The way through the wilderness of Edom. So the king of Israel went, and the king of Judah, and the king of Edom." This "king of Edom" was not a native Edomite, but a deputy (1 Kings 22 : 47) appointed, probably, by Jehoshaphat (2 Kings 8 : 20), and formed a party to the expedition in the capacity of a vassal, rather than as an independent prince. "And they fetched a compass of seven days' journey: and there was no water for the host and for the cattle that followed them. And the king of Israel said, Alas! that the Lord hath called these three kings together to deliver them into the hand of Moab." When such a man of God as Jehoshaphat identifies himself with such a man as the king of Israel, distress must needs come upon them, that victory may be recognized as an act of God's sovereign grace, and not a spark of honor left to the follower of Jeroboam's calves.

"But Jehoshaphat said, Is there not here a prophet of the Lord, that we may enquire of the Lord by him?" Elisha is here, said one of the king of Israel's servants. "And Jehoshaphat said, The word of the Lord is with him. So the king of Israel, and Jehoshaphat, and the king of Edom went down to him." Even wicked men will cry to God in the hour of their calamity, yet without change of heart. But Elisha had as little respect for or fear of Jehoram, as Elijah his master had had for his idolatrous predecessors. "And Elisha said unto the king of Israel, What have I to do with thee? get thee to the prophets of thy father, and to the prophets of thy mother. And the king of Israel said unto him, Nay: for the Lord hath called these three kings together, to deliver them into the hand of Moab. And Elisha said, As the Lord of hosts liveth, before whom I stand, surely, were it not that I regard the presence of Jehoshaphat the king of Judah, I would not look toward thee, nor see thee."

Then, as the minstrel played, "the hand of the Lord came upon him," and he ordered the valley to be filled with ditches, saying, "Thus saith the Lord, Ye shall not see wind, neither shall ye see rain: yet that valley shall be filled with water, that ye may drink, both ye, and your cattle, and your beasts. And this is but a light thing in the sight of the Lord: He will deliver the Moabites also into your hand." And so, "It came to pass, in the morning, when the meat-offering was offered, that, behold, there came water by the way of Edom, and the country was fillled with water."

This sudden and abundant water supply was, probably, as has been suggested, caused by heavy rains on the eastern mountains of Edom, so far away that no signs of the storm were visible to the invaders. In any case it was God's doing, whatever the physical forces used by Him to bring it about. Faith never gives itself concern about the scientific explanation of such occurrences. God could have created the water, had He so ordained. And "He giveth not account of any of His matters," either to adoring, wondering

faith, or caviling, questioning unbelief. A starving
man need not concern himself as to how, or where, the
food set before him was obtained by his benefactor.
It is his to eat, and be thankful. And any to whose
ears the report of this benevolence comes, should, also,
not be occupied with questions concerning the manner
or means by which the philanthropist was enabled to
do the beggar this kindness. Their business should
be to admire and laud the spirit of disinterested love
and mercy that prompted the deed of generosity.

"And when all the Moabites heard that the kings
were come up to fight against them, they gathered all
that were able to put on armour, and upward, and
stood in the border." When the morning dawned
they saw the water, as the sun shone upon it, in the
ditches, and it appeared to their eyes red as blood.
"And they said, This is blood: the kings are surely
slain, and they have smitten one another; now therefore, Moab, to the spoil." They probably supposed
that the Edomites had turned mutinous at the last,
and in their effort to free themselves of Hebrew domination, had caused the mutual destruction of the confederate armies. But alas, for them and their over-
sanguine conclusion. When they approached the
Israelitish camp, "The Israelites rose up and smote
the Moabites so that they fled before them." Their
defeat was thorough and crushing, as it was unexpected. Israel seems now to have exceeded in un-
merciful persuit and pressure upon the king of Moab,
who, in desperation, "took his eldest son that should
have reigned in his stead, and offered him for a burnt
offering upon the wall. And there was great indigna-

tion against Israel: and they departed from him, and returned to their own land."

This was Jehoshaphat's second act of affinity with the ungodly, and like the first, it ended in failure, or was entirely barren of results. If even sinners wish success in their undertakings they should be careful not to admit into their partnership God's children, for God's hand may be upon His own for discipline, and ill fortune will attend them. Neither Ahab, nor Jehoram gained anything by having the godly Jehoshaphat as their ally—so jealous is God of His people's associations.

How strange, yet sadly true it is, that the history of a country is largely the history of its *wars*. The maxim holds good, not only of the land of Israel, but of its kings especially. Omit the records of their warfare, and there would be little to say of any of them. How it all tells of man's fall and ruin, and of God's righteous government.

The second important incident recorded of Jehoram's life is in connection with the invasion of his territory by the king of Syria. "Then the king of Syria warred against Israel, and took counsel with his servants, saying, In such and such a place shall be my camp. And the man of God sent unto the king of Israel, saying, Beware that thou pass not such a place; for thither the Syrians are come down. And the king of Israel sent to the place which the man of God told him and warned him of, and saved himself there, not once nor twice." The prophet seems to look upon Jehoram here with somewhat less disfavor than when on the expedition against the Moabites.

(See also 2 Kings 3 : 13.) He seems to have been pursued by the king of Syria, and there may have been some change in his conduct too, which Elisha would be quick to take note of, and encourage in every possible way—so gracious is God in His governmental dealings with the sons of men.

On learning how Jehoram obtained the information by which he was enabled to repeatedly escape the ambushments set for him, the king of Syria sent to apprehend the revealer of his military secrets. In answer to His servant's prayer, the Lord smote the Syrians with blindness, and the man they were bent on arresting led them into the very midst of their enemy's capital. "And the king of Israel said unto Elisha, when he saw them, My father, shall I smite them? shall I smite them?" But, in New Testament spirit, he answers, "Thou shalt not smite them; wouldest thou smite those whom thou hast taken captive with thy sword and with thy bow? Set bread and water before them, that they may eat and drink, and go to their master. And he prepared great provision for them: and when they had eaten and drunk, he sent them away, and they went to their master." The Syrians had heard before that "the kings of the house of Israel" were "merciful kings" (1 Kings 20 : 31); they were now given a demonstration of the mercy of Israel's God through His prophet's intervention. And it was not without some effect, nor at once forgotten, for we read, "So the bands of Syria came no more into the land of Israel." Such is the power of grace, over hardened, heathen soldiers, even.

"And it came to pass after this, that Ben-hadad

king of Syria gathered all his host, and went up, and besieged Samaria." This does not in any way contradict what is stated in the preceding verse (2 Kings 6: 23, 24). Josephus says, "So he [Ben-hadad] determined to make no more *secret* attempts upon the king of Israel" (Ant. ix. 4, § 4). He afterwards made open war upon him, by legitimate methods; no more by marauding bodies and ambushments.

Alas, Israel's heart was hardened, so that, in the famine accompanying the siege, instead of turning to Jehovah, some of the inhabitants in their terrible extremity turned to the horrible deed of eating even their own offspring! See Lev. 26: 26–29; Deut. 28: 52, 53; which was finally fulfilled under the Romans.

"And as the king of Israel was passing by upon the wall, there cried a woman unto him, saying, Help, my lord, O king. And he said, If the Lord do not help thee, whence shall I help thee? out of the barn-floor, or out of the winepress? And the king said unto her, What aileth thee?" And then he has told into his ears the terrible tale of women deliberately agreeing to boil and eat their own children! "And it came to pass, when the king heard the words of the woman, that he rent his clothes; and he passed by upon the wall, and the people looked, and, behold, he had sackcloth within upon his flesh. Then he said, God do so and more also to me, if the head of Elisha the son of Shaphat shall stand on him this day." He had sackcloth on his flesh, but murder in his heart. Alas, what power of Satan over man's heart and mind is manifested in this! The heart of the king rises in bitter passion against God, and His prophet will serve to vent the rage of his unrepentant, unsubdued heart. It is not the only occasion in history where rulers have put the blame of national calamities upon God; and how often men's hearts rise against God, rather than humble themselves in repentance, under the pains of what they cannot change or overcome. (See Rev. 16 : 10, 11.)

The king therefore sent an executioner to make good his hasty threat. His motive in following after his executioner is not clear. Was it to see the accomplishment of his murderous design, or regret at his reckless order?

" But Elisha sat in his house, and the elders sat with him; and the king sent a man from before him: but ere the messenger came to him, he said to the elders, See ye how this son of a murderer hath sent to take away my head? Look, when the messenger cometh, shut the door, and hold him fast at the door : is not the sound of his master's feet behind him? And while he yet talked with them, behold, the messenger came down unto him: and he (the king) said, Behold, this evil is of the Lord, what [why, N. Tr.] should I wait for the Lord any longer?" He had professedly been waiting upon the God of Elisha, and now when deliverance seems as far off as ever, throws it all up, as much as saying, It is useless to look to the Lord for deliverance; and the unbelief and passion of his heart break out.

But human extremity is the divine opportunity; and when the unbelieving king breaks out in fretful despair, the faith of God's prophet shines out, proclaiming full relief and abundance on the morrow. "Then Elisha

said, Hear ye the word of the Lord; Thus saith the
Lord, To-morrow about this time shall a measure of
fine flour be sold for a shekel, and two measures of
barley for a shekel, in the gate of Samaria." And as
the man of God foretold, so it came to pass. A miraculous noise from the Lord frightened the besieging
army, supposing it to be a mighty host's arrival. "For
the Lord had made the host of the Syrians to hear a
noise of chariots, and a noise of horses, even the noise
of a great host: and they said one to another, Lo,
the king of Israel hath hired against us the kings of
the Hittites, and the kings of the Egyptians, to come
upon us. Wherefore they arose and fled in the
twilight, and left their tents, and their horses, and
their asses, even the camp as it was, and fled for
their life." Lepers, in the night, bring the welcome
news to the king, who delays the deliverance by his
unbelief, sending even to the Jordan, a score of
miles away, for proofs of the report. Thus was Samaria relieved.

As for Syria, the dynasty of the first two Benhadads
was soon after ended with the strangling of the king
on his sick-bed by his prime minister Hazael, who
reigned in his stead. News of this revolution, probably, encouraged Jehoram to attempt the recovery of
Ramoth-Gilead, which his father, fourteen years before,
had attacked in vain, with fatal consequences to
himself. "And he [Jehoram, king of Judah] went
with Joram the son of Ahab to the war against Hazael
king of Syria in Ramoth-Gilead; and the Syrians
wounded Joram. And king Joram went back to be
healed in Jezreel of the wounds which the Syrians had

E

given him at Ramah [or Ramoth], when he fought against Hazael king of Syria."

How he was shortly after slain by Jehu his commander-in-chief, will be dwelt upon in the review of that king's life. (See Jehu; also Jehoram king of Judah.) The dynasty of Omri (the most powerful of the nine that ruled over Israel) ended with his life. His character was neither strong, nor very marked in anything. He appears to have had leanings toward the worship of Jehovah; but as a patron, rather than in heart-subjection to Him as the one true God of heaven and earth. He evidently looked upon Elisha's miracles as matters of speculation, in idle curiosity inquiring of the prophet's disgraced servant Gehazi. "And the king talked with Gehazi the servant of the man of God, saying, Tell me, I pray thee, all the great things that Elisha hath done." These marvellous signs of Jehovah were to him material for entertainment, merely, as the miracles of Elisha's great Antitype were to Herod. (See Mark 6: 14, 20; Luke 9: 9; 23: 8.) He was the counselor of Jehoram king of Judah, to his destruction (2 Chron. 22: 4, 5); and such was his unpopularity with his subjects that Jehu had but little difficulty in effecting a revolution, and supplanting him upon the throne after his murder.

He appears to have been, in spiritual matters, one of those undecided, neutral characters, who puzzle most observers, and who never seem to know themselves just where they stand, or belong. He put away the Baal statue, made by his father Ahab, but never become a real believer in Jehovah. The reading of the inspired record of his life leaves the impression on one's mind that he was, in all matters of faith, both skeptical and superstitious. God, who knew him and his ways perfectly, has caused it to be recorded of him, "He wrought evil in the sight of the Lord." As such, we and all posterity know him. And as such he shall be manifested in the coming day, when "great," as well as "small," shall stand before the throne to be judged, "every man, according to his works."

JEHU

(Jehovah is He.)

2 Kings, chaps. 9 and 10.

Contemporary Prophet: ELISHA.

"The great God that formed all things both rewardeth the fool, and rewardeth transgressors."—*Proverbs
26 : 10.*

"AND Elisha the prophet called one of the children of the prophets, and said unto him, Gird
up thy loins, and take this box of oil in thy
hand, and go to Ramoth-gilead: and when thou com-
est thither, look out there Jehu the son of Jehoshaphat
the son of Nimshi, and go in, and make him arise up
from among his brethren, and carry him to an inner
chamber; then take the box of oil, and pour it on his
head, and say, Thus saith the Lord, I have anointed
thee king over Israel. Then open the door, and flee,
and tarry not."

Twenty years before, he had (probably) been anointed by Elijah* (1 Kings 19 : 16), as David was anointed

---

* Both the announcement to Hazael that he would be king
over Syria, and the anointing of Jehu to Israel's kingdom, seem
rather to have been left by Elijah to his successor Elisha, to be
done at God's appointed time. In both Hazael and Jehu
Elisha's appointment take immediate effect, as Elijah's mantle
thrown upon Elisha had also taken immediate effect. See 1
Kings 19 : 19–21; 2 Kings 8 : 10–15; 9 : 1–3 and 11–14. —[*Ed.*

by Samuel long before his anointing by the people
(2 Sam. 2 : 4).

The anointing of the king over Israel was not an
established custom, or rule. It was done when the
circumstances were out of the ordinary, or when there
might be some question as to his title to the crown.
Saul and David were both anointed by Samuel; the
one as *first* king, the other as head of a new line
(1 Sam. 9 : 16; 16 : 12). Zadok the priest and Nathan the prophet jointly anointed Solomon, because
of the faction under Adonijah (1 Kings 1 : 34). The
rebel son Absalom was also anointed (2 Sam. 19 : 10).
So was the boy-king Joash (2 Kings 11 : 12); so, too,
was the wicked and ill-fated Jehoahaz (2 Kings 23 :
30). See also Judges 9 : 8, 15. "In the case of Jehu,
in whom the succession of the kingdom of Israel was
to be translated out of the right line of the family of
Ahab, into another family, which had no [legal] right
to the kingdom, but merely the appointment of God,
there was a necessity for his unction, both to convey
to him a title, and to invest him in the actual possession of the kingdom " (Burder).

Joram's army still lay siege to Ramoth-gilead, where
his general Jehu commanded the forces. "So the
young man, even the young man the prophet, went to
Ramoth-gilead. And when he came, behold, the captains of the host were sitting; and he said, I have an
errand unto thee, O captain. And Jehu said, Unto
which of all us? And he said, To thee, O captain.
And he arose, and went into the house; and he poured
the oil on his head, and said unto him, Thus saith the
Lord God of Israel, I have anointed thee king over

the people of the Lord, even over Israel. And thou shalt smite the house of Ahab thy master, that I may avenge the blood of My servants the prophets, and the blood of all the servants of the Lord, at the hand of Jezebel. For the whole house of Ahab shall perish: and I will cut off from Ahab every male, and him that is shut up and left in Israel: and I will make the house of Ahab like the house of Jeroboam the son of Nebat, and like the house of Baasha the son of Ahijah: and the dogs shall eat Jezebel in the portion of Jezreel, and there shall be none to bury her. And he opened the door, and fled." At last, after more than fifteen years' delay, the blood of Naboth, crying, like Abel's, for vengeance from the ground, was about to be requited. God, when judging men, is never in haste. He allowed Jezebel to outlive, not only her husband, but his two successors. She was powerless, evidently, to continue her former high-handed practices after Ahab's death; and it was a part of her punishment to live to see his dynasty overthrown and the extinction of his and her house begun.

"Then Jehu came forth to the servants of his Lord: and one said unto him, Is all well? wherefore came this mad fellow to thee? And he said unto them, Ye know the man, and his communication.* And they said, It is false: tell us now. And he said, Thus and thus spake he to me, saying, Thus saith the Lord, I have anointed thee king over Israel. Then they hasted, and took every man his garment, and put it under him on the top of the stairs (an ancient custom,

* Translated "babbling" in Prov. 23 : 29.

see Matt. 21 : 7), and blew with trumpets, saying, Jehu
is king . . . And Jehu said, If it be your minds, then
let none go forth nor escape out of the city to go to
tell it in Jezreel."

Impatient to be in actual and acknowledged possession of the kingdom, and without a thought of waiting,
even for the briefest season, upon God, Jehu is off
with Bidkar his captain on his thirty-five mile journey
to Jezreel. "So Jehu rode in a chariot, and went to
Jezreel; for Joram lay there. And Ahaziah king of
Judah was come down to see Joram. And there stood
a watchman on the tower of Jezreel, and he spied the
company of Jehu as he came, and said, I see a company. And Joram said, Take a horseman, and send
to meet them, and let him say, Is it peace? So there
went one on horseback to meet him, and said, Thus
saith the king, Is it peace? And Jehu said, What
hast thou to do with peace? turn thee behind me.
And the watchman told, saying, The messenger came
to them, but he cometh not again." Another messenger is despatched to meet the advancing cavalcade.
And with like result, only the watchman this time
adds, in his report, "The driving is like the driving
of Jehu the son of Nimshi; for he driveth furiously."
Eager to be at his work of extirpation, the newly-
anointed executioner-king makes all speed, as if the
solemn, fearful work of destruction to which he had
been commissioned was to him an exciting pleasure,
instead of a painful task of stern necessity, as it must
have been had he been in true fellowship with God in
his work of overthrow and retributive judgment upon
the house of Ahab. God has no pleasure in the death

of the sinner. The taking of human life, whether done by divine appointment or otherwise, should be, and is, one of the saddest and most solemn acts that it is possible for man to perform. Jehu's ready willingness betrayed how little his soul really entered into the awful nature of his charge; and, what is more lamentable, the gravity of the guilt that had occasioned it.

"And Joram said, Make ready! And his chariot was made ready. And Joram king of Israel and Ahaziah king of Judah went out, each in his chariot, and they went out against (to meet, N. Tr.) Jehu, and met him in the portion of Naboth the Jezreelite. And it came to pass, when Joram saw Jehu, that he said, Is it peace, Jehu? And he answered, What peace, so long as the whoredoms of thy mother Jezebel and her witchcrafts are so many? And Joram turned his hands, and fled, and said to Ahaziah, There is treachery, O Ahaziah. And Jehu drew a bow with his full strength, and smote Jehoram between his arms, and the arrow went out at his heart, and he sunk down in his chariot." It was but the sudden beginning of a speedy end; for it is but "a short work" that God makes with men when He makes inquisition for apostasy and blood. "Then said Jehu to Bidkar his captain, Take up and cast him in the portion of the field of Naboth the Jezreelite: for remember how that, when I and thou rode together after Ahab his father, the Lord laid this burden upon him; surely I have seen yesterday the blood of Naboth, and the blood of his sons (see Josh. 7 : 24), saith the Lord; and I will requite thee in this plat, saith the Lord. Now therefore take and cast him into the plat of ground, according to the word of the Lord." They slew Ahaziah king of Judah also (see AHAZIAH), as he was seeking to escape. "And Jehu followed after him, and said, Smite him also in the chariot."

Jezebel's turn comes next: "And when Jehu was come to Jezreel, Jezebel heard of it; and she painted her face, and tired her head, and looked out at a window. And as Jehu entered in at the gate, she said, Had Zimri peace, who slew his master?" Her innate vanity manifested itself up till the last. She probably knew her end had come; but instead of preparing her soul, she adorned her body (soon to be eaten by dogs), darkening, according to Eastern custom, her brows and eyelashes with antimony, that she might appear queenly and beautiful even in death. Her daring spirit, even with her last breath, taunts her slayer by reminding him of Zimri's end, who, like Jehu (as she would make it appear), "slew his master." * "And he lifted up his face to the window, and said, Who is on my side? who? And there looked out to him two or three eunuchs. And he said, Throw her down. So they threw her down: and some of her blood was sprinkled on the wall, and on the horses: and he trode her under foot. And when he was come in, he did eat and drink, and said, Go, see now this cursed woman, and bury her: for she is a king's daughter. And they went to bury her: but they found no more of her than the skull, and the feet, and the palms of her hands.

---

* The New Translation makes her say, "Is it peace, Zimri, murderer of his master?"

Wherefore they came again, and told him. And he said, This is the word of the Lord, which He spake by His servant Elijah the Tishbite, saying, In the portion of Jezreel shall dogs eat the flesh of Jezebel : and the carcase of Jezebel shall be as dung upon the face of the field in the portion of Jezreel ; so that they shall not say, This is Jezebel "—i. e., there should be no tomb to mark the resting-place of her remains.

Thus miserably perished this wretched woman, a foreigner in Israel, who did her utmost to make her Tyrian Baal-worship the established religion of her husband's kingdom, and hesitated not to slay any who dared oppose her propaganda, or interfere with her desires or designs in any way. She is made (as we believe) a type of papal Rome in Rev. 3 ; and a more suitable character to represent that system of idolatry, corruption and murder, the history of the ages does not supply. And her tragic death is as the shadow cast before of that coming event foretold in Rev. 17 : 17—Babylon's end, "the judgment of the great⎪whore," whose idolatries and crimes have stained the earth.

"And Ahab had seventy sons in Samaria. And Jehu wrote letters, and sent to Samaria, unto the rulers of Jezreel, to the elders, and to them that brought up Ahab's children, saying, Now as soon as this letter cometh to you, seeing your master's sons are with you, and there are with you chariots and horses, a fenced (fortified) city also, and armor ; look even out the best and meetest of your master's sons, and set him on his father's throne, and fight for your master's house." It was seemingly a bold challenge, though in reality only his manner of frightening them into subjection. He knew well the character of those with whom he had to deal; besides, there does not appear to have been much love or loyalty to the reigning dynasty. So the fervid reformer knew he had little to fear from them. " But they were exceedingly afraid, and said, Behold, the two kings stood not before him : how then shall we stand? And he that was over the house, and he that was over the city, the elders also, and the bring-ers up of the children, sent to Jehu, saying, We are thy servants, and will do all that thou shalt bid us; we will not make any king : do thou that which is good in thine eyes." Thus these spiritless elders and rulers of Jezreel tamely surrender everything to Jehu. When Jezebel sent her imperious letter to them, commanding them to falsely accuse and then murder Naboth, they abjectly complied without the slightest show of resist-ance or conscience, putting to death their righteous fellow-townsman. A cringing obedience might well have been expected by Jehu from such men.

" Then he wrote a letter the second time to them, saying, If ye be mine, and if ye will harken unto my voice, take ye the heads of the men your master's sons, and come to me to Jezreel by to-morrow this time. Now the king's sons, being seventy persons, were with the great men of the city, which brought them up. And it came to pass, when the letter came to them, that they took the king's sons, and slew sev-enty persons, and put their heads in baskets, and sent him them in Jezreel. And there came a messenger, and told him, saying, They have brought the heads of the king's sons. And he said, Lay ye them in two heaps at the entering in of the gate until the morning.

And it come to pass in the morning, that he went out, and stood, and said to all the people, Ye be righteous: behold, I conspired against my master, and slew him: but who slew all these?" It was a crafty stroke of policy on Jehu's part to have the principal men of the capital slay the residue of Ahab's posterity. Their act, he shrewdly divined, would create a breach between themselves and any sympathizers with the extinct dynasty, or their royal relatives across the border; thus effectually destroying the last remaining opposition to his course, and settlement upon the throne. True, though his motives were purely political, he gives his wholesale executions a religious coloring, making capital of God's word and principle of retribution in regard to Ahab and his house: "Know now that there shall fall unto the earth nothing of the word of the Lord, which the Lord spake concerning the house of Ahab: for the Lord hath done that which He spake by His servant Elijah. So Jehu slew all that remained of the house of Ahab in Jezreel, and all his great men, and his kinsfolks, and his priests, until he left him none remaining."

The sword of judgment, so far as the expressed purpose of Jehovah was concerned, should have been confined to the house of Ahab. But a reckless and ambitious hand was wielding it, and it devoured beyond the allotted limits:

"And he arose and departed, and came to Samaria. And as he was at the shearing house (shepherd's meeting-place, N. Tr.) in the way, Jehu met with the brethren of Ahaziah king of Judah, and said, Who are ye? And they answered, We are the brethren of Aha-

ziah ; and we go down to salute the children of the
king and the children of the queen. And he said,
Take them alive. And they took them alive, and slew
them at the pit (well, N. Tr.) of the shearing house,
even two and forty men ; neither left he any of them."
It was not any part of Jehovah's commission to Jehu
to slay these, or any of the descendants of king Jehoshaphat. God had not required this at his hands ;
and in his unwarranted slaughter of these brethren of
Ahaziah he all but exterminated the house of David,
leaving the rule of the kingdom to the infamous Athaliah. Jehu probably cared little for this. His thought,
probably, was to prevent any uprising against himself
from the royal family of Judah. The possible consequences of his ruthless act in reference to the continu-
ance of David's line (until Messiah) gave him no concern. As to the butchered princes, they reaped the
melancholy consequences of their intimacy with a
family doomed by God to destruction for their apostasy and wickedness. Let Christians take warning,
and obey the call of God to His own, so unmistakably
imperative and plain, " Come out from among them,
and be ye separate " (2 Cor. 6 : 17).

Jehu's self-complacency is manifested on his meeting with Jehonadab the son of Rechab. He patron-
izingly took him into his chariot, giving him his hand
(signifying a pledge, in the East; see Ezra 10 : 19), and
saying, "Come with me, and see my zeal for the
Lord." His ostentatious display of his reforming
zeal revealed how little he had God's glory in mind in
the midst of all his feverish activity and abolition—in
sad contrast to Him who always hid Himself and

sought His Father's glory only.   He too had a zeal; but, oh, of what a different character from that of Jehu!   "The zeal of Thy house consumes Me," He could say.   But Jehu's zeal, on the contrary, consumed and destroyed everybody and everything that stood in the way of his own advantage or aggrandizement, but never touched himself.   He appears to have been a total stranger to real exercise of soul.   God ordained him as His executioner, and, as has been aptly said, "Never was a more fitted instrument for the work whereunto he was appointed than Jehu."   And he had his reward.   It was for this world alone; and the fourth generation of his children saw its end.

"And when he was come to Samaria, he slew all that remained unto Ahab in Samaria, till he had destroyed him, according to the saying of the Lord, which He spake by Elijah."   He then turned his attention to the priests of Baal.   A monk, at the dawn of the Reformation, remarked, "We must root printing out, or it will root *us* out."   Jehu felt the same toward the Baal-worship in his newly-acquired kingdom; hence it must be rooted out.   Baal had formed a powerful link between Ahab's family and his worshipers, and might be a menace to his tenure of the throne; his priests must therefore share the fate of that family under whose powerful patronage they had flourished in established security the past thirty-six years.   "And Jehu gathered all the people together, and said unto them, Ahab served Baal a little; but Jehu shall serve him much."   He then gathers, by subtilty, all the priests and followers of Baal into their place of worship.   There is a measure of righteousness in his doings, however, for he takes pains to have none of the servants of Jehovah mixed up with the devoted worshipers of Baal. "And it came to pass, as soon as he (they, N. Tr.) had made an end of offering the burnt-offering, that Jehu said to the guard and to the captains, Go in, and slay them; let none come forth. And they smote them with the edge of the sword; and the guard and the captains cast them out, and went to the city (some read buildings, or citadel) of the house of Baal. And they brought forth the images out of the house of Baal, and burned them. And they brake down the image of Baal, and brake down the house of Baal, and made it a draught house unto this day."

"Thus Jehu extirpated Baal out of Israel. Only, the sins of Jeroboam the son of Nebat, who made Israel to sin, from them Jehu departed not, [from] the golden calves that were in Bethel, and that were in Dan. And Jehovah said to Jehu, Because thou hast executed well that which is right in My sight, and hast done unto the house of Ahab according to all that was in My heart, thy children of the fourth generation shall sit on the throne of Israel. But Jehu took no heed to walk in the law of Jehovah the God of Israel with all his heart; he departed not from the sins of Jeroboam, who made Israel to sin" (2 Kings 10: 28–31, N. Tr.).

While he is God's faithful, and, as we have seen, over-zealous instrument, there is nothing lovely, and little that is commendable, in the *character* of Jehu. He served God's purpose as an executioner, but with that he stopped. He could slay "with all his heart," but took no heed to walk in the law of the Lord with earnestness. He could break down the gross and vile worship of Baal, yet go on in the calf-worship of Jeroboam. It is easier to serve God in outward things than to acquire the character which He loves, enthroning Him in the heart, and giving the spiritual intelligence of His mind. How different was David from Jehu! He too was God's instrument for judgment, but how different was his way of carrying it out! God did not, nor did He let Israel, forget his heartless slaughter, saying to the prophet Hosea, a hundred years later, " Call his name Jezreel; for yet a little while, and I will avenge the blood of Jezreel upon the house of Jehu" (Hos. 1 : 4).

The great lesson to be drawn from this remarkable man's life is that of being constantly on our guard, as servants of God, lest we be found doing His work— whether it be in the exercise of discipline, or the accomplishment of reformation—in a spirit of unbrokenness and without due exercise of heart and conscience before Him who is "a God of judgment," and by whom "actions are *weighed*."

" Now the rest of the acts of Jehu, and all that he did, and all his might, are they not written in the book of the chronicles of the kings of Israel? And Jehu slept with his fathers : and they buried him in Samaria. And Jehoahaz his son reigned in his stead. And the time that Jehu reigned over Israel in Samaria was twenty and eight years."*

---

* For further and excellent reflections on the character of Jehu, see a pamphlet called " The Zeal of Jehu," published by R. T. Grant, Los Angeles, Cal.

JEHOAHAZ

(Jehovah-seized.)

2 Kings 13 : 1–9.

Contemporary Prophets: ELISHA, JONAH.

"When the righteous are in authority, the people rejoice : but when the wicked beareth rule, the people mourn."—*Proverbs 29 : 2.*

"IN the three and twentieth year of Joash the son of Ahaziah king of Judah, Jehoahaz the son of Jehu began to reign over Israel in Samaria, and reigned seventeen years. And he did that which was evil in the sight of the Lord, and followed the sins of Jeroboam the son of Nebat, which made Israel to sin; he departed not therefrom." There is no variation from the same sorrowful formula usually used in describing the moral conduct of these Israelitish kings: "He did that which was evil in the sight of the Lord." His ways may not have appeared sinful in the sight of his fellows; but God, who "seeth not as man seeth," pronounced it "evil," and sent upon him and his subjects the chastisement their wicked idolatry deserved.

"And the anger of the Lord was kindled against Israel, and He delivered them into the hand of Hazael king of Syria, and into the hand of Ben-hadad the son of Hazael, all their days." Hazael's conquest of the

kingdom had begun in the days of Jehu, Jehoahaz'
father : "In those days the Lord began to cut Israel
short : and Hazael smote them in all the coasts of Israel ; from Jordan eastward, all the land of Gilead, the
Gadites, and the Reubenites, and the Manassites, from
Aroer, which is by the river Arnon, even Gilead and
Bashan" (2 Kings 10 : 32, 33). Jehu, though so
"swift to shed blood" in the beginning of his reign,
was more slow to take the sword in defence of the
land and people of God toward its close. Men of this
class are seldom really "good soldiers." They may be
exceedingly active in obtaining the position they love
and covet, while very careless about the true interests
of the people of God. There is no hint of his having
made the slightest attempt to resist these inroads of
the king of Syria in his dominion. He probably remained timorously passive at Samaria while the en-
croachments on God's territory were being made.
The Black Obelisk records that he ("Jahua") sent
gold and silver to Shalmaneser I. at this time, probably to invoke the Assyrian's aid against Hazael. Certainly valor was not characteristic of Jehu. Impetu-
osity is not courage, nor must we mistake enthusiasm
for the earnestness of conviction. To boast when
putting on the harness is an easy matter ; the wise will
wait until the time to put it off (1 Kings 20 : 11) ; and
then the truly wise will glory only in the Lord.

"And Jehoahaz besought the Lord, and the Lord
harkened unto him : for He saw the oppression of Israel, because the king of Syria oppressed them. And
the Lord gave Israel a saviour, so that they went out
from under the hand of the Syrians : and the children

of Israel dwelt in their tents, as beforetime. Nevertheless they departed not from the sins of the house
of Jeroboam, who made Israel to sin, but walked
therein: and there remained the grove (Asherah, N.
Tr.) also in Samaria." In this parenthetic paragraph
we see how Elisha's prophecy of Hazael's pitiless oppression of the children of Israel was fulfilled (2 Kings
8: 12). Well might the man of God, who so dearly
loved Israel, weep as before him stood the destined
perpetrator of these cruelties against his people—God
even thus seeking to turn them back to repentance
from their idolatries. This bitter chastisement appears to have had a salutary effect upon Jehoahaz, for
he "besought Jehovah." When the "goodness" of
God fails to bring men to repentance, His "severity"
is required, and used. See Ps. 78: 34; Hos. 5: 15.
"Accordingly God accepted of his repentance," Josephus says; "and being desirous rather to admonish
those that might repent, than to determine that they
should be utterly destroyed, He granted them deliverance from war and dangers. So the country having
obtained peace, returned to its former condition, and
flourished as before" (Ant. ix. 8, § 5). This restoration to prosperity began under Joash son of Jehoahaz,
and culminated during the reign of his grandson Jeroboam II.* So prayer is frequently answered after the
petitioner has passed away. Let none say, then, like
the wicked of old, in reference to God, "What profit

---

* A *temporary* deliverance may have been granted as 2 Kings
13: 4, 5, seems to imply; and the reason of being only temporary given in the 6th verse: "Nevertheless they departed
not from the sins of the house of Jeroboam" etc.—[*Ed.*

should we have, if we pray unto Him?" (Job 21 : 15.)*
What profit? Ah, true prayer is always heard at the
Throne: "Whatsoever we ask, we know that we have
the petitions that we desired of Him" (1 John 5 : 15).

"Hazael king of Syria oppressed Israel all the days
of Jehoahaz" (2 Kings 13 : 22). There was no respite
until Joash's day. This must have been a test to Jehoahaz' faith, if his repentance was really the result of
"godly sorrow" for his and the nation's sins. But
when has faith, untried, ever flourished? Stagger not,
then, nor stumble, beloved fellow-believer, at "the trial
of your faith." God "harkened" to Jehoahaz, though
he died with Hazael busy at his work of devastation
in his realm. "Neither did he leave of the people to
Jehoahaz but fifty horsemen, and ten chariots, and ten
thousand footmen; for the king of Syria had destroyed
them, and had made them like the dust by threshing."
See Amos 1 : 3.

"Now the rest of the acts of Jehoahaz, and all that
he did, and his might, are they not written in the book
of the chronicles of the kings of Israel? And Jehoahaz slept with his fathers; and they buried him in Samaria: and Joash his son reigned in his stead."

---

* The very need of the creature, even though unintelli-
gent, is like a prayer—an appeal to God : " Who provideth
for the raven his food? *when his young ones cry unto God*"
(Job. 38: 41).—[*Ed.*

JOASH (or, JEHOASH)

(Jehovah-gifted.)

2 Kings 13 : 10–25 ; 14 : 8–16.

Contemporary Prophet : JONAH (?)

———————

"A man shall not be established by wickedness ; but the root of the righteous shall not be moved."—*Proverbs 12 : 3.*

———————

"IN the thirty and seventh year of Joash king of Judah began Jehoash the son of Jehoahaz to reign over Israel in Samaria, and reigned sixteen years" (2 Kings 13 : 10). It is evident from a comparison of the figures of this verse with those given in verse one of same chapter, and first verse of the chapter following, that Joash (Jehoash, abbreviated) reigned jointly with his father (a thing not uncommon in ancient times) during the last two years of the latter's life. This readily explains an otherwise inexplicable chronological difficulty, and it is quite likely that the seeming discrepancies of chronology in Scripture (those most difficult of solution) could—excepting a few which undoubtedly owe their origin to errors of transcription—be as simply and as satisfactorily explained.

"And he did that which was evil in the sight of the Lord ; he departed not from all the sins of Jeroboam the son of Nebat, who made Israel to sin : but he walked therein." Josephus calls him a "good man"

(Ant. ix. 8, § 6).   This misjudgment of the character
of Joash is probably based on the incident of his visit
to the dying prophet Elisha.   A little manifestation of
religious, or even semi-religious, sentiment goes a long
way, with some persons, in accounting people "good."
It has been supposed by some that Joash reformed, or
repented, toward the end of his life (founded partly,
perhaps, on his mild treatment, toward the close of his
reign, of Amaziah, when he had it in his power to
take that combative meddler's life—see AMAZIAH), and
that Josephus refers to this latter period of his reign.
But the words, " *He departed not* from the sins of Jeroboam," forbid all thought of any real, or lasting repent-
tance at any period of his life.   God is more anxious
to record, than any of His people are to read, any good
in any of these monarchs' lives.   He has noted none
in Joash's ; and where He is silent, who will dare to
speak ?

The episode of Joash's visit to the dying prophet
has been alluded to ; we quote it here in full : " Now
Elisha was fallen sick of his sickness whereof he died.
And Joash the king of Israel came down unto him,
and wept over his face, and said, O my father, my
father ! the chariot of Israel, and the horsemen thereof.
And Elisha said unto him, Take bow and arrows.
And he took unto him bow and arrows.   And he said
to the king of Israel, Put thy hand upon the bow.
And he put his hand upon it : and Elisha put his
hands upon the king's hands.   And he said, Open the
window eastward.   And he opened it.   Then Elisha
said, Shoot.   And he shot.   And he said, The arrow
of the Lord's deliverance, and (even, N. Tr.) the arrow

of deliverance from Syria : for thou shalt smite the Syrians in Aphek, till thou have consumed them. And he said, Take the arrows. And he took them. And he said unto the king of Israel, Smite upon the ground. And he smote thrice, and stayed. And the man of God was wroth with him, and said, Thou shouldest have smitten five or six times ; then hadst thou smitten Syria till thou hadst consumed it : whereas now thou shalt smite Syria but thrice."

The application of all this is simple. Joash could not but realize that the prophet's departure from them would be a serious loss to the nation. And in calling him "the chariot of Israel, and the horsemen thereof," he meant that the prophet's presence in their midst was to them what chariots and horsemen were to other nations—their main defence.* And by putting his dying hands upon those of the king, Elisha meant him to understand the truth of what God said more than three hundred years later, through the prophet Zecha-

---

* The whole narrative here brings vividly to mind the departure of Elijah, when the chariot and horses of fire bore him away as by a whirlwind to heaven, and Elisha exclaimed, "My father, my father, the chariot of Israel, and the horsemen thereof !" King Joash (fully acquainted, no doubt, with the circumstances of Elijah's carrying away to heaven) repeats Elisha's very words at the taking away of his master, Jehovah's faithful and honored servant. Like many another disobedient heart unreconciled to God, king Joash has a sense of the loss that Elisha's death would be to the kingdom—Jehovah's *defence*, as well as His reproofs, was departing. Yet Elisha (like Elijah dropping his mantle) would leave a blessing and help for poor Israel, limited only by Israel's and their king's unbelief.—[*Ed.*

riah, "Not by might [or forces, or army], nor by power, but by My Spirit, saith the Lord of hosts" (Zech. 4 : 6). "Without Me, ye can do nothing," this would be in New Testament phraseology. The shooting of the arrow eastward, toward the territory conquered by Syria, signified Joash's victory over Ben-hadad's forces at Aphek ("on the road from Syria to Israel in the level plain east of Jordan ; a common field of battles with Syria."—*Fausset*). See 1 Kings 20 : 26. Only Joash's lack of faith, manifested in his half-hearted smiting the ground with arrows but thrice, prevented his destroying the Syrians utterly. And it was unto him according to his faith. "And Jehoash the son of Jehoahaz took again out of the hand of Ben-hadad the son of Hazael the cities which he had taken out of the hand of Jehoahaz his father by war. *Three times* did Joash beat him, and recovered the cities of Israel."

Like Asa [see], he had the opportunity given him to end the power of Syria (2 Chron. 16 : 7), which from its beginning had been such a plague to both Judah and Israel. But, like Asa, he let it pass, and the work was left to the Assyrian, who destroyed both it (Syria) and them (Israel and Judah).

"And the rest of the acts of Joash, and all that he did, and his might wherewith he fought against Amaziah king of Judah, are they not written in the book of the chronicles of the kings of Israel? And Joash slept with his fathers; and Jeroboam sat upon his throne: and Joash was buried in Samaria with the kings of Israel."

JEROBOAM II.

(Whose people is many.)

(2 Kings 14 : 23–29.)

Contemporary Prophets: HOSEA; AMOS.

"The froward is abomination to the Lord : but His
secret is with the righteous."—*Proverbs 3 : 32.*

"IN the fifteenth year of Amaziah the son of Joash
king of Judah, Jeroboam the son of Joash king of
Israel began to reign in Samaria, and reigned
forty and one years. And he did that which was evil
in the sight of the Lord : he departed not from all the
sins of Jeroboam the son of Nebat, who made Israel
to sin." His was the longest and most prosperous of
any of the reigns of the kings of Israel. "He restored
the coast of Israel from the entering of Hamath unto
the sea of the plain, according to the word of the Lord
God of Israel, which He spake by the hand of His
servant Jonah, the son of Amittai, the prophet, which
was of Gath-hepher." This was the beginning of the
ministry of the sixteen prophets whose writings have
been preserved to us. Jonah was the earliest of these
probably, and appears to have been Elisha's immediate successor. His prophecy referred to here, of the
enlargement of Israel's coast (border), must have been
a very pleasant one to him—a much more welcome
work than his commission toward the Ninevites. But
God's servants have no choice. They know "the love
of Christ," and, constrained by that same love, it is

their joy to tell it; but they also know "the terror of the Lord"; and knowing this, they do their utmost to "persuade" and warn men of "the wrath to come." It is not grace only that came by Jesus Christ, but "grace *and truth.*' And the truth must be made known to men, however unpleasant or unthankful the task. But if done as unto God, it can never be a disagreeable or unwelcome undertaking to the spirit, however painful or unpleasant to the flesh. See 1 Cor. 9: 16, 17.

The increase of Israel's territory under Jeroboam II. was considerable; his prosperity in this way corresponding with his name—*whose people is many*. "'The entering in of Hamath' indicates that the long valley between Lebanon and Anti-lebanon was the point of entrance into the land of Israel for an invading army" (*Fausset*). "The sea of the plain" was the Dead Sea (Josh. 3: 16), making the total distance of his kingdom, north and south, almost two hundred miles. He was, no doubt, the "savior" promised under the unfortunate reign of Jehoahaz (2 Kings 13: 5). "For the Lord saw the affliction of Israel, that it was very bitter: for there was not any shut up, nor any left, nor any helper for Israel. And the Lord said not that He would blot out the name of Israel from under heaven: but He saved them by the hand of Jeroboam the son of Joash." This was not for any goodness that He saw in them or Jeroboam their king, but "because of His covenant with Abraham, Isaac, and Jacob" (2 Kings 13: 23).

"Now the rest of the acts of Jeroboam, and all that he did, and his might, how he warred, and how he recovered Damascus, and Hamath, which belonged to

Judah, for Israel, are they not written in the book of
the chronicles of the kings of Israel?"   Damascus
and Hamath were both capitals of two once powerful
kingdoms, and though once subjugated by David
(1 Chron. 18 : 3–6), their recovery to Israel under Jeroboam, more than one hundred and fifty years after
their revolt from Judah, speaks eloquently for the success and power of his arms against those hostile nations on his northern border.   Hamath, called "the
great" in Amos 6 : 2, was the principal city of upper
Syria, and an important strategic point, commanding
the whole valley of the Orontes leading to the countries on the south.

Israel was blessed with the ministries of both
Hosea and Amos during Jeroboam's reign.   From
their writings it will readily be seen that though there
was political revival under his rule, there was no real
moral or spiritual awakening among the people.   Amos
was looked upon as a troubler to the peace of the
kingdom, and admonished by Amaziah the priest of
Bethel to flee away to the land of Judah, "and there
eat bread, and prophesy there," as if God's prophet
were nothing more than a mere mercenary like himself.   He also accused the prophet before the king of
having conspired against his life.   Jeroboam appears
to have paid little or no attention to this charge, being,
perhaps, too sensible a man to believe the accusation,
knowing the jealous, self-seeking spirit of the arch-
priest of the nation.   See Amos 7 : 7–17.

"And Jeroboam slept with his fathers, even with
the kings of Israel; and Zachariah his son reigned in
his stead."

ZACHARIAH

(Jah has remembered.)

2 Kings 15 : 8–12.

Contemporary Prophet: AMOS.

"Righteousness keepeth him that is upright in the way : but wickedness overthroweth the sinner."—*Proverbs 13 : 6.*

"IN the thirty and eighth year of Azariah king of Judah did Zachariah the son of Jeroboam reign over Israel in Samaria six months." There appears to be (from a comparison of dates) a period unaccounted for, of about eleven years, between Jeroboam's death and the beginning of his son Zachariah's reign. This is not surprising when we see what quickly followed his accession to the throne. "And he did that which was evil in the sight of the Lord, as his fathers had done : he departed not from the sins of Jeroboam the son of Nebat, who made Israel to sin. And Shallum the son of Jabesh conspired against him, and smote him before the people, and slew him, and reigned in his stead."

Anarchy probably prevailed during the above-noted interregnum. Hosea, whose prophecy dates about this time (as regards Israel, see Hos. 1 : 1), seems to allude frequently to this season of lawlessness and revolution. See his prophecy, chaps. 7 : 7 ; 10 : 3, 7 ;

13 : 10—the last of these reads in the New Translation, "Where then is thy king?" etc. The people were probably unwilling to have Zachariah succeed his father to the throne. He appears to have been quite unpopular with the mass of the nation, for Shallum slew him without fear "*before the people.*" But God has said next to nothing as to this parenthetic period, and we dare not say more. To speculate here would be worse than folly, since God's wisdom has chosen to give us no record of it; and where no useful end is gained, He always hides from the gaze of the curious the sins and errors of His people. Contemporary Scripture-dates, however, show that such an interval must have elapsed between the close of Jeroboam's and the beginning of his son's reign, though God has passed over the interregnum in silence.*

The assassination of Zachariah ended the dynasty of Jehu, five generations in all, and extending over a period of more than a hundred years. But at last God avenged "the blood of Jezreel upon the house of Jehu" (Hos. 1 : 4). God's eyes were upon "the sinful kingdom" (Amos 9 : 8), and its sinful kings; and from the time of Jeroboam's death, declension set in, ending, less than seventy years later, in its final overthrow and dissolution. Prophetic ministry was from

---

* "The English laws of to-day do not recognize the validity of Charles the First's deposition and execution, nor that of any laws in Parliament or decisions delivered by judges between 1641 and 1660. That whole period of nineteen years is treated as a legal blank, and Charles the Second's reign is counted in the statute-book from his father's death—no reckoning being made of Oliver Cromwell's sovereignty."

this time greatly increased. "Such is the way of our gracious God," an unknown writer says, "that when judgment is near to approach, then testimony is multiplied." How much it was needed in Israel the prophecies of Hosea and Amos abundantly testify.

"And the rest of the acts of Zachariah, behold, they are written in the book of the chronicles of the kings of Israel. This was the word of the Lord, which He spake unto Jehu, saying, Thy sons shall sit upon the throne of Israel unto the fourth generation. And so it came to pass." And thus was it written by the prophet, "At daybreak shall the king of Israel utterly be cut off" (Hos. 10: 15, N. Tr.).

Zachariah's name—*Jah has remembered*—was strikingly significant. God did not forget the wholesale slaughter of men—many of them, perhaps, better than their executioner. Though a century had passed, Jah remembered, and made the inevitable "inquisition for blood," upon the fifth and final member of the murderer's succession.

SHALLUM

(*Requital.*)

2 Kings 15 : 13–15.

Contemporary Prophet: AMOS (?).

"An evil man seeketh only rebellion : therefore a cruel messenger shall be sent against him."—*Proverbs 17 : 11.*

"SHALLUM the son of Jabesh began to reign in the nine and thirtieth year of Uzziah king of Judah; and he reigned a full month in Samaria. For Menahem the son of Gadi went up from Tirzah, and came to Samaria, and smote Shallum the son of Jabesh in Samaria, and slew him, and reigned in his stead." This assassin was not allowed to live long in his ill-gotten power—only for a brief four weeks—and then met the just reward of his crime. His name (a very common one in Israel) means *recompense*, or *retribution;* and as he requited his predecessor, so did Menahem his successor recompense him. It is the old principle of governmental just retribution in kind exemplified. This assassination of two rulers, Zachariah and Shallum, within the space of half a year, speaks loudly of the state of anarchy prevailing in the kingdom at the time. It was, as the prophet testified, "blood toucheth blood" (Hos. 4 : 2). The great prosperity and ex-

pansion under Jeroboam II. appears to have corrupted
the people and caused them to give free rein to their
evil desires and violence.   See Hos. 4 : 7.   Those in
authority, instead of checking this spirit of lawlessness,
found pleasure in it.   "They make the king glad with
their wickedness, and the princes with their lies"
(Hos. 7 : 3).   Dissipation to surfeit marked the conduct of these princes, under this monarchy: "In the
day of our king, the princes made themselves sick
with the heat of wine" (Hos. 7 : 5, N. Tr.).   The de-
moralized condition of public affairs can scarcely be
wondered at, when the king himself encouraged the
disdain of the lawless : "He stretched out his hand to
scorners" (*Ibid.*).   Disintegration and bloodshed followed, as a natural consequence.   Out of the political
chaos and disorder following the death of this, Israel's
most powerful king, came forth the undesired Zachariah, and his murderer, Shallum.   So wickedness
brings its own reward, whether it be in a nation, a
family, or an individual.

"And the rest of the acts of Shallum, and his conspiracy which he made, behold, they are written in the
book of the chronicles of the kings of Israel."

MENAHEM

(*Comforter.*)

2 Kings 15 : 16–22.

"By the blessing of the upright the city is exalted : but it is overthrown by the mouth of the wicked."— *Proverbs 11 : 11.*

MENAHEM, Josephus asserts, and not without reason, was general of the Israelitish forces. His coming up from Tirzah to slay Shallum, and afterwards starting "from Tirzah" (where the main army was posted, probably) on his expedition of slaughter against Tiphsah, implies as much. "Then Menahem smote Tiphsah, and all that were therein, and the coasts thereof from Tirzah : because they opened not to him, therefore he smote it ; and all the women therein that were with child he ripped up." Tiphsah was originally one of Solomon's northeastern border cities, on the Euphrates (1 Kings 4 : 24). It was doubtless recovered to Israel under Jeroboam II., and was probably in revolt when so cruelly attacked by the war-king Menahem. "Situated on the western bank of the Euphrates, on the great trade road from Egypt, Syria and Phenicia to Mesopotamia, it was important for Menahem to rescue it" (*Fausset*). He, in all likelihood, expected by his brutal treatment of the Tiphsahites to strike terror to all who were likely to oppose his tenure of the crown.

"In the nine and thirtieth year of Azariah king of Judah began Menahem the son of Gadi to reign over Israel, and reigned ten years in Samaria. And he did that which was evil in the sight of the Lord: he departed not all his days from the sins of Jeroboam the son of Nebat, who made Israel to sin. And Pul the king of Assyria came against the land: and Menahem gave Pul a thousand talents of silver, that his hand might be with him to confirm the kingdom in his hand. And Menahem exacted the money of Israel, even of all the mighty men of wealth, of each man fifty shekels of silver, to give to the king of Assyria. So the king of Assyria turned back, and stayed not there in the land." This is the first mention of the dreaded "Assyrian" in Scripture. Assyriologists are not perfectly agreed as to just who this "Pul" of Scripture was. The name (that form of it, at least) is not found on any of the Assyrian monuments. A "Phulukh" is mentioned in the Nimrud inscription, with whom some would identify him. Berosus mentions a Chaldean king named Pul, who reigned at just this time, and where the wise cannot among themselves agree we must not venture even to put forth an opinion, but pass on to that concerning which there can be no doubt—his invasion of the land, and the enormous price paid by Menahem for peace. Some suppose that Pul regarded Menahem's reduction of Tiphsah as an attack upon his territory; hence his march against his kingdom; but it is more probable that it was a mere plundering incursion, as most of these ancient military expeditions were, especially those of Assyria. The burden of the levy fell upon the rich, which needs not excite much sympathy when we learn from the prophets Amos and Micah how their riches were obtained. See Amos 4: 1; 5: 11, 12; 8: 4–6; Micah 2: 2; 6: 10–12.

"And the rest of the acts of Menahem, and all that he did, are they not written in the book of the chronicles of the kings of Israel? And Menahem slept with his fathers; and Pekahiah his son reigned in his stead." Though he probably reigned as a military dictator merely, he evidently died in peace, as the expression "slept with his fathers" implies. The expression "his fathers" implies too that he was an Israelite, though his name Menahem does not sound like Hebrew. It is found nowhere else in Scripture, nor is that of his father (Gadi, *fortunate*)—a peculiar and somewhat remarkable, if not significant, circumstance. A competent and spiritually-minded Semitic philologist would, we believe, find an ample and productive field for original research here, as well as in many other portions of Old Testament Scripture, especially the opening chapters of 1 Chronicles.

Menahem's name appears on the monuments of Tiglath-pileser, though it is thought by some, for various reasons, that the Assyrian chroniclers confused the name of Menahem with that of Pekah—his son's slayer. But this, like everything of merely human origin, is uncertain. Only in divinely-inspired Scripture have we absolute exactitude and certainty; for He who was "the Truth" declared, "the Scripture cannot be broken." Hence they "are most surely believed among us" (Luke 1: 1).

PEKAHIAH

(Jah has observed.)

2 Kings 15 : 23–26.

"The righteousness of the upright shall deliver them : but transgressors shall be taken in their own naughtiness."—*Proverbs 11 : 5.*

" IN the fiftieth year of Azariah king of Judah, Pekahiah the son of Menahem began to reign over Israel in Samaria, and reigned two years. And he did that which was evil in the sight of the Lord : he departed not from the sins of Jeroboam the son of Nebat, who made Israel to sin. But Pekah the son of Remaliah, a captain of his, conspired against him, and smote him in Samaria, in the palace of the king's house, with Argob and Arieh, and with him fifty men of the Gileadites : and he killed him, and reigned in his room." Azariah (Uzziah), during his long reign of more than half a century, saw the death of five of Israel's kings, three of whom were assassinated, besides an interregnum of anarchy lasting at least eleven years. This marked contrast is what the prophet referred to, probably, when he wrote, "Ephraim encompasseth Me about with lies, and the house of Israel with deceit, but Judah yet walketh with God [El], and with the holy things of truth" (Hos. 11 : 13, N. Tr.). This does not mean that all Judah's ways pleased the Lord, but that, unlike apostate Israel, they still, as a State, maintained the truth of Jehovah, as revealed in the law and symbolized in the temple's worship and service.

Pekahiah's slayer was his captain (*shalish*, aide-de-camp, probably; "the general of his house," Josephus says), Pekah, with two of his followers, and a company of fifty Gileadites. These Gileadites ("fugitives of Ephraim," Judges 12 : 4*) appear to have been a rough, wild class, a kind of Hebrew highlanders, and ready in Pekahiah's day for any and all manner of villainy. See Hos. 6 : 8. They slew the king in his very palace ("with his friends at a feast;" Josephus' Ant. ix. 11, § 1), so bold were they. His name, *Jah has observed*, implies that God had looked upon the murder of Shallum by his father Menahem, and in the death of Pekahiah his son requited it (2 Chron. 24 : 22). His name, like his father's and grandfather's, does not occur anywhere else in Scripture.

"And the rest of the acts of Pekahiah, and all that he did, behold, they are written in the book of the chronicles of the kings of Israel." His death ended the seventh dynasty of the Israelitish kings.

---

* "Fugitives of Ephraim," however, was an unrighteous taunt of the proud Ephraimites to their Manassite brethren. Gilead was a direct descendant of Manasseh, eldest son of Joseph, and head of a large, powerful family, to whom Moses gave the conquered territory east of Jordan called Gilead. See Num. 32 : 39–41 ; Deut. 3 : 13.

PEKAH

(*Watch.*)

2 Kings 15 : 27–31.

Contemporary Prophet: ODED.

"Righteousness tendeth to life : so he that pursueth
evil pursueth it to his own death."—*Proverbs 11 : 19.*

"IN the two and fiftieth year of Azariah (Uzziah)
king of Judah, Pekah the son of Remaliah began
to reign over Israel in Samaria, and reigned
twenty years. And he did that which was evil in the
sight of the Lord: he departed not from the sins of
Jeroboam the son of Nebat, who made Israel to sin."
How painfully this oft-recurring testimony, like a sad
refrain, falls upon the ear! But this is the last time.
Under Hoshea, Pekah's slayer and successor, God
made "to cease the kingdom of the house of Israel"
(Hos. 1 : 4). And he, though he wrought iniquity, did
it "not as the kings of Israel that were before him"
(2 Kings 17 : 2).

"In the days of Pekah king of Israel came Tiglath-
pileser king of Assyria, and took Ijon, and Abel-beth-
maachah, and Janoah, and Kedesh, and Hazor, and
Gilead, and Galilee, all the land of Naphtali, and carried them captive to Assyria." This occurred after
Pekah's unprovoked and dastardly attack on Jerusalem, in concert with Rezin king of Damascus. See

AHAZ. And the king of Assyria's invasion and devastation of his land was his just reward for his "fierce anger" and "evil counsel" against the house of David, which he sought to overthrow by conspiracy and revolution. See Isa. 7 : 4–6.

He slew in his "fierce anger" one hundred thousand Jews in one day (2 Chron. 28 : 6); and God requited him in kind; for as he had so treacherously shed man's blood, by man was his blood also treacherously shed. "And Hoshea the son of Elah made a conspiracy against Pekah the son of Remaliah, and smote him, and slew him, and reigned in his stead, in the twentieth year of Jotham the son of Uzziah."

Josephus says Hoshea was "a friend" of Pekah's (Ant. ix. 13). In his death the prophecy of Isaiah (chap. 7 : 16) was fulfilled. His name, meaning *watch*, is from a root, "to open" (as the eyes); figuratively, to *be observant* (*Strong*). But watch as he might, his very friend in whom he trusted became, in the ordering of God, his slayer; so impossible is it for the wicked to escape their merited retribution from the hand of Him who has said, "Vengeance is Mine; I will repay." Read Amos 9 : 1–5.

"And the rest of the acts of Pekah, and all that he did, behold, they are written in the book of the chronicles of the kings of Israel."

HOSHEA

(*Deliverer.*)

2 Kings 15 : 30 ; 17 : 1-6.

"Scornful men bring a city into a snare : but wise men turn away wrath."—*Proverbs 29 : 8.*

" IN the twelfth year of Ahaz king of Judah began Hoshea the son of Elah to reign in Samaria over Israel nine years." He was the last of the nineteen kings who ruled (or, rather, misruled) Israel. An interregnum of at least eight years (see HEZEKIAH) occurred between the murder of Pekah, his predecessor, and his actual assumption of the throne. Why this kingless interval, we have no means of knowing, nor how the time was occupied. Josephus, even if we could always trust him, gives us no help here (the usual way of re-writers, or would-be improvers, of Scripture history), for he passes the subject over in silence.

But God's word has chronicled Hoshea's wickedness thus : "And he did that which was evil in the sight of the Lord, but not as the kings of Israel that were before him." There is nothing in the last clause of the above that could be construed to Hoshea's credit, for the Assyrian plunderers had in all probability removed and carried away the golden calves of Dan and Bethel. See Hosea 10 : 5-8. If he did not worship

them, or other abominations, it was not because he
" abhorred idols " (Rom. 2 : 22).

But his evil doings, whatever their character, speedily brought the Assyrian, "the rod of God's anger,"
upon him and his iniquitous subjects. "Against him
came up Shalmaneser king of Assyria ; and Hoshea
became his servant, and gave him presents." He
who conspired against his weaker Israelitish master
attempted the same (to his sorrow) with his powerful
Gentile lord. "And the king of Assyria found conspiracy in Hoshea : for he had sent messengers to So
king of Egypt, and brought no present to the king of
Assyria, as he had done year by year : therefore the
king of Assyria shut him up, and bound him in prison."
What follows, in reference to the siege of Samaria,
occurred, in point of time, before Hoshea's imprison-
ment, though recorded after. "Hoshea's imprison-
ment was not *before* the capture of Samaria, but the
sacred writer first records the *eventual* fate of Hoshea
himself, then details the invasion as it affected Samaria and Israel" (*Fausset*). "Then the king of Assyria
came up throughout all the land, and went up to Samaria, and besieged it three years. In the ninth year
of Hoshea the king of Assyria took Samaria, and carried Israel away into Assyria, and placed them in Ha-
lah and in Habor by the river of Gozan, and in the
cities of the Medes." This siege and capture of Samaria are recorded on the monuments of Assyria just as
they are narrated here in 2 Kings 17. What finally
became of Hoshea is not revealed, unless he is the
king meant in the prophet's poetic allusion, "As for
Samaria, her king is cut off as the foam upon the wa-

ter" (Hos. 10: 7).   His name means *deliverer*, and may have a prophetic significance, as a gracious reminder to the now long scattered nation, of that great "Deliverer" who shall "come out of Zion" (God's grace) "and turn away ungodliness from Jacob." And then, and so, " all Israel shall be saved "(Rom. 11 : 26).

A brief review of Israel's course and its consequences is now given us: as in 2 Chron. 36: 15–23 the end of *Judah's* kingdom is given us, with a glimpse, there, of coming mercy to a remnant.

So instructive and touching is the inspired review given of Israel's downward course, in the passage following what has been already quoted (in reference to the siege and capture of Samaria), that we cannot forbear repeating it here in full:

" And it was so, because the children of Israel had sinned against Jehovah their God, who had brought them up out of the land of Egypt, from under the hand of Pharaoh king of Egypt, and had feared other gods ; and they walked in the statutes of the nations that Jehovah had dispossessed from before the children of Israel, and of the kings of Israel, which they had made.   And the children of Israel did secretly against their God things that were not right ; and they built them high places in all their cities, from the watchmen's tower to the fortified city.   And they set them up columns [or statutes] and Asherahs on every high hill and under every green tree ; and there they burned incense on all the high places, as did the nations that Jehovah had carried away from before them, and they wrought wicked things to provoke Jehovah to anger ; and they served idols, as to which Jehovah had said to them, Ye shall not do this thing. And Jehovah testified against Israel and against Judah, by all the prophets, all the seers, saying, Turn from your evil ways, and keep my commandments, my statutes, according to all the law which I commanded your fathers, and which I sent to you through My servants the prophets. But they would not hear, and hardened their necks, like to the neck of their fathers, who did not believe in Jehovah their God. And they rejected His statutes, and His covenant which He had made with their fathers, and His testimonies which He had testified unto them ; and they followed vanity and became vain, and [went] after the nations that were round about them, concerning whom Jehovah had charged them that they should not do like them. And they forsook all the commandments of Jehovah their God, and made them molten images, two calves, and made an Asherah, and worshiped all the host of the heavens, and served Baal; and they caused their sons and their daughters to pass through the fire, and used divination and enchantments, and sold themselves to do evil in the sight of Jehovah, to provoke Him to anger. Therefore Jehovah was very angry with Israel, and removed them out of His sight. There remained but the tribe of Judah only. Also Judah kept not the commandments of Jehovah their God, but walked in the statutes of Israel which they had made. And Jehovah rejected all the seed of Israel, and afflicted them, and delivered them into the hands of spoilers, until He had cast them out of His sight. For Israel had rent [the kingdom] from the house of David; and they had made Jeroboam the son of Nebat king; and

Jeroboam violently turned Israel from following Jehovah, and made them sin a great sin.   And the children
of Israel walked in all the sins of Jeroboam which he
did; they did not depart from them: until Jehovah
had removed Israel out of His sight, as He had said
through all His servants the prophets, and Israel was
carried away out of their own land to Assyria, unto
this day" (2 Kings 17: 7–23, N. Tr.).

It has been truly observed that "the most dis-
mal picture of Old Testament history is that of the
kingdom of Israel."   Of the nine distinct dynasties
that successively ruled the dissevered tribes, three
ended with the total extirpation of the reigning family.
The kingdom continued for a period of about two
hundred and fifty years, and the inspired records of
those eventful two-and-a-half centuries of Israel's
kings and people furnish us with little more than repeated and fearful exhibitions of lawlessness and evil.
Out of the nineteen kings that reigned from the great
schism to the deportation to the land of Assyria, only
seven died natural deaths (Baasha, Omri, Jehu, Jehoahaz, Jehoash, Jeroboam II., and Menahem); seven
were assassinated (Nadab, Elah, Joram, Zachariah,
Shallum, Pekaiah, and Pekah); one committed suicide (Zimri); one died of wounds received in battle
(Ahab); one was "struck" by the judgment of God
(Jeroboam); one died of injuries received from a fall
(Ahaziah); and the other, and last (Hoshea), apparently was "cut off as foam upon the water."   To this not
unmeaning array of facts must be added two prolonged
periods of anarchy, when "there was no king in

Israel," every man doing, in all likelihood, "that which was right in his own eyes."

The kingdom of Judah continued for more than a century and a quarter after the kingdom of Israel had ceased to exist, making its history fully one-third longer than that of the ten tribes. Then it too, like its sister-kingdom, fell into disintegration and decay, and was given up to the first universal empire, under the renowned Nebuchadnezzar. This world-monarchy began the "times of the Gentiles," during which "the Most High ruleth over [not 'in,' as in A. V.] the kingdom of men, and giveth it to whomsoever He will" (Dan. 4 : 25)—setting up over it, at times, even "the basest of men" (as Belshazzar, the last Darius, Alexander, Nero, etc.). Since that day empire has superseded empire, dynasty has supplanted dynasty, and king succeeded king, as God has said, "I will overturn, overturn, overturn it! This also shall be no [more], until He come whose right it is; and I will give it [to Him]" (Ezek. 21 : 27, N. Tr.). It is "till He come," which, we hope, will be very soon; and then the eye of weeping, waiting Israel "shall see the King in His beauty."

But before this, one, "the wilful king," the "profane, wicked prince of Israel" (the Antichrist), must come. And from his unworthy head shall be removed the mitre-crown (see Ezek. 21 : 25, 26, N. Tr.), to be placed, with many others, on the once thorn-crowned brow of Him who is the King of kings and Lord of lords. That, Christian reader, will be our highest joy and glory, to see Him, our Lord and Saviour Jesus Christ, honored and owned by all, as God's "First-born, higher than the kings of the earth."

> "The Ruler over men shall be just,
> Ruling in the fear of God;
> And He shall be as the light of the morning,
> Like the rising of the sun,
> A morning without clouds,
> When, from the sunshine after rain,
> The green grass springeth from the earth.
>
> * * * * *
>
> For this is all my salvation,
> And every desire" (2 Sam. 23 : 3-5, N. Tr.).

"Amen.   Even so, come, Lord Jesus."